family handyman

BIG BOOK

OF PROJECTS

fh family handyman

A FAMILY HANDYMAN BOOK

Copyright © 2022 Home Services Publications,
a subsidiary of Trusted Media Brands, Inc.
2915 Commers Drive, Suite 700
Eagan, MN 55121

ISBN 978-1-62145-874-6 (hardcover)
ISBN 978-1-62145-875-3 (paperback)
ISBN 978-1-62145-894-4 (e-pub)

Component number 118300112H

We are committed to both the quality of our products and the service we provide to our customers. We value your comments, so please feel free to contact us at TMBBookTeam@TrustedMediaBrands.com.

For more Family Handyman products and information, visit our website: www.familyhandyman.com

Printed in U.S.A. (hardcover)
10 9 8 7 6 5 4 3 2 1

Printed in China (paperback)
10 9 8 7 6 5 4 3 2 1

Text, photography and illustrations for *Big Book of Projects* are based on articles previously published in *Family Handyman* magazine (familyhandyman.com).

WARNING

All do-it-yourself activities involve a degree of risk. Skills, materials, tools and site conditions vary widely. Although the editors have made every effort to ensure accuracy, the reader remains responsible for the selection and use of tools, materials and methods. Always obey local codes and laws, follow manufacturer's operating instructions and observe safety precautions.

Photo and Illustration Credits

10, 20, 21, 45, 61, 63, 65, 75, 87, 90, 113, 159, 176, 177, 214, 217, 231, 232, 235, 244, 254, 255: Frank Rohrbach III; 15, 104, 207: Don Mannes; 26, 197: Mario Ferro; 32: Trevor Johnston; 40: Matt Boley; 79, 125, 222: Bruce Kieffer; 119: Paul Perreault; 153, 154: Artisan Hardware; 257: Eugene Thompson; 268, 269: Jeff Gorton

SAFETY FIRST—ALWAYS!

Tackling home improvement projects and repairs can be endlessly rewarding. But as most of us know, with the rewards come risks. DIYers use chain saws, climb ladders, and tear into walls that can contain big and hazardous surprises.

The good news is, armed with the right knowledge, tools and procedures, homeowners can minimize risk. As you go about your projects and repairs, stay alert for these hazards:

ALUMINUM WIRING

Aluminum wiring, installed in about 7 million homes between 1965 and 1973, requires special techniques and materials to make safe connections. This wiring is dull gray, not the dull orange characteristic of copper. Hire a licensed electrician certified to work with it. For more information, go to cpsc.gov and search for "aluminum wiring."

SPONTANEOUS COMBUSTION

Rags saturated with oil finishes, like Danish oil and linseed oil, and with oil-based paints and stains can spontaneously combust if left bunched up. Always dry them outdoors, spread out loosely. When the oil has thoroughly dried, you can safely throw them in the trash.

VISION AND HEARING PROTECTION

Safety glasses or goggles should be worn whenever you're working on DIY projects that involve chemicals, dust, and anything that could shatter or chip off and hit your eye. Sounds louder than 80 decibels (dB) are considered potentially dangerous. Sound levels from a lawn mower can be 90 dB, and shop tools and chain saws can be 90 to 100 dB.

LEAD PAINT

If your home was built before 1979, it may contain lead paint, which is a serious health hazard, especially for children 6 and under. Take precautions when you scrape or remove it. Contact your public health department for detailed safety information or call (800) 424-LEAD (5323) to receive an information pamphlet. Or visit epa.gov/lead.

BURIED UTILITIES

A few days before you dig in your yard, have your underground water, gas and electrical lines marked. Just call 811 or go to call811.com.

SMOKE AND CARBON MONOXIDE (CO) ALARMS

The risk of dying in reported home structure fires is cut in half in homes with working smoke alarms. Test your smoke alarms every month, replace batteries as necessary and replace units that are more than 10 years old. As you make your home more energy efficient and airtight, existing ducts and chimneys can't always successfully vent combustion gases, including potentially deadly carbon monoxide (CO). Install a UL-listed CO detector, and test your CO and smoke alarms at the same time.

FIVE-GALLON BUCKETS AND WINDOW COVERING CORDS

Anywhere from 10 to 40 children a year drown in 5-gallon buckets, according to the U.S. Consumer Products Safety Commission. Always store them upside down and store ones containing liquid with the covers securely snapped.

According to Parents for Window Blind Safety, hundreds of children in the United States are injured every year after becoming entangled in looped window treatment cords. For more information, visit pfwbs.org.

WORKING UP HIGH

If you have to get up on your roof to do a repair or installation, always install roof brackets and wear a roof harness.

ASBESTOS

Texture sprayed on ceilings before 1978, adhesives and tiles for vinyl and asphalt floors before 1980, and vermiculite insulation (with gray granules) all may contain asbestos. Other building materials made between 1940 and 1980 could also contain asbestos. If you suspect that materials you're removing or working around contain asbestos, contact your health department or visit epa.gov/asbestos for information.

CONTENTS

BEGINNER PROJECTS

INTERMEDIATE PROJECTS

ADVANCED PROJECTS

BEGINNER PROJECTS

SUMMER SANCTUARY

///

TURN AN UNUSED CORNER OF A DECK OR PATIO INTO A SHADY RETREAT FOR SITTING.

This corner arbor turns empty space into a leafy green sanctuary. Use it to create shade and privacy, to screen an unattractive view, or to add color to a concrete patio or wood deck—even a second-floor deck. Our arbor is covered with mandevilla, a tropical vine great for walls and trellises, too.

The entire arbor is made from pressure-treated wood, but coating it with a penetrating stain and hiding the fasteners make the project look more like a nice piece of furniture than decking. The stain will also help keep the arbor from cracking and warping as it weathers.

Using pressure-treated wood keeps the cost reasonable, too. The project can be built over two weekends—or one if you don't stain it.

Treated wood lasts almost forever, but it can be gnarly to work with. Take your time picking through the lumber pile for good pieces. Look for dry (lighter) pieces without too many knots. You'll need straight pieces for the uprights and benches, but you can use nice-looking, moderately warped pieces for the planters. Let the lumber sit for a few weeks so it all shrinks uniformly. Remember to put the best sides out when you assemble the planters and benches.

WHAT IT TAKES	
TIME 2 weekends	**SKILL LEVEL** Beginner
TOOLS Basic hand tools, circular saw, drill driver	

3 SIMPLE COMPONENTS

**2 trellis grids + 3 planter boxes + 2 bench seats =
A garden arbor that's easy to build and simple to customize**

To build this project, just cut lumber to length and screw the parts together. If you can handle a tape measure, a saw and a drill, you can do it. Customization is easy, too: Build shorter seats to suit a small space or add components to surround a big space. If you don't need shade or privacy, leave off the trellis.

TRELLIS

PLANTER BOX

BENCH SEAT

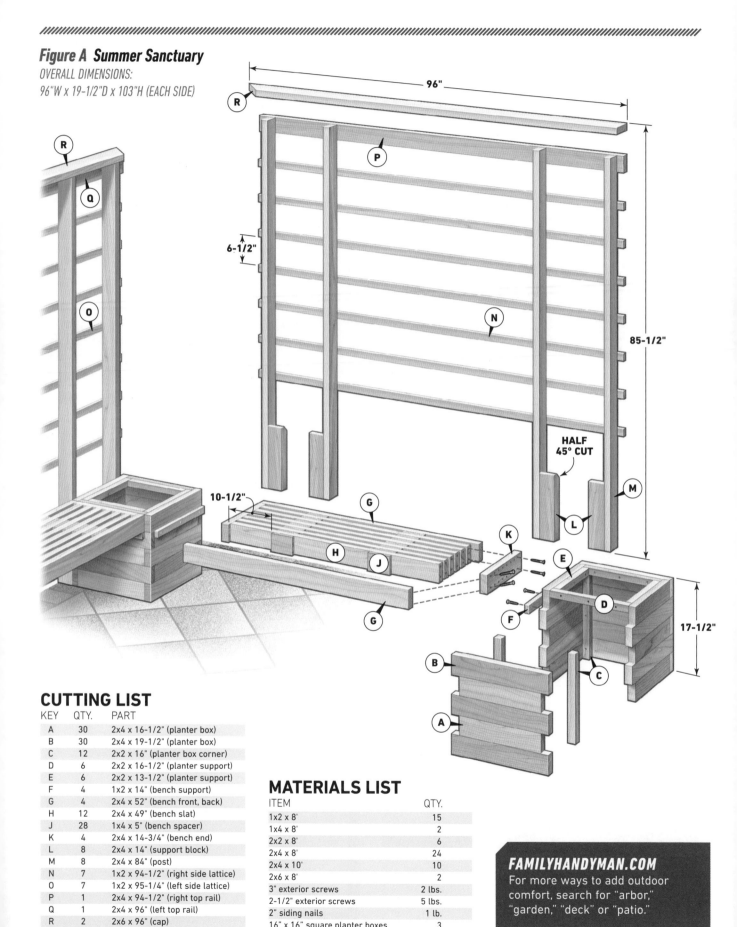

Figure A **Summer Sanctuary**

OVERALL DIMENSIONS:
96"W x 19-1/2"D x 103"H (EACH SIDE)

96"

6-1/2"

85-1/2"

HALF 45° CUT

10-1/2"

17-1/2"

CUTTING LIST

KEY	QTY.	PART
A	30	2x4 x 16-1/2" (planter box)
B	30	2x4 x 19-1/2" (planter box)
C	12	2x2 x 16" (planter box corner)
D	6	2x2 x 16-1/2" (planter support)
E	6	2x2 x 13-1/2" (planter support)
F	4	1x2 x 14" (bench support)
G	4	2x4 x 52" (bench front, back)
H	12	2x4 x 49" (bench slat)
J	28	1x4 x 5" (bench spacer)
K	4	2x4 x 14-3/4" (bench end)
L	8	2x4 x 14" (support block)
M	8	2x4 x 84" (post)
N	7	1x2 x 94-1/2" (right side lattice)
O	7	1x2 x 95-1/4" (left side lattice)
P	1	2x4 x 94-1/2" (right top rail)
Q	1	2x4 x 96" (left top rail)
R	2	2x6 x 96" (cap)

MATERIALS LIST

ITEM	QTY.
1x2 x 8'	15
1x4 x 8'	2
2x2 x 8'	6
2x4 x 8'	24
2x4 x 10'	10
2x6 x 8'	2
3" exterior screws	2 lbs.
2-1/2" exterior screws	5 lbs.
2" siding nails	1 lb.
16" x 16" square planter boxes	3

FAMILYHANDYMAN.COM
For more ways to add outdoor comfort, search for "arbor," "garden," "deck" or "patio."

1 CUT ALL THE PIECES
Cut the planter box pieces and the bench parts quickly and accurately using a stop block.

STOP BLOCK

ONE SCREW PER 2x4

INSIDE CORNERS

SPACER BLOCKS

2 BUILD THE FRONT AND BACK
Assemble the front and back of the planters against a square. Use spacer blocks to align the planter box corners perfectly.

3 ATTACH THE SIDES
Stand the front and back, then attach the sides, screwing through the planter box corners. Predrill to avoid splits.

4 APPLY STAIN FIRST
Stain the bench and trellis parts and the completed planter boxes before assembly to save time and mess.

ASSEMBLE THE PLANTER BOXES

Each planter box is made by alternating 10 short and 10 long lengths of 2x4 and joining the inside corners with 2x2s. The overall size is based on 16-in.-square plastic planters (actual size 15-1/2 in.) sold at home centers. If you can't locate that exact size or you prefer a different style, make the planter supports **(D and E)** larger or smaller, or build a base inside the planter box to support the planter. You can also change the size of the planter box.

Use a stop block to cut all the pieces quickly and accurately **(Photo 1)**. Set three long and two short pieces against a square clamped to the worktable, using short spacer blocks for alignment **(Photo 2)**. Predrill the 2x2 corners with a No. 8 countersink bit to avoid splitting the wood. One 2-1/2-in. screw per 2x4 is sufficient.

Make a front and back for each planter box, then set them upright and join them with interlocking 2x4 pieces, attaching them from the inside **(Photo 3)**. Although screwing from the inside is fussier, it enables you to avoid the cracks that often occur when pressure-treated wood is screwed near the ends. Finally, screw on the bench supports **(Figure A)**.

Stain the boxes and other pieces now to avoid drips on the patio or deck and to make it easier to coat the bench pieces on all sides **(Photo 4)**.

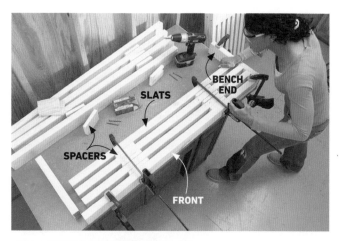

5 ATTACH THE FRONT AND END
Clamp the bench front and bench end against a square corner. Screw the bench pieces together from the back to keep fasteners hidden.

6 ATTACH BOXES TO THE ENDS
Set the benches on the bench supports, then fasten the planter boxes to the bench ends.

7 USE SHIMS TO LEVEL
Shim the planter boxes to level the benches. Install hidden legs to hold the planter level, then remove the shims.

8 SCREW ON THE POSTS
Attach the posts to the sides of the support blocks with three screws each.

CONSTRUCT THE BENCHES

Clamp the front and one of the sides of the bench to a square edge. Clamp the first set of spacers and the first 2x4 slat to the front piece, then drive two 3-in. screws through the slat and the spacer into the front piece. Continue fastening, clamping the slats in position to keep them aligned before screwing them **(Photo 5)**. Check to make sure the bench stays flat as you assemble it. Toe-screw the bench ends to the front of the bench, then drive two screws into the end of each slat **(see Figure A)**.

ASSEMBLE THE ARBOR

Put the benches in place flush with the back of the planter boxes **(Photo 6)**. Screw the benches and planter boxes together with four 2-1/2-in. screws. Then screw on each planter support inside the planter box with three 2-1/2-in. screws. Level the planter boxes if necessary, adding hidden 2x2s or 2x4s for legs **(Photo 7)**.

Screw support blocks to the backs of the planter boxes 3 in. from the corners, then attach the posts **(Photo 8)**. Cut the posts 7 ft. long plus the distance (if any) the planter boxes were shimmed up so that the posts sit on the ground but are level with each other at the top. Drive two additional screws into the posts from inside the planter boxes. Don't worry if the boxes are still wobbly. The top rail and cap lock everything together.

Set the top 2x4 rails on the ground next to the posts, leaving

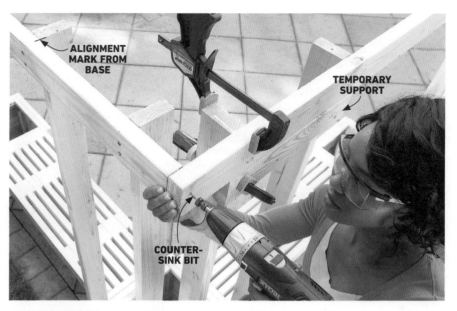

ALIGNMENT MARK FROM BASE

TEMPORARY SUPPORT

COUNTER-SINK BIT

a 1-1/2-in. overhang at the outside ends. Mark the position of each post on the top rail, then clamp the rails flush with the tops of the posts. Fasten the rails with 3-in. screws to the posts and to each other **(Photo 9)**.

Nail on the lattice, overhanging it 1-1/2 in. on the outside edges and butting the pieces at the corner **(Photo 10)**.

Screw on the 2x6 cap pieces to finish the structure, mitering them at the inside corner and screwing the two sides together. Drop in the plastic planter boxes (these are sold at home centers or garden supply stores), fill them with dirt, and plant a mix of climbing flowers and vines.

9 ATTACH THE TOP RAILS
Screw the right and left top rails to the posts. Mark the post spacing first to keep the posts plumb.

OVERHANG

TEMPORARY SUPPORT

SIDING NAILS

10 SECURE THE LATTICE
Mark the bottom edges of the lattice pieces on each post, and then nail the lattice pieces to the posts with siding nails.

BRICK-LINED WALKWAY

ADDING A BRICK PAVER BORDER TO YOUR FRONT SIDEWALK TRANSFORMS A DULL AND UTILITARIAN CONCRETE PATH INTO AN ELEGANT ENTRANCE TO YOUR HOME.

SOD

TRENCH FOR FILL

1 REMOVE SOD AND DIG

Dig a trench to provide space for the compacted fill. The fill provides a stable base to keep the brick border from shifting.

SCREED

GRAVEL FILL

2 ADD GRAVEL AND LEVEL

Level the gravel about 3-1/2 in. below the top of the sidewalk to allow room for the bricks and about an inch of sand. A 2x4 with a scrap of plywood screwed to it makes a perfect notched screed board.

The curb appeal of this project can easily add more to the value of your home, much more than the project costs, making it an addition that looks great and is a good investment of both your time and money.

For our project here, we installed a deep compacted gravel base under the bricks. If you don't want to do that, you could certainly save a lot of work by simply digging a small trench and laying the bricks right on the soil. But there's a trade-off to that method: The bricks will probably have to be realigned every summer. Our method takes longer, but it guarantees the walkway will look attractive and function well for decades.

Figure A **Brick Edging details**

BRICK PAVER

EDGING

GRAVEL

SAND

1"

8"

14"

FAMILYHANDYMAN.COM
For more curb appeal projects and ideas, search for "curb appeal."

PLANNING AND PREPARATION

For this project, you'll need bricks, compactable gravel for the base, washed sand and plastic paver edging to hold the bricks in place. If you're lucky enough to have a full-service landscape supplier in your area, you can order all your materials there. Otherwise, look for pavers and plastic paver edging at home centers, garden centers or brickyards. Find gravel at a landscape supplier or at a sand and gravel quarry. Don't forget to ask about delivery charges.

Clay pavers have a rich, authentic look, but cement pavers are a little less expensive. Both types are durable and long-lasting. Most pavers are 4 x 8 in.

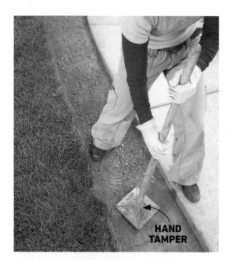

HAND TAMPER

SCREED FOR SAND

SAND

3 USE A TAMPER

Pound the gravel with a hand tamper until the layer feels solid. The level will drop as the gravel settles, but that's OK because you'll add sand later to make up for it.

4 ADD SAND AND LEVEL

Add a layer of sand on top of the gravel to create a flat bed for the brick. Bricks should protrude about 1/4 in. above the sidewalk when set on the screeded sand.

5 PLACE THE BRICKS

Set the bricks on the sand bed. Don't worry if the tops aren't even. You'll tamp them down later to level them out and make them fit so they're flush to the sidewalk.

and about 2-1/4 in. thick, but other sizes are available. Measure the total linear feet of edging you plan to install and multiply by 3 to arrive at the number of 4-in.-wide brick pavers you'll need. The plastic paver edging needed to hold the bricks in place may seem expensive, but the edging is necessary to keep the bricks from drifting. Use the total linear feet of border to order edging. You'll also need enough 10-in.-long spikes to install one every 12 inches.

To ensure that the bricks remain stable and won't tip when you wheel a lawn mower over them, the new compacted base should be 6 in. wider than the brick and extend 6 in. below the bottom of the brick. This means you'll dig a 14-in.-wide by 8-in.-deep trench for typical brick pavers. To determine how much gravel you'll need for this size trench, multiply the linear feet of trench by 0.02. The result is the number of cubic yards of gravel needed.

Order gravel that ranges in size from 3/4 in. down to a powder

(called 3/4-in.-minus). For our project, which was 60 linear feet, we ordered 1-1/4 cu. yds. of 3/4-in.-minus crushed limestone. Have the gravel dumped on the driveway where it's easier to shovel up. You'll also need a 1-in. layer of sand under the bricks. It's usually cheaper and easier to simply order bags of sand rather than have a small quantity delivered. Divide the linear feet of border by 5 to determine how many 50-lb. bags of sand you'll need.

We rented a sod cutter to slice a neat layer of grass from along the edge of the sidewalk, but a flat shovel will also work. In addition to a shovel and rake, you'll need a wheelbarrow, a tamper (you can rent this), and some scraps of lumber and basic carpentry tools to construct the screeds **(Photos 2 and 4)**.

If your sidewalk is straight and you only have a few bricks to cut, you can use a diamond blade mounted in a circular saw to cut the bricks. If your sidewalk is curved or you anticipate a lot of

cutting, you should rent a brick saw **(Photo 7)**.

DIG THE TRENCH

Two days before you start digging, call your local one-call number and ask to have the buried utility lines along your sidewalk located and marked (call 811 or visit 811.com to find your local one-call number). When you're sure it's safe to dig, start by removing a 14-in.-wide layer of grass along the sidewalk. If your grass is in good shape, slice it off carefully so you can use it to patch in along the new border. A sod cutter simplifies this job and leaves you with neat rolls of sod that are easy to reuse. But if your grass isn't worth saving, just dig it out and plan to buy a few rolls of sod instead.

MATERIALS LIST

ITEM

3/4-in.-minus gravel

Sand

Brick pavers

Plastic paver edging

10-in. paver spikes

GAP

6 MARK FOR CUTTING

For fitting the bricks around a curve, set the bricks in place and estimate how much to cut off to close the gaps between bricks. Draw each cutting line with a permanent marker.

Next, dig a 14-in.-wide by 8-in.-deep trench along the sidewalk to accommodate the gravel, sand and pavers **(Photo 1)**. You're going to have a lot of dirt to get rid of. Ask around the neighborhood to see if someone needs fill for a low spot, or consider building a raised-bed garden or decorative earth berm. As a last resort, you can rent a 10-cu.-yd. trash bin to dispose of the dirt. When you're done digging, rake the bottom of the trench smooth and compact it with the hand tamper.

Because the purpose of the gravel fill is to provide a stable base, you must compact it well. Start by spreading a 3-in.-deep layer of gravel in the trench. Pound every square inch with the hand tamper until it's tightly packed. Then add another 3 in. of fill and drag a screed across the top to create a surface that's parallel to the top of the sidewalk **(Photo 2)**.

Construct a screed by screwing a 14-in.-wide scrap of plywood to a 32-in. length of 2x4. The plywood should extend below the 2x4 by the thickness of the brick paver plus 3/4 in. Tamp the fill again after leveling it with the screed **(Photo 3)**.

Then spread a layer of sand a little deeper than 1 in. over the base. If the sand is dry, dampen it with mist from the hose. This will help hold the sand in place as you scrape away the excess to install the paver edging **(Photo 8)**.

Construct another screed and use it to level the sand **(Photo 4)**. Figure the depth of the notch by subtracting 1/4 in. from the thickness of a brick. Set a paver on the screeded sand to test the depth. The paver should protrude about 1/4 in. above the surface of the sidewalk. You'll make the pavers flush later by tamping them down into the sand bed **(Photo 9)**.

SET THE PAVERS

Since there's a good chance you'll have to cut the last brick to fit, start with a full brick in the most visible location and plan to finish in the least conspicuous spot. If your edging turns a right angle corner, start at the corner and work out. **Photo 5** shows how to get started. You'll have to cut the pavers to go around curves. To figure out how much to cut from each, arrange a half dozen pavers along the curve with the ends touching and estimate the gap between them. If the curve is very gradual, you can simply cut every third or fourth paver to fit. For steeper curves, mark the cuts **(Photo 6)** and cut along the marks with a brick saw **(Photo 7)**. Cut and install several

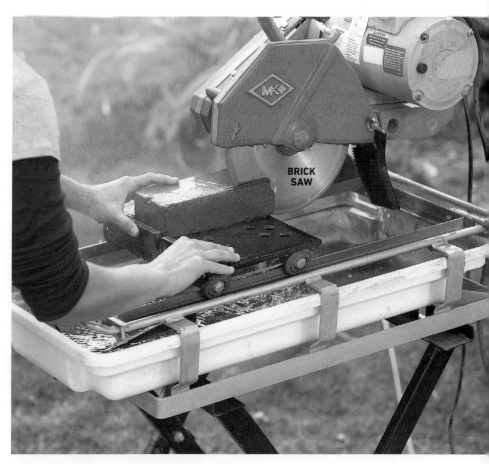

BRICK SAW

7 FOR LOTS OF CUTTING, RENT A SAW

To speed up the work or if you have a lot of bricks to cut, rent a brick saw. Water spraying on the diamond blade keeps dust to a minimum and speeds cutting.

pavers, then repeat the process to finish the curved section.

Next, install plastic paver edging behind the bricks to hold them in place. Start by scraping the extra sand out from behind the bricks so the edging will rest on the compacted fill. The edging we used required us to cut the outermost band with tin snips to allow the edging to bend around the curve. Press the edging against the bricks and drive 10-in. spikes every 12 in. to hold the edging in place (**Photo 8**).

At this point, the bricks should protrude slightly above the surface of the sidewalk. **Photo 9** shows how to use a scrap of lumber and hand maul to embed the bricks in the sand and make them flush with the surface of the sidewalk. Embed all the bricks. Then spread sand over them and work it into cracks with a broom. Be sure the sand is dry or it won't settle into the cracks. Tamp the bricks again with a 2x6 board and hand maul. The vibration will cause the dry sand to fill the cracks and lock the bricks tightly together.

Complete the project by filling the trench behind the bricks with some of the soil you removed earlier. Leave the soil slightly below the surface of the lawn to allow room for the sod. You may have to experiment a little to get the level just right. Set the sod in place and trim it to fit with a utility knife.

Photo 10 shows how we ran the bricks alongside the step. This technique works whether you have one or several steps. In some cases, you may have to remove an additional strip of sod alongside the steps and regrade the soil slightly so the lawn lines up with the edge of the bricks, but it's a neat-looking solution that's worth the extra effort.

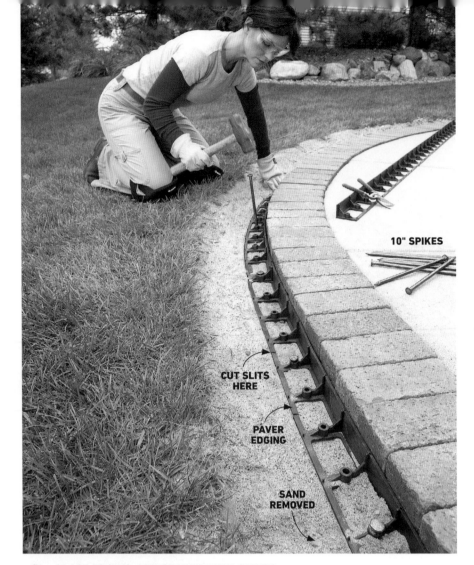

10" SPIKES

CUT SLITS HERE

PAVER EDGING

SAND REMOVED

8 PLACE EDGING AND SECURE WITH SPIKES
Hold the bricks securely in place with plastic paver edging. Press the plastic edging against the bricks and secure it with spikes. The edging bends easily once you cut the plastic band located along the outside edge.

9 LEVEL BRICKS
Level the tops of the brick pavers with a board and hand maul. Tamp them down so the tops are flush to the surface of the sidewalk.

10 SLOPE FOR TRANSITION
Slope bricks alongside steps to make an attractive transition. Follow the grade of the adjacent lawn to determine the slope.

EASY GARDEN ARCH

A SMALL PROJECT MAKES A BIG IMPRESSION IN YOUR YARD.

WHAT IT TAKES

TIME	**SKILL LEVEL**
1 day	Beginner

TOOLS
Basic hand tools, circular saw, drill, handsaw, jigsaw

Figure A Easy Garden Arch
OVERALL DIMENSIONS: 90"H x 78"W

HEADER
1-1/2" x 7-1/4" x 78"

5-1/2"

12"

NOTCH
7-1/4" x 1-1/2"

3-1/2"
SCREWS

43"

POST
5-1/2" x 5-1/2" x 10'

30"

CONCRETE

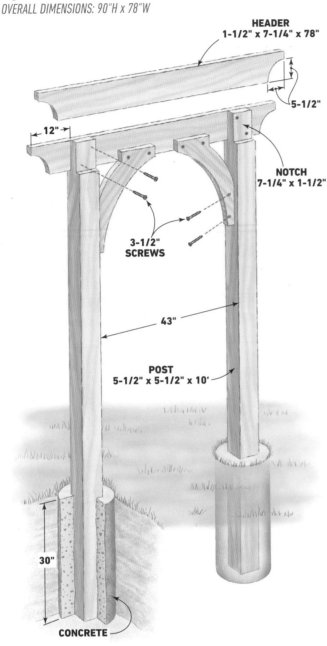

AN ARCH MADE FROM SIX PARTS

Building an arch is one of the easiest ways to give your landscape a striking centerpiece. And this arch is easier than most. Made from just six parts, it can be built in less than a day—even if you're a rookie carpenter. The design is versatile, too: The arch can become a gateway in a fence, frame a walkway through a hedge, or stand alone in your yard or garden. You can stain it for a rustic look or paint it for a more formal look.

1 CUT NOTCHES
Notch the tops of the beams. Cut as deep as you can from both sides with a circular saw, then finish the cuts with a handsaw.

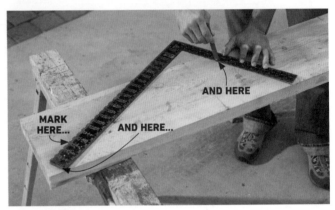

AND HERE

MARK HERE...

AND HERE...

2 LOCATE A BRACKET
Mark where to cut a bracket without fussy measurements or geometry—just align a framing square with the edges of a 2x10 and make three marks.

3 MARK THE ARCS AND CUT OUT THE BRACKETS
Draw perfect curves fast using a tape measure to guide your pencil. Cut out the bracket and use it as a pattern for the other bracket.

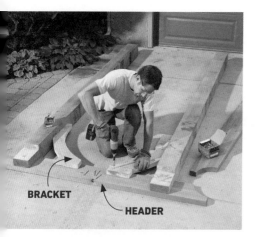

BRACKET

HEADER

SHIMS

STRETCHER

Figure B Bracket detail

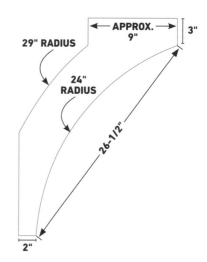

29" RADIUS

APPROX. 9"

3"

24" RADIUS

26-1/2"

2"

4 ATTACH THE POSTS

Screw through the posts and brackets into the header. That way, one header will have no visible screws. Screw through the second header into the posts.

CUT THE PARTS

To get started, cut notches in the tops of the beams with a circular saw **(Photo 1)**. If you're using rough-sawn lumber as we did, you may have to change the length and depth of these notches to suit your 2x8 headers. (The dimensions of rough-sawn lumber vary.) Set the cutting depth of your circular saw to 1-1/2 in. to make the crosscuts for the notches. Then set your saw to full depth to make the other cuts.

Next, cut the 2x8 headers to length and mark arcs at the ends as shown in **Figure A**. To mark the curves, use the bottom of a 5-gallon bucket or any circle that's 10 to 11 in. in diameter. Cut the curves with a jigsaw.

The curved brackets may look complicated, but they're easy to mark since they're based on a standard framing square. After

MATERIALS LIST

ITEM	QTY.
6x6 x 10' (posts)	2
2x8 x 8' (headers)	2
2x10 x 8' (brackets)	1
2x4 x 8' (stretcher, stakes, braces)	3
Concrete mix (60-lb. bags)	3
3" and 3-1/2" screws	As needed

5 LEVEL AND PLUMB

Set the arch level and plumb before you pour concrete. Wedge shims under the stretcher until the header is level, then plumb and brace the posts.

marking with the square **(Photo 2)**, set a nail in a sawhorse 20 in. from the edge of the board. Carefully adjust the position of the board until both corner marks of the bracket are 24 in. from the nail. Then, holding your pencil at the 24-in. mark on the tape measure, draw an arc. To draw the second arc, move your pencil to the 29-in. mark **(Photo 3)**. Cut the straight edges of the brackets with a circular saw and the arcs with a jigsaw. If the curves are a bit wavy, smooth them with an orbital or belt sander. Don't be too fussy. Small imperfections won't be noticed.

PUT IT ALL TOGETHER

Mark one header 12 in. from both ends and lay out the posts, aligned with the marks. Take measurements at the other end to make sure the posts are perfectly parallel. Drive 3-1/2-in. screws through the posts and into the header. At the tops of the brackets, drive 3-in. screws at a slight angle so they won't poke through the face of the header **(Photo 4)**. Set 1-1/2-in.-thick blocks under the other ends of the brackets. Then

drive screws at an angle through the sides of the brackets and into the posts. Drill 1/8-in. pilot holes so you don't split the brackets. Set the second header in place and screw it to the posts. Note: The brackets aren't centered on the posts, so there's a 1-in. gap between the second header and the brackets.

SET IT UP

A few days before you dig the postholes, call 811 to have underground utility lines marked. You'll set the arch posts into 10-in.-dia. holes 30 in. deep. But before you move the arch into place, screw on a temporary 2x4 "stretcher" 30 in. from the post bottoms. Then round up a helper or two and set the posts into the holes. Patiently level and plumb the arch, using stakes and 2x4s to brace it **(Photo 5)**. Be careful not to nudge the posts out of position as you fill the holes with concrete. Let the concrete harden for at least four hours before you finish the wood. We brushed on two coats of clear penetrating wood finish to deepen the color of the wood and repel moisture.

STONE FIRE RING

CREATE A SIMPLE, DURABLE AND SAFER GATHERING PLACE FOR FAMILY AND FRIENDS.

An outdoor fire pit is a natural gathering spot for family and friends, whether for a cookout or casual conversation on a cool evening.

You can make those gatherings more comfortable and safe by building a simple fire ring with retaining wall stone. To complete the setting, surround the ring with flagstone that more comfortably accommodates chairs and benches and eliminates the inevitable mud pit that comes with wet weather.

This project requires no special tools or skills. In fact, the primary tool for this project is a strong back! You'll be lifting and moving heavy stone, both for the fire ring and for the surround. Rent or borrow a two-wheel dolly to ease the load if you have to move the stone far. A manual sod cutter (rented; **Photo 2**) simplifies the digging, but it also takes some strength to operate. A good shovel is easier to use but quite a bit slower.

WHAT IT TAKES	
TIME 1 day	**SKILL LEVEL** Beginner
TOOLS Shovel, sod cutter, two-wheel dolly	

SITE PLANNING AND RING ASSEMBLY

Begin your planning with a call to your local building department to learn about fire restrictions. Many regions require burning permits and restrict the size of a fire ring.

Choose an area about 18 ft. in diameter and relatively flat. Be sure to locate the fire ring away from trees, bushes and buildings. Burning wood snaps and pops, sending sparks into the air.

Drive a pipe at the center and mark out a 9-ft. radius circle **(Photo 1)**. Remove the sod or plant material and enough dirt so the paving stones you've chosen are flush with the surrounding grass when set in 1 in. of sand **(Photos 2 and 3)**. The sod cutter shown here operates with a firm stomp on the crossbar. It takes practice and strength to cut smoothly. Be sure to wear heavy boots and gloves.

Although you want your fire ring to sit level, the surrounding flagstone sitting area can follow the contours of the yard, its edges blending with the sod **(Photo 3)**. However, if you have from 1 to 3 ft. of rise over the 18-ft. dia. of the sitting area, consider excavating the high side to keep the sitting area reasonably level. Then build a small retaining wall to hold back the soil. The retaining wall becomes a sitting area as well as a shelf and counter.

Granite retaining wall stones are shown here for the ring. They are a uniform size and easy to fit together tightly, and their weight (about 70 lbs.) makes them stable. Other types of retaining wall stone, including concrete, will work, too.

MATERIALS LIST

ITEM	QTY.
Granite retaining wall stones (6-1/2 x 8 x 14 in.)	24
Flagstone (Chilton)	200 sq. ft.
Sand (delivered)	1-1/2 yds.

1 MARK THE CIRCLE
Drive a pipe into the ground at the fire ring's center. Loop a string over the stake; measure out 9 ft. and mark this point with tape. Hold a can of marking spray paint at the tape and spray the circle.

2 REMOVE THE SOD
Cut away the sod with a sod cutter. Follow the perimeter and then cut away the inside of the circle. Leave the pipe in place.

3 GET THE PROPER GRADE
Remove enough dirt so that the top of the flagstone sits 1 in. below the surrounding sod. The sod cutter works well for shaving down the grade, but a flat shovel works well, too.

LANDSCAPE SPIKE

STRING LINE AT SOD HEIGHT

2" SPACE

6" LANDSCAPE SPIKE

70-LB. BLOCKS

21" RADIUS

4 SPREAD AND LEVEL THE SAND

Drive a 6-in. landscape spike beside the center pipe until it's 2 in. below the sod level. Drive six additional spikes about 3 ft. away from the center, spacing them evenly around the center. Level the top of each spike with the center one, then spread sand in the circle flush with the tops of the spikes.

5 PLACE THE FIRST ROW

Draw a 21-in. radius circle with the string and marking paint. Lay the first row of retaining wall stones (12 in our case) along the line, minimizing the gaps between them. Twist each stone back and forth a few times in the sand to firmly set it. Make the tops level.

Lay the stones in a circle to determine how large to make the ring. There's no exact rule here. A 42-in. inner diameter works well, but you can adjust the size according to preference and code. Measure the radius of the circle and then mark this circle at the center of your fire ring **(Photo 5)**.

It's important to set the stones on a level bed of sand to keep the base stones stable and the joints tight. Stretch a string tightly across the circle to establish the height of the sod, and follow **Photo 4** to create the sand bed. Use a carpenter's level to accurately align the tops of the first row of stones **(Photo 5)**. Minimize the gaps between stones. The second

row goes up fast—you simply set it on top of the first **(Photo 6)**.

LAY THE SITTING AREA

Many types of materials will make a nice sitting area: various gravels; stone, brick or concrete pavers; flagstones; or even poured concrete. Irregular flagstones with grass planted between them offer an attractive, informal look and are easy to lay and maintain. Just run the lawn mower over the stones to trim the grass.

Set the flagstones in a bed of sand, letting them follow the contour of the ground **(Photos 7 and 8)**. To minimize tripping, make an effort to keep the edges flush. If you want a finished look right

away, meticulously cut and fit sod between the stones, although it's easier to fill the gaps with topsoil and sow grass seed. Or, instead of grass, you might consider ground covers suitable for your climate.

Finally, add about 4 in. of sand or gravel to the inside of the fire ring to raise the level of the fire. This will make it easier to tend.

RING HEIGHT

To avoid pinched toes or fingers, limit the height of the ring to about 12 in., or two rows of stone. If you go higher, keep in mind that the stones can slip off and fall, especially if you use smaller, less stable stones.

TWIST STONE INTO PLACE

RAKED SAND

6 LAY THE SECOND ROW

When the first row is complete, set the second row of stones on top of it. Each stone should be centered on a joint of the first row.

7 SET THE FIRST SITTING AREA STONE

Spread 1 in. of sand over the sitting area. Fit the first flagstone tightly to the fire ring. Twist it into the sand to firmly set it, adding or removing sand to stabilize it.

SLEDGE-HAMMER

BREAK LARGER STONES AS NEEDED

TOPSOIL

8 COMPLETE THE SITTING AREA

Fit and set stones out to the circle's edge. Keep the flagstone edges flush to one another and leave 2- to 4-in. spaces in between. You can break larger flagstones with a sledgehammer. Caution: Wear eye protection when breaking stone.

9 PLACE SOD BETWEEN THE STONES

Fill the spaces between the stones with topsoil about 1/2 in. below the top. Then cut sod with a knife to fit between the stones. Press the sod firmly into the soil and keep the sod damp until it has rooted.

GARDEN TOOL CUBBY

BUILD A HOUSE TO HOLD SMALL GARDEN TOOLS AND SUPPLIES, AND PLACE IT IN YOUR YARD SO IT'S HANDY WHEN YOU NEED THEM.

Keep tools and supplies next to your garden with this small storage house. It takes only a few hours to build and can be made with pine or rough-sawn cedar, as shown here.

Cut flat, dry 1x12s to the sizes in the Cutting List. Nail and glue the sides, base and back together, then attach the rafters and gables. Fasten the shorter roof panel on one side, leaving 7/8-in. overhangs in the front and back. Caulk the top edge, then nail on the longer panel.

Place the hinge mortises into the door and side, and hang the door. Stain or paint the wood inside and out to seal it. Then use green branches for nature-inspired handles, nailing them in place.

Make a rustic door handle from a tree branch. Nail the crosspieces to the door with brad nails, then notch the back of the handle so it sits flat on the crosspieces and nail it in place.

Figure A Garden Tool Cubby
OVERALL DIMENSIONS: 23-1/2"H x 18"W x 11-1/4"D

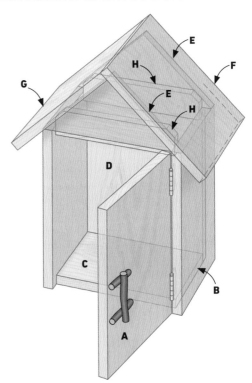

CUTTING LIST

KEY	QTY.	PART
A	1	11" x 15-3/4" door
B	2	9-1/2" x 15-7/8" sides
C	1	11-1/4" x 8" bottom
D	1	11-1/4" x 15-7/8" back
E	2	12-3/4" x 6-1/2" gables
F	1	11-1/4" x 12-3/4" long roof panel
G	1	11-1/4" x 12" short roof panel
H	2	11-1/4" x 2-1/2" rafters

Note: All dimensions are for 3/4"-thick wood

MATERIALS LIST

ITEM	QTY.
1x12 x 8' cedar or pine	2
4x4 x 8' post	1
2" x 2" mortise hinges	1 pr.
Magnetic catch	1
1-1/2" galvanized finish nails	1 lb.

WHAT IT TAKES

TIME	SKILL LEVEL
1/2 day	Beginner

TOOLS
Basic hand tools, chisel, circular saw or handsaw

KIDS CLIMBING WALL

//

KIDS GOT YOU CLIMBING THE WALLS? GET THEM CLIMBING THIS WALL! IT'S EASY TO BUILD AND PROMISES TO KEEP THE YOUNGSTERS HAPPILY OCCUPIED.

This folding A-frame climbing wall is an easy project to build that will introduce your kiddos to new heights of play while keeping them busy and active. When it's not in use, it can be compactly stored out of the way in a garage or shed.

WHAT IT TAKES	
TIME 1 day	**SKILL LEVEL** Beginner
TOOLS Basic hand tools, circular saw, drill, jigsaw	

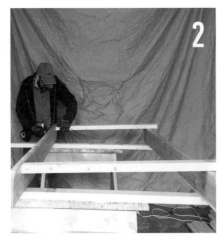

CHOOSE YOUR WOOD

Make sure your boards are straight, flat and have four good edges. Avoid splits or blow outs on the ends. We chose to work with cedar 2x6 and pine 1x6 for affordability and weight. Pressure-treated lumber is too heavy. You could go with all cedar, but that gets expensive in a hurry.

1 MAKE THE LEGS

Cut 45-degree angles at the end of each 2x6 leg. Make a mark 6 in. from the opposite end of the 45-degree angle cut, 1 in. from the short edge of the leg. Set a nail on the mark.

Using string with a loop around the nail, hold your pencil on the string at the end of the leg and draw a radius.

Remove the nail; drill a 1/2-in. hole on the mark you made. Then cut the radius with a jigsaw. Use the one complete leg as a template for the other three legs and repeat the process.

2 CUT THE CROSS BRACES AND ASSEMBLE THE FRAMES

Cut two 2x4s to 44 in. each, and then cut two more at 40-5/8 in. Because we want one side of the A frame to nest into the other, we subtracted 3 in. (the thickness of two 2x6s) plus 3/8 in. to account for the spacer washers.

Using 3-in. screws, install each pair of cross braces on the long edges of the legs, 5 in. from the top radius and 6 in. from the bottom.

Nest the narrower frame inside the other frame; line up the 1/2-in. holes. With a hammer, knock 3/8-in. carriage bolts in from the outside of the legs, setting two spacer washers between each pair of legs. Install a washer and lock nut on the threaded end of each bolt. Be sure you don't overtighten the lock nut; you want it just snug so the two legs will pivot smoothly.

3 CUT AND INSTALL THE FACE BOARDS

Cut 15 pieces of 1x6 at 47 in. and another 15 at 45-1/2 in.

Starting at 2 in. below the top radius, install the face boards using 1-5/8-in. deck screws. Use two screws on each side, right and left, of every board. Keep the screws 1 in. back from the board edges to avoid splitting. Keep boards tight to each other and square to the frame as you work your way toward the bottom.

4 CUT HOLES AND INSTALL SCREW EYES FOR THE CLIMBING ROPE

At the top of the narrow wall face, measure 10-3/4 in. from each side and 2-1/4 in. down from the top board. At these marks, drill two 1-1/4-in. holes using a spade bit.

With a 1/4-in. drill bit, make two pilot holes below the center of the two 1-1/4-in. holes into the top 2x4 cross brace. These holes will receive the 5/16 x 1 x 3-in. screw eyes. Also, keep the pilot holes centered in the top edge of the 2x4 cross brace.

Install the screw eyes so they line up with the 1-1/4-in. holes. You may need to place a screwdriver in the eye of the screw for extra torque when threading it in.

Thread each 8 ft. length of rope through the face holes into screw eyes and tie off.

5 INSTALL CLIMBING HOLDS

Using a 1/2-in. drill bit, make 20 random holes in the wide wall side. Use your judgement for spacing; it never hurts to have a few extra holes for creating different layouts.

Each hold should have two mounting holes. Install each

MATERIALS LIST

ITEM	QTY.
1-5/8" deck screws (self piloting)	Varies
1" rope	16 ft.
1x6 x 8' board	15
2x4 x 8'	4
2x6 x 8'	4
3" exterior wood screws	As needed
3/8" carriage bolts	2
3/8" locking nuts	2
3/8" washers	6
4-1/2 x 12" J bolts	As needed
5/16 x 1 x 1-1/2" screw eyes	4
5/16 x 1 x 3" screw eyes	2
Kids climbing holds	20

hold snugly with one bolt at first. Then position the hold to your liking and drill again through the remaining mounting hole to install the second bolt.

6 INSTALL SCREW EYES FOR GROUND STAKES

Drill four 1/4-in. pilot holes at the foot of each leg about 1-1/2 in. from the edge and 3 in. up from the tip of the 45-degree angle. Thread in the 5/16 x 1 x 1-1/2-in. screw eyes that will receive the 12-in. J bolts for anchor stakes.

7 FINISHING TOUCHES

Sand off any rough or splintered edges on the frames. Make sure there are no high screw heads. Find a good level spot in your yard, roughly 8 ft. square and free of obstacles. With another adult, move the climbing wall into place.

Hold the kids back until you set the desired angle and drive

in the ground stakes. Then turn them loose! Be sure to spot-check the younger ones until they get the hang of it. If you already have a swing set or a play set in your

yard, you'll find this climbing wall is the perfect addition. It's a great way to keep your kids stimulated and to burn off some energy.

PRO TIP

This process will go much faster with a drill/driver or impact driver coupled with a socket or hex-head, depending on what type of bolt your holds require. (The climbing holds we ordered came with a 1/2-in. drill bit and a hex-driver bit).

STONE WALLS

MODULAR BLOCK SYSTEMS STACK UP SO EASILY THAT YOU CAN BUILD A HANDSOME, FREESTANDING WALL IN A WEEKEND.

Building a low stone wall is a simple project that will have a big impact on the front of your house. The welcoming structure will draw guests to your front door, or it can complement other yard features like patios, walkways, flower beds and arbors. But natural stone walls are expensive, and the irregular shapes and sizes of stones make them tricky to lay. A wide variety of natural-looking concrete modular blocks are available at landscaping centers. These modular wall blocks offer significant cost savings and simple installation techniques. We'll show you how to assemble one of these systems, as well as a natural stone cap, from start to finish.

CHOOSING BLOCKS AND GRAVEL

Measure the desired length of your wall and take that figure to a landscape supplier. The staff will help you calculate how many blocks you'll need based on the style you select. Order the gravel footing material at

WHAT IT TAKES	
TIME 1 weekend	**SKILL LEVEL** Beginner
TOOLS Circular saw with diamond blade, hand maul or sledgehammer, hand tamper, levels (2 ft. and 4 ft.), shovel, sod cutter (rent), wheelbarrow	

1 MARK THE LOCATION OF THE WALL

Lay out the stone on the ground to best shape the curved wall. Then mark the footprint of the wall 6 in. from both sides of the stones with marking paint.

COLUMN BASE

MARKING PAINT

2 DIG A TRENCH

Dig a trench 10 in. deep, keeping the bottom roughly level. Fine-tune the trench depth using a level and board so the blocks in each wall line up.

LEVEL BOTH WAYS

3 ADD CRUSHED LIMESTONE

Dump in 4 in. of crushed limestone, pack it, then pack in an additional 4 in. Flatten the surface and level it both ways.

4 CHECK EACH STONE FOR LEVEL

Level each successive stone with the previous one. Lower high ones by tapping lightly with a sledgehammer. Add more fill beneath low blocks.

the same time so you can have it delivered with the wall blocks. Your choice of gravel will depend on what's offered at the landscape center. The key is to select a granular material that's easy to shovel and to level, and one that will compact when you tamp it. We used Class II fill, a coarsely ground limestone combined with finer granules that packs and drains well and is easy to level. With moisture and compaction, it forms a semi-solid footing.

If Class II isn't available, you can use any type of 1/2- to 3/4-in. crushed gravel. But avoid rounded stone because it won't compact. The staff can advise you on the best available material.

Figure the footing volume by multiplying 1.6 ft. (trench width) by 0.66 ft. (8 in. depth) by the length of the trench. That'll give you the volume in cubic feet. Divide that by 27 to get the cubic yards you'll need to order.

LAY OUT THE FOOTINGS AND DIG THE TRENCH

Straight walls are easy to lay out—just use marking paint to outline a trench 6 in. wider than the width of the blocks. But if you're planning on a curved wall, first lay a row of

MATERIALS LIST

ITEM

Concrete modular blocks and block locking pins
Natural stone (cap)
Gravel footing material
Construction adhesive
Marking paint

Figure A Stone Wall details

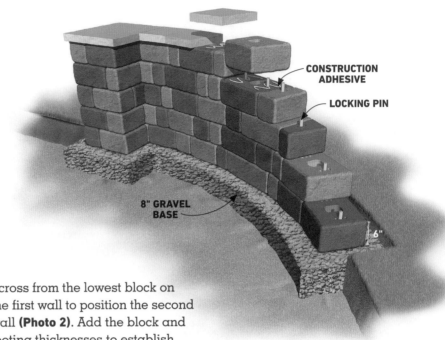

CONSTRUCTION ADHESIVE

LOCKING PIN

8" GRAVEL BASE

6"

blocks on the ground and adjust the pieces until you get the even, gradual curve that you want. Then use marking paint to mark the trench outline 6 in. from both sides of the blocks **(Photo 1)**. Remove the overlying sod and dig the trench to a depth that'll allow for 8 in. of gravel plus one-third the thickness of the first row of blocks. Our blocks were 6 in. high, so we dug down 10 in. Setting the first row of blocks slightly below the ground looks best and locks the wall into place. As you dig, check the bottom of the trench with a 4-ft. level to keep a reasonably consistent, level grade. The gravel will take care of minor variations. If your yard has a slope, begin your trench at the low end. (For steeper slopes, see "Building on Slopes" above.)

Ideally, this depth will get you through the topsoil and into solid subsoil (clay, sand or a mixture). Topsoil can settle and cause the wall to sag or lean over time. So if digging a few extra inches gets you down to subsoil, it's worth the trouble. Pack any disturbed soil at the bottom of the trench with a hand tamper before you pour in the footing material.

It looks best to match the horizontal joint lines with the lines on nearby walls. Our two walls flank a sidewalk, so we leveled

across from the lowest block on the first wall to position the second wall **(Photo 2)**. Add the block and footing thicknesses to establish the trench bottom. Use the same method later when you're packing in the footing material so the first row matches the other wall.

KEEP THE WALL TRUE

If you're using crushed gravel as your footing, just pour it in, level it, pack it and start the wall. But if the footing material contains clay or is crushed limestone like ours, add the footing in two 4-in.-deep "lifts" (layers) **(Photo 3)**. Roughly rake the first lift flat, then mist it with a garden sprayer and compact it with the hand tamper. Dampening the footing makes the material compact easier and better. Overlap each tamper footprint, working from one end of the trench to the other. Tamp it twice.

Use more care when you're leveling the second layer. Rake it flat and use a level to fine-tune the grade before tamping. Use a shorter level to ensure the footing is level across the width so the wall won't lean. Aim for a grade that varies no more than 1/8 in.

LAY THE BLOCK

The first row of blocks is critical to your wall's appearance. Small variations will create gaps and cause the wall to lean. Start your wall at ends that abut other walls or sidewalks. Alternate block sizes for variety. Be patient and level each block perfectly both ways before you set the next one **(Photo 4)**. Light taps from a sledgehammer will slightly nest blocks into the footing to help the leveling. But don't pound too hard; you could crack the block. If a block is too high to level by light tapping, remove the block and scrape away some of the gravel. If a block is too low, sprinkle in footing material, retamp and try again.

Building the rest of the wall usually takes less time than setting the base course. With each row, dry-lay the blocks with pins (no adhesive), choosing widths so the blocks straddle (offset) the seams below. This takes a bit of picking, choosing and switching sizes. You

ADHESIVE

OFFSET
JOINTS

DRY
FITTING

BLOCK
PINS

STRAIGHTEDGE

GARDEN
SPRAYER

DIAMOND
BLADE

5 SET THE NEXT ROW
Dry-fit the entire next row with locking pins. Remove each block, apply a few beads of adhesive under each and set it.

6 FIT THE CAPSTONES
Start at one end; butt the capstones together. Lay a straightedge across the joint; mark cut lines on both stones.

7 CUT AND SET THE CAPSTONES
Cut the miters with a diamond saw blade and set the capstones with beads of adhesive.

also want to get a good random mix of colors. The instructions will tell you how many pins are needed and where they should be placed. Use a screwdriver to scrape away any concrete "crumbs" that may be plugging holes.

When you're happy with the look of each row, remove the blocks one at a time, add a few beads of adhesive and set the block back into place. Keep the adhesive from the edges; it could ooze out and be visible. Use polyurethane adhesive tubes for dry blocks (or the adhesive recommended by the manufacturer). If blocks are damp, use a liquid polyurethane glue like Gorilla Glue or Elmer's Ultimate Glue—either will stick and cure on damp surfaces.

ADD THE TOP CAPSTONES

Follow the manufacturer's directions if you're capping the wall with modular units. Usually that's just a matter of fitting and gluing down the cap blocks without pins. But fitting natural stones calls for cutting as well, especially on a curved wall. The trick for tight joints is to set the stones into place and scribe the cutting lines **(Photo 6)**.

Start by laying the first stone, scribing and cutting an angle on the end if it's needed where the wall abuts a wall or column.

Cutting stone is easier than it sounds. Rest the stone on the grass. Use a diamond blade in a circular saw and follow the line with the blade, as if you were cutting wood. The stone we used was soft enough to cut in one pass with the blade all the way down. Harder stones may need several passes: first a shallow cut, then deeper cuts. It's a dusty, noisy process, so wear a dust mask, safety glasses and hearing protection. Reduce dust by having a helper aim a thin stream of water from a garden sprayer into the part of the blade that generates the most dust **(Photo 7)**.

Center the second capstone on the wall and butt it against the first. Center a straightedge over the joint. Draw cutting lines on each stone. Adjust the lines if needed to minimize waste. After cutting, set the stones in place. Add the next stone and repeat the process. Move the stones around a bit to close up small gaps, but not too much or variations in the overhangs will be obvious.

CHOOSING MODULAR BLOCK

Realistic cast wall materials rival natural stone in looks, but not, fortunately, in cost (or in tricky fitting techniques!). In fact, a modular block wall costs considerably less than a natural stone wall. Manufacturers mimic the natural appearance of stone by varying the sizes, colors and textures of each block. You mix up the blocks while assembling the wall to better mimic the random sizes of natural stone.

BLOCK PINS

Most systems offer blocks that are finished on all four sides. You'll need them for corners, especially if you build columns at the wall ends. Be sure to include capstone for the top of your wall. Most manufacturers offer thinner cast versions of the blocks for this. We decided to use natural Indiana limestone and then cut it to fit to add to the natural appearance of the wall **(Photo 7)**. However, be aware that the cost of a natural top cap can rival the cost of the block wall itself!

WHAT IT TAKES

TIME
8 hours over several days

SKILL LEVEL
Beginner

TOOLS
Basic hand tools, pressure washer (own or rent), scraper

DECK REVIVAL

A FRESH FINISH MAKES WEATHERED WOOD LOOK LIKE NEW AGAIN.

Remember how great your deck looked when it was new? Well, you can restore that look with a new finish. The basic process is simple: Remove the old finish with a chemical stripper, wash the wood with a cleaner (often called a "brightener") and apply a new finish, which may be a stain, sealer or waterproofer. You'll spend at least eight hours on this project, spread over a couple of days. Here's how to get faster, better results.

1 MAKE REPAIRS FIRST

If you have cracked or rotted deck boards or railings, replace them before you strip the deck. Putting new wood through the same stripping, cleaning and staining process as the old wood will produce a better match when the job is done. Even you may not be able to tell the new wood from the old!

2 SAVE TIME WITH A PRESSURE WASHER

To prep a deck for a fresh coat of stain, you'll have to clean it and strip away the old stain. You can get great results with a stiff brush and elbow grease, but a gas or electric pressure washer will save you hours of labor. Most pressure washers have a tank or intake tube that will add stripper or cleaner to the water as you spray.

Keep in mind that a pressure washer can damage wood. Start gently in an inconspicuous area, at a setting no higher than 1,000 psi, and hold the wand at least 12 in. from the wood. Increase the pressure or hold the wand closer if needed, but check for gouging and "fuzz" before you move on to the rest of the deck.

3 STAIN RAILINGS FIRST

Work from the top down, starting with the rail, followed by balusters and posts. Rollers and foam paint applicators are great tools for applying stain fast. But also keep a paintbrush handy; you'll need it to smooth out runs and drips. If you drip onto the deck (you will!), immediately brush the drips to avoid spotting.

MATERIALS LIST
ITEM

Deck cleaner
Replacement boards
Stain
Staining pad
2-mil plastic sheeting
Spray bottle
Stripper

4 PROTECT PLANTS

Some deck cleaners and strippers are formulated to be harmless to plants. But refinishing pros tell us that these products are often less effective than stronger cleaners. And since protecting plants is quick and easy, there's no need to avoid the most effective products. Just give nearby plants a good soaking and then cover them with 2-mil plastic sheeting. On a sunny day, plastic covering can "cook" your plants, so keep the covered-up time to a minimum. Spread the plastic right before you begin to clean and remove it immediately after.

5 SCRAPE BEFORE YOU STRIP

Stripping off the old finish is the slowest—and most tedious—part of deck refinishing. And since you never know how well a stripper will work until you try it, do a little experiment: Apply some stripper to a small area where the old stain is in fairly good condition. While you're waiting for the stripper to loosen the stain, hit another area with a paint scraper. Don't try to scrape off all the stain; just get most of it off. Then use stripper to remove the remaining stain on the scraped area. You just might find that a combination of light scraping followed by stripper is much faster and easier, especially on areas where the stain is in good shape.

6 RINSE EVERYTHING, THEN WAIT

Be sure to thoroughly rinse all the wood after you're done

stripping off the old stain. That not only washes away any leftover debris but also neutralizes stripper residue. Also rinse down any nearby surfaces that the stripper may have drifted onto.

After the final rinse, wait for the wood to dry thoroughly. Drying times depend on the weather, but expect to wait at least 48 hours. If it rains, you'll have to wait another two days. That's frustrating, but dryness is critical. Most stains won't penetrate or adhere well to damp wood. If you rush the job, the new stain will flake off and

you'll have to repeat the whole project. **EXCEPTION:** Some stains can be applied to damp wood. One example is Thompson's WaterSeal Waterproofing Stain.

7 APPLY STAIN WITH A SPRAYER

If you have lattice or other hard-to-coat surfaces, put some stain in a spray bottle. To avoid runs, set the spray at a wide pattern and apply a light coating; you can always add more stain if the color is too light. Keep a paintbrush handy so you can smooth out runs.

WHAT IT TAKES

TIME
2 hours

SKILL LEVEL
Beginner

TOOLS
Basic hand tools, circular saw, drill, jigsaw, level, table saw (optional)

BUILD-A-BOX BIKE RACK

//
GET YOUR BIKE UP AND OUT OF THE WAY WITH JUST
A COUPLE OF HOURS OF WORK.

Finding space to store your bike can be challenging
enough if you have a garage, but if you're an
apartment dweller, you likely get tired of tripping over
it. This simple project gets your bike off the floor and
out of your way, and it even has an accessory drawer
for tools, gloves and other gear. Plus, you can take the
rack with you when you move, and it leaves just two
tiny holes in the wall—no worries about losing your
damage deposit! It's a great starter project, so
be creative and have fun.

A DRAWER
FOR YOUR
STUFF

ADD A KNOB

Before you start, set your bike on the floor and
test different heights for the optimal setback from
windows or doors. If it will be in a traffic area,
allow enough room to walk by it. Also measure
your bike to be sure the frame will fit the rack's
12-in. width. You may have to modify the rack for
some kids' and women's bikes.

Figure A Bike Rack
OVERALL DIMENSIONS: 16"L x 12"W x 7"H

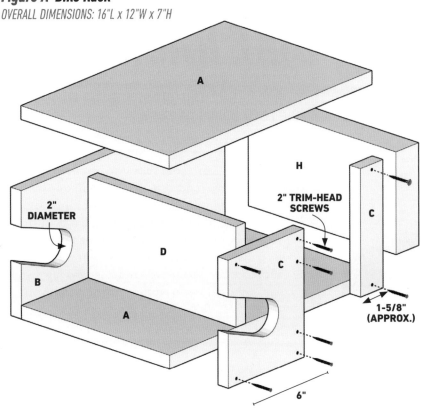

2"
DIAMETER

2" TRIM-HEAD
SCREWS

1-5/8"
(APPROX.)

6"

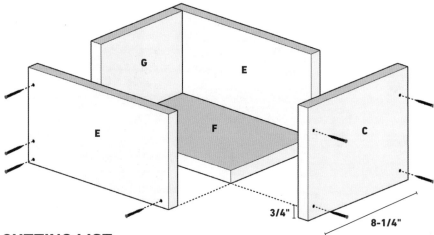

3/4"

8-1/4"

BUYING MATERIALS

Any type of plywood will work for this project, so your choice depends on the look you want. Birch plywood is a good option if you plan to paint the bike rack. Any plywood you buy at a home center will have "voids" in the core that will show up as gaps in the cut edges, but you can easily patch those gaps with wood filler. You'll also need a short scrap of 2x6. Most home centers have a scrap pile where you can get cutoffs super cheap.

BUILDING TIPS

A table saw and miter saw are best for cutting parts, but a circular saw also works. For a guide to perfect cuts with a circular saw, go to familyhandyman.com and search for "saw guide."

Figure B Cutting Diagram

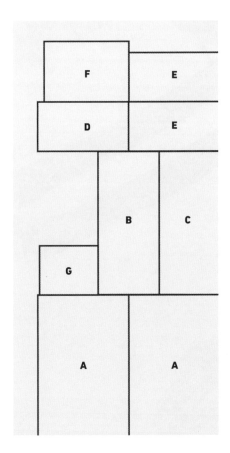

CUTTING LIST

KEY	QTY.	PART
A	2	3/4" plywood 3/4" x 10-1/2" x 16" Top and base
B	1	3/4" plywood 3/4" x 7" x 16" Side
C	1	3/4" plywood 3/4" x 7" x 16" (cut into 3) Drawer front and side pieces
D	1	3/4" plywood 3/4" x 5-1/2" x 10-1/2" Divider
E	2	3/4" plywood 3/4" x 5-1/2" x 10-1/2" Drawer sides
F	1	3/4" plywood 3/4" x 9-3/4" x 6-3/4" Drawer bottom
G	1	3/4" plywood 3/4" x 5-1/2" x 6-3/4" Drawer back
H	1	2x6 board 1-1/2" x 5-1/2" x 10-3/8" Cleat

MATERIALS LIST

ITEM	QTY.
3/4" x 2' x 4' plywood	1
2x6 board, at least 10-1/2" long	1
2" trim-head screws	23
Wood glue	7
Drawer pull/knob	1
3" construction screw	2

1 MARK THE TUBE SLOTS

With all your parts cut according to the Cutting List, mark the sides **(B and C)** as shown above. Center a caulk tube on the crosshairs and draw a circle. Draw parallel lines from the top and bottom of the circle.

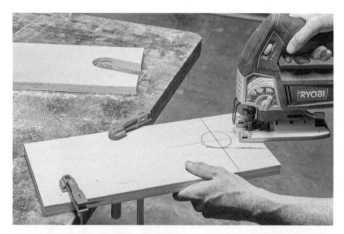

2 CUT THE SLOTS

To create the tube slots, use a jigsaw to follow the lines you made in the previous step.

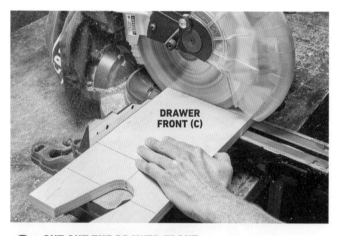

3 CUT OUT THE DRAWER FRONT

Cut side **C** to form three parts: the drawer front and the two side pieces. Locate the cuts so the drawer front is exactly 8-1/4 in. wide.

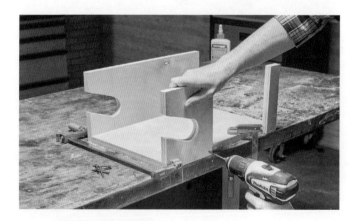

4 ATTACH THE SIDES

Glue, clamp and screw side **B** to the base. Then glue and screw the two side pieces (from **C**) to the base.

5 INSERT THE DIVIDER

Set the divider **(D)** flush and square with the side pieces. Clamp the assembly, and glue and screw the divider into the box.

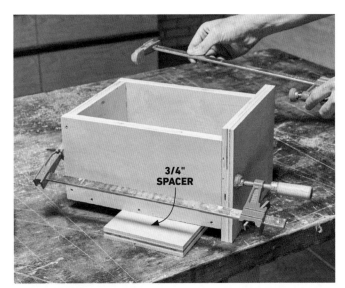

6 ATTACH THE TOP
Glue and screw the top into place. Due to differences in plywood thickness, expect a small gap between the top and the divider **(D)**.

7 ASSEMBLE THE DRAWER
Glue and screw the drawer box together. Then rest the box on a scrap of 3/4-in. plywood spacer and attach the drawer front.

8 SCREW THE CLEAT TO A STUD
Mark the stud with masking tape. Screw the top screw into the cleat **(H)** with a 3-in. construction screw. Fine-tune the cleat to make sure it's level, then add the second screw.

9 ATTACH THE RACK TO THE CLEAT
Hold the rack tight against the wall and drive four screws (two on the top, two on the bottom) into the 2x6 cleat.

- Bar clamps that open to at least 12 in. are helpful for this project, but they are definitely not essential.
- Most trim-head screws are self-drilling, but to avoid splitting the plywood, it's best if you first drill pilot holes.

FINISHING
You can finish your bike rack any way you wish—paint it to match your walls, customize it as we did or even just don't finish it. We started with a base of white enamel paint and then added pieces of plastic laminate, which we cut with a utility knife and applied with contact cement.

If you want to paint your rack, we recommend priming it first, then using acrylic paints available at any crafts store. Apply water-based polyurethane if you'd like a glossy finish that's smooth to the touch.

EASY KITCHEN SHELF

THIS IS SIMPLE FOR ANYONE TO BUILD—AND FUN TO CUSTOMIZE!

Lots of kitchens have a little wall space that would be perfect for a storage or display shelf. Plenty of bathrooms do, too, so we wanted to design a shelf that anyone with basic tools could build. This one is a great project for a beginning woodworker, and because it's so easy to adapt to different uses, a more advanced DIYer can have a lot of fun customizing it.

TOOLS AND WOOD
You'll need a jigsaw, a drill and two accessories for the drill. The first is a No. 8 combination drill bit and countersink (see "Low-Tech Woodworking" on

the next page). The second is a small sanding drum **(see Photo 3)**. The only other tool you might need is a nail set for setting the heads of finish nails below the surface of the wood. Obviously, if you have a band

WHAT IT TAKES	
TIME	**SKILL LEVEL**
1/2 day	Beginner

TOOLS
Basic hand tools, drill with a combination bit and countersink and a sanding drum, jigsaw, nail set

LOW-TECH WOODWORKING

This is a low-tech project. A jigsaw and a cordless drill are the only power tools you need, though there are more accurate and faster options. You'll also need some basic hand tools and two specialized accessories for the drill: a sanding drum and a combination drill bit/countersink. (See the text for more info.)

COMBO DRILL/COUNTER-SINK

SANDING DRUM

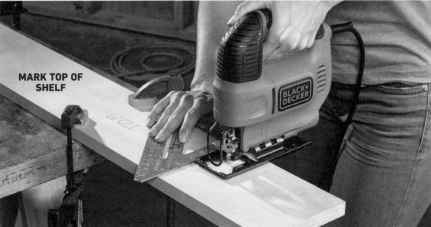

MARK TOP OF SHELF

1 CUT THE SHELF TO LENGTH

Use a fresh blade and a square to guide your cut. A miter saw is the best tool for the job, but if you don't have access to one, you can substitute almost any other saw.

saw and a miter saw, they will make this project a piece of cake.

You can build this shelf from just about any type of wood. Resist the urge to use the least expensive knotty pine, unless that's the look you're after. Knotty pine will be harder to work with and to paint. Instead, get clear pine, poplar or any other knot-free board. If you're planning to paint the shelf, avoid oak. We used alder.

CUT OUT THE SHELF AND BRACKETS

Begin by cutting the shelf to length with a jigsaw (Photo 1). Then cut a piece 6 in. long from which you can cut the two brackets (Photo 2). Jigsaws often make a rougher cut on the top surface, so label that "top." The roughness will be hidden by the edging, even if the top of the shelf is visible after hanging it. But use a fine-tooth blade and set your oscillating feature (if your saw has it) to zero.

You can create the curve for the brackets from the pattern, or use the bottom of a coffee can or a small plate. The exact curve isn't important. After the brackets are cut, smooth the sawn edges with a file, sanding block and the sanding drum in your drill (Photo 3). You can stop sanding at about 150 or 180 grit.

ADD EDGING STRIPS

Start edging the shelf by cutting the end strips to length. Instead of measuring, just hold the molding

MATERIALS LIST

ITEM	QTY.
1x6 clear paint-grade softwood or hardwood	3'
7/16" x 1-1/4" pine stop molding	3'
1-1/4" drywall or utility screws	4
3/4" x 3/4" corner braces or brackets	2
Plastic or metal screw-in drywall anchors	2
Aerosol paint	1 can
Sandpaper	As needed
Wood glue	As needed

Figure A Easy Kitchen Shelf exploded view

OVERALL DIMENSIONS: 20-7/8"W x 5-15/16"D x 1-1/4"H

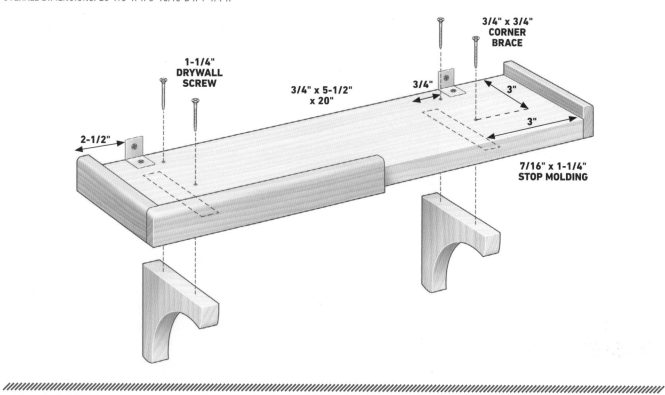

3/4" x 3/4"
CORNER BRACE

1-1/4"
DRYWALL SCREW

3/4" x 5-1/2"
x 20"

3/4"

3"

3"

2-1/2"

7/16" x 1-1/4"
STOP MOLDING

Figure B Bracket

OVERALL DIMENSIONS: 3/4"W x 5-1/2"D x 4-3/4"H

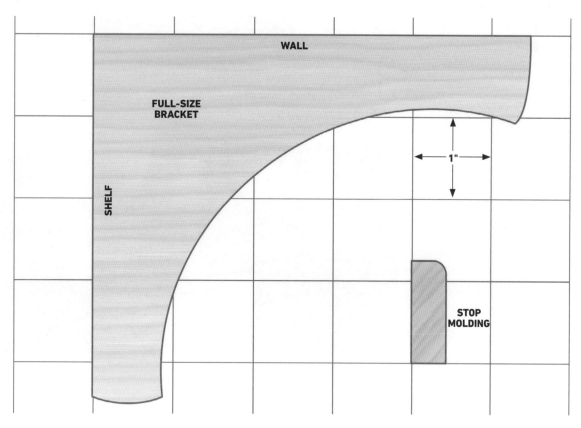

WALL

FULL-SIZE BRACKET

SHELF

1"

STOP MOLDING

to the end of the shelf and mark it for cutting. It won't hurt if it's a hair too long. Mark one edge of the shelf as the front edge, then nail on the side strips **(Photo 4)**, keeping the front edge flush. Make sure the rounded edge faces out, put a thin bead of glue on the shelf edge before nailing and keep the bottom edge as flush as you can. If the strips are a little long in back, you can easily sand or file off the excess, and if they stick out a little on the bottom edge, that can be sanded off, too. Finally, nail on the edging strip in front.

Now set the nails and put a little painter's putty on them. When the putty is dry, sand the edging so the corners are smooth and the bottom edge is flush with the shelf. The bottom of the shelf will have a seam between the shelf and the edging. It's pretty much impossible to eliminate that seam permanently. Expansion and contraction of the wood will open it up even if you caulk or putty it, so don't be too much of a perfectionist. However, if your cut on the 1x6 is particularly rough, some putty there will help clean things up.

SCREW THE BRACKETS TO THE SHELF

The next step is to drill some screw holes in the shelf for attaching the brackets. The idea is simple: two screw holes on each side of the shelf so you can screw down into the brackets. Here's what to do: First, hold a bracket where you want it to be, but on the top of the shelf. Trace around the bracket, then do the same thing for the other bracket. Mark the screw locations and drill screw holes in the shelf from the top, using your combination countersink/drill bit. Now hold a bracket in position on the bottom of the shelf, making

2 CUT THE CURVED BRACKETS
For a curve like this, a smooth continuous cut is more important than following the line exactly. Any bumps or blips that occur will be hard to sand out.

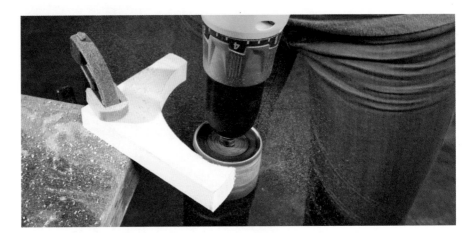

3 SAND THE CURVES WITH A SANDING DRUM
The trick is to go against the direction of the rotation of the drill, with the drill going fast. If you make a gouge, angle the drum slightly to remove it.

4 NAIL ON THE EDGING
The edging is a stock molding from home centers. It keeps stuff from falling off the shelf and covers the rough ends.

sure the back edge is flush with the back edge of the shelf and that the screw holes are centered on the bracket. You can do it by eye, but if that's hard, put the two screws in their holes and use the points of the screws to guide you. Drive the screws by hand into the bracket **(Photo 5)**, then repeat with the other bracket. Now is a good time to step back and admire your work, because you're almost done. But if for some reason you messed this part up, just drill new holes and fill the old ones with putty. You can shift the position of the brackets if you want.

PAINT YOUR SHELF

Begin this part of the project by unscrewing the brackets. It's always easier to paint a project well if you can do the parts separately. Sand the pieces thoroughly to about 150 to 180 grit, removing sharp edges and corners but not rounding them over too much. Wipe off the sanding dust with a rag and vacuum the parts thoroughly. Now set up your painting area. We highly recommend using spray paint for this project because it'll get you the smoothest finish.

Cover your work surface with paper or plastic, and set your shelf on strips or blocks to get it up off the surface. The shelf is pretty easy to paint, but go light on the edges to avoid drips. After the first coat of paint is thoroughly dry, sand it lightly with fine sandpaper just enough to take off any roughness. Wipe and vacuum, then apply two final coats.

There's a trick to painting the brackets: Drive a long screw in one of the holes and use it as a little handle. That way you can spray the whole piece evenly in one shot **(Photo 6)**. Then carefully set it down on a couple strips of

wood to dry. When the paint is dry, reassemble your shelf.

HANG YOUR SHELF

Use small angle brackets to hang your shelf **(Photo 7)**. Normally the top of a shelf is above eye level and the small brackets are hidden, especially with items on the shelf. If your brackets are more exposed, give them a little spray paint to match the shelf and paint the part that goes on your wall to match your wall. They'll be barely noticeable. Generally, though, this step isn't necessary.

To hang the shelf, use drywall anchors. Don't worry about hitting studs; there shouldn't be enough weight on this shelf to require it. Just put the shelf where you want it to go, make sure it's level, mark through the brackets where the anchors will go and install the anchors. If it seems as if you need a third hand to manage everything, you could draw a level line on the wall where the shelf will go. With the anchors in place, use the screws that came with the anchors to attach the shelf.

5 SCREW THE BRACKETS TO THE SHELF
Notice that we've traced the shape of the bracket on the top of the shelf to help position the screw holes. We used a combination countersink/drill bit for the holes.

6 SPRAY-PAINT THE SHELF PARTS
You'll get better results by unscrewing the brackets and painting everything separately. A screw in the top of the bracket is a handy handle.

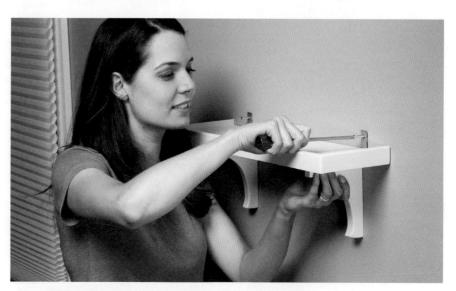

7 HANG YOUR SHELF WITH SMALL ANGLE BRACKETS
For a light-duty shelf like this one, you don't need to screw it to studs. Just make sure the shelf is level and use drywall anchors in the wall.

WHAT IT TAKES

TIME
4-5 days

SKILL LEVEL
Beginner

TOOLS
Basic hand tools, drill driver, paintbrushes, roller arms, spray-painting equipment (optional)

MATERIALS LIST

ITEM

Rosin paper
Grease remover
Sandpaper
Tack cloth
Primer
Green abrasive pad
Paint
Cone filter
Shellac in a spray can

PAINT CABINETS

//

USE THIS GUIDE TO LEARN THE PROPER TECHNIQUES AND TOOLS FOR A PROFESSIONAL-LOOKING FINISH.

If you want to upgrade your kitchen without spending a lot of money, painting your kitchen cabinets is the perfect DIY solution. Water-based paints like acrylic alkyds and acrylic urethanes have made it much easier to get a durable, professional-looking result. These finishes can be cleaned up with water and don't make your house smell like a chemical factory. And quality tools like mini rollers and good consumer-grade sprayers allow even beginners to get pro results.

1 PROTECT COUNTERTOPS WITH ROSIN PAPER

Painting cabinets is a messy job, and the last thing you want is paint all over your countertops. An easy way to protect your countertops, backsplash and floor is to cover them with inexpensive rosin or brown builder's paper. When you're done in the kitchen, you'll have plenty of paper left for future painting projects.

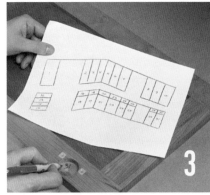

2 REMOVE DOORS, DRAWER FRONTS AND HARDWARE

We've all seen painting projects where the hinges and hardware are covered with paint and paint is slopped over drawer interiors. It's tempting to leave the doors in place for painting, but you'll get much neater and more professional-looking results by removing them along with all the hardware. On many modern cabinets, drawer fronts can be removed from the drawer by backing out a few screws. But if your drawer fronts are part of the drawer and can't be removed, use masking tape to cover the drawer sides and bottom if you don't want to paint them.

NOTE:
Want to speed up the project? Choose a fast-drying primer for the first coat. Read the label for information on recoating time and to make sure the primer is compatible with the paint you're planning to use.

PRO TIP
Water-based paint has come a long way, and some top-quality acrylic alkyd hybrids rival oil-based paint. Still, many pro painters prefer oil-based paint, especially for priming. Oil-based paint dries slowly and levels well. This gives you more working time and fewer brush marks. Also, when they're dry, oil-based primers, like Benjamin Moore Fresh Start Enamel Underbody, sand easily to provide a perfect base for your finish coat.

3 LABEL DOORS

Start by making a quick sketch or two showing all the doors and drawers. Number them however you want. Then as you remove the doors and drawers, label them with the corresponding numbers. Write each number under the hinge location where it won't be visible. Then cover the numbers with masking tape to protect them while you're painting.

4 GET THE GREASE OFF

Even the best paint won't stick to greasy cabinets. So the first critical step in preparing your cabinets for paint is to clean them with a grease-cutting solution. Dishwashing liquid will work, but a dedicated grease remover like TSP substitute is even better. Mix according to the instructions and scrub the cabinets. Then rinse them with clear water and wipe them dry with a clean rag.

5 DON'T GO OVERBOARD ON SANDING CABINETS

You should sand cabinets before painting them to give the new paint a good surface to grip. But you don't need to sand to bare wood. If your cabinets have a factory finish, sand lightly with 120-grit sandpaper or a sanding sponge. If the surface is rough from a previous paint job or poor varnishing job, start with coarser 100-grit paper to remove bumps. Then sand again with 120-grit to get rid of any sanding marks.

6 CONSIDER FILLING OPEN GRAIN

Some types of wood, like oak, have grain with many open pores. The pores show through finishes and are especially noticeable under paint. It's OK to leave the grain showing, but if you want a grain-free look, you have to fill the pores before painting. There are a few methods. You can apply several coats of a high-build primer, sanding between coats until the pores are filled. Or you can fill the grain with spackling as shown here. If your cabinets have a lot of curves and molded edges, filling them with spackling is more difficult. Then when the filler dries, sand and prime to finish the job.

7 VACUUM AND THEN USE A TACK CLOTH

To ensure a smooth paint job and good adhesion, it's critical that you remove all the sanding dust from the doors, drawer fronts and cabinet frames. Start by vacuuming everything using a soft bristle brush attachment. This removes loose dust, but you still need to get rid of the rest.

The traditional painter's method is to use tack cloths. You can buy them in packs at home centers. To use a tack cloth, completely unfold it and loosely bunch it up. Wipe it gently over the surface to pick up dust. Shake it out frequently and re-form the bundle to use it again. When the cloth has lost its dust-grabbing ability, throw it away and get a new one.

8 SUPPORT DOORS ON STANDOFFS

At paint stores or home centers you can buy plastic painter's pyramids or tripods that work great for supporting doors while you paint them. Or you can make your own standoffs: Drive 2-in. screws through 3-in.-square scraps of plywood. If you don't mind having a few barely visible dimples on the back of each door, you can paint both sides of a door at once using standoffs.

Here's how: Paint the back first, leaving the edges unpainted

so you'll have a spot to put your fingers when you turn the door over. Then flip the door over and rest it on the screw tips. Now you can paint the door edges and front, then let the door dry. If you look hard, you can spot tiny indentations where the screws contact the wet paint, but they're inconspicuous.

9 DOUBLE-CHECK FOR DEFECTS AFTER PRIMING

The first paint-prep step after cleaning grease from cabinets is usually filling unwanted holes, dents and dings with spackling or wood filler. After sanding, getting rid of dust and priming the cabinets, it's a good idea to check everything with a bright light to spot and fill any remaining holes or dents. It's usually easier to spot these problems after priming.

We prefer filling with an oil-based spackling compound like MH Ready Patch because it sticks well and dries hard for a

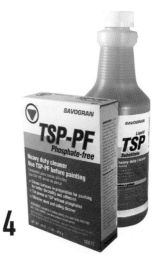

durable repair. But other fillers will also work. The downside of this additional round of spackling is that you'll have to reprime the patched areas.

10 SAND LIGHTLY BETWEEN COATS

Dust can settle in paint or primer as it dries. To achieve the smoothest final coat, sand between coats of primer or paint with 220-grit sandpaper or an extra-fine sanding sponge. Then vacuum and wipe with a tack cloth as usual before recoating.

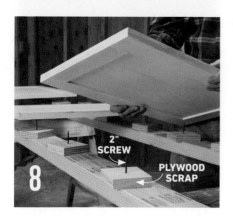

120-GRIT SANDING SPONGE

5

OAK DOOR

SPACKLING COMPOUND

6

TACK CLOTH

7

2" SCREW

PLYWOOD SCRAP

8

9

10

11

12

NOTE:
If you like to paint with a brush, you can speed things up by first applying the paint with a mini roller. Roll on the paint. Then drag the paint bristles lightly over the surface to even out the coat and eliminate roller marks.

FOAM MINI ROLLER

11 PAINT WITH A MINI ROLLER

A good painter can work wonders with a brush, but for most of us a mini roller is a great alternative. Mohair, microfiber or foam are good choices. Foam gives the smoothest finish but doesn't hold much paint, so you'll be reloading frequently. Experiment with the different types on the insides of doors to see which works best.

12 IMPROVE THE PAINT FLOW

If your paint seems too thick and isn't leveling out after it's applied, try mixing in a paint conditioner like Floetrol. Read the instructions carefully to determine the correct proportion of conditioner to paint. You'll find that conditioned paint is often easier to apply and dries to a smoother finish.

13 STRAIN YOUR PAINT

Some pros suggest that even fresh paint should be strained before use to remove any small lumps that could mar the paint job. If you don't want to go to this extreme, you should at least filter any leftover paint you plan to use and any paint from a can that's been used. You can buy paper cone filters in any paint department.

14 SCUFF UP PROFILES WITH A PAD

When you're sanding a smooth finish to get a better surface for paint, use a green abrasive pad on the molded profiles. Sandpaper doesn't conform well enough to get into the intricate spots. An abrasive pad does.

15 BUY A TOP-QUALITY BRUSH

If you decide to paint with a brush, splurge on a good one. For cabinets, a 2-in. brush is perfect. Keep it clean and it will last for many jobs. Paint stores usually offer the widest selection and the best advice.

13

14

15

PRO TIP
When using water-based paints, it's easier to clean your brush if you dampen it with water before you start painting.

16

PRO TIP
If you are paint-
ing frame-and-
panel doors,
follow the direc-
tion of the wood
grain with your
finishing brush-
strokes. The
vertical stiles
should receive
the last brush-
strokes running
from top to
bottom.

17

16 WIPE THE EDGES

When you're painting the edge of a cabinet door, it's easy to apply too much paint and create a buildup along the edge. To avoid a dried ridge of paint along the door edge, smooth out any paint that's lapped over onto the adjoining surface with a paintbrush or small sponge brush.

17 WORRIED ABOUT ADHESION? TRY ACRYLIC URETHANE

An acrylic urethane product such as Rust-Oleum's XIM UMA has many properties that make it a perfect choice for priming kitchen cabinets. First, it sticks tenaciously to almost any surface. In fact, you could even paint over plastic laminate cabinets when you prime with acrylic urethane. Second, it cures to a very hard and durable finish, and you can cover it with your choice of paint.

Another option to consider: You could use acrylic urethane paint such as Benjamin Moore's Insl-X Cabinet Coat as the final coat. This paint is formulated specifically for use on cabinets.

18 CONSIDER SPRAY-PAINTING

With a little practice and a good sprayer, you can achieve factory-finish quality by spraying your doors. A pro-quality airless sprayer will work best to spray unthinned water-based finishes. But you can also get great results with a high-volume, low-pressure (HVLP) sprayer as long as you thin the paint according to the instructions and apply several thin coats rather than one thick one.

19 SPOT-PRIME WITH SHELLAC

Pigmented shellac in a spray can such as BIN is perfect for spot-priming places you missed or areas patched, sanded and needing primer. Shellac adheres to most finishes, plus it dries fast and covers well.

NOTE:
Read the label and choose paint that's formu-lated for painting woodwork and cabinets. And remember that glossier sur-faces highlight imperfections, so unless you're a very meticu-lous painter, consider an eggshell or a satin sheen.

18

19

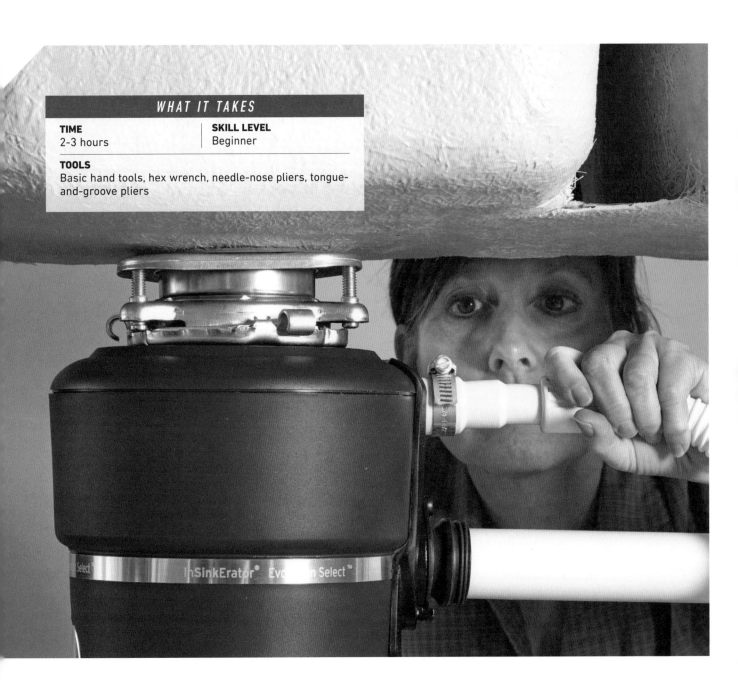

WHAT IT TAKES

TIME
2-3 hours

SKILL LEVEL
Beginner

TOOLS
Basic hand tools, hex wrench, needle-nose pliers, tongue-and-groove pliers

REPLACE A GARBAGE DISPOSAL

HERE ARE 13 WAYS TO AVOID LEAKS AND MISTAKES.

When you flip the switch to turn on the garbage disposal and all you get is a hum—or a loud, metal-on-metal grinding noise—you know something's wrong. Maybe it's just trash stuck in the disposal, but there's also a chance that the unit is dead, kaput, never to dispose again.

Fortunately, replacing a disposal isn't hard, even if you haven't done much plumbing. Manufacturers provide clear instructions that tell you most of the things you need to know—but not everything. We talked to veteran plumbers and collected their best tips for a smooth, trouble-free installation.

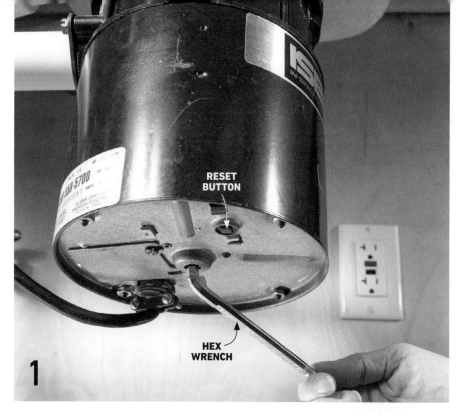

RESET BUTTON

HEX WRENCH

1

SINK FLANGE

FIBER GASKET

BACKUP FLANGE

UPPER MOUNTING RING

SNAP RING

LOWER MOUNTING RING

2

1 *IS IT REALLY BROKEN?*

A disposal that seems dead might be revived with an easy fix. Here are three things to try:

■ Look for a jam. Something too tough to grind, such as a piece of glass, could be jamming the motor. Turn off the power and water, then unplug the disposal. (If it's hardwired, turn off the power at the breaker.) Remove the rubber baffle inside the drain—most baffles just lift out—and shine a flashlight into the hole. Then fish out the obstruction with a pair of tongs or needle-nose pliers.

■ Turn the motor manually. You'll need a hex wrench. Some disposals come with one bent at a convenient angle, but if you don't have it, you can buy one at a hardware store or use a standard Allen wrench. Rotate the wrench back and forth as shown above until the motor turns a full revolution, then remove the wrench and switch on the motor.

■ Press the reset button. If your motor has overheated from working too long, wait 5 minutes

for it to cool down and push the reset button (it's usually located on the underside of the disposal). It's possible the motor may also have overheated because of a jam. If the motor doesn't start after manually turning it, try pushing the reset button.

2 *FIGURE IT OUT FIRST*

When you buy a new disposal, the box will contain all the parts you need to install it. But before you jump into removing the old unit, take a few moments to familiarize yourself with all of the

various parts. Assemble them in the correct order and try out the locking mechanism. Understanding how everything fits together ahead of time will make the installation job go much more smoothly and you'll be less likely to make an error.

3 *UNDERSTANDING DISPOSAL SYSTEM ANATOMY*

If you have a double sink, the best way to plumb a disposal is to run its discharge tube directly to a tee below the opposite sink. The tube must drop about 1/4 in. in order to drain properly.

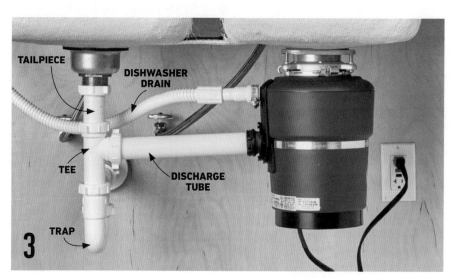

TAILPIECE

DISHWASHER DRAIN

TEE

DISCHARGE TUBE

TRAP

3

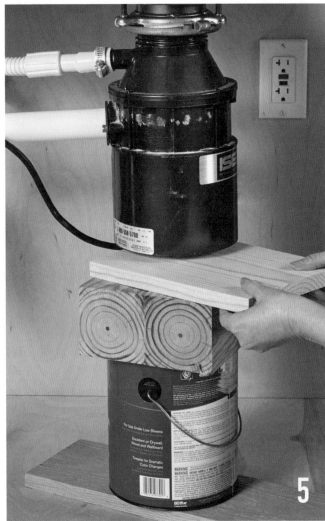

4 KNOCK OUT THE KNOCKOUT!

Everyone who's installed a few disposals is aware of this mistake: forgetting to remove the dishwasher knockout before hanging the unit.

If you have a dishwasher, the first thing you should do after removing the disposal from the box is to punch out the knockout with a hammer and a screwdriver. Fish out the knockout by reaching down inside the disposal. You don't want this plastic disc to be the first thing that the disposal tries to grind up!

This is also the best time to add the cord and plug to your disposal. It's really awkward to add these after the disposal is installed.

5 SUPPORT THE WEIGHT

Garbage disposals can weigh 15 lbs. or more. That's a lot of weight to catch suddenly with one hand while you're turning the lower mounting bracket with the other hand.

Before you unhook anything, assemble a support under the unit using a paint can and scraps of wood. Leave a 1/4- to 1/2-in. gap under the unit so it can drop a bit. Use the same support to help you install the new disposal.

6 DON'T FORGET THE CORD

Surprise! Most new disposals don't come with a cord and plug. If your old unit has a cord and plug, you can remove the whole assembly and reinstall it on the new unit. (Instructions are included with the new disposal.) Or you can simply buy a new cord and plug when you buy the disposal. They're usually located together in the store.

If you're not comfortable making electrical connections, you can buy a disposal that already has a cord attached. Ask at your home center or appliance store, or search online for "garbage disposal with cord attached."

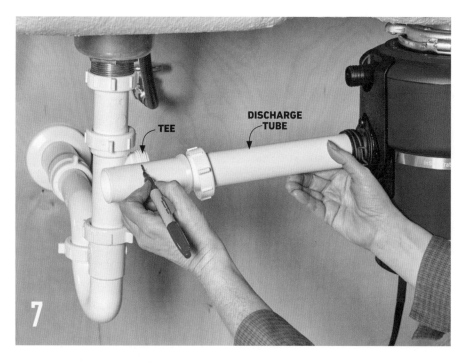

TEE

DISCHARGE TUBE

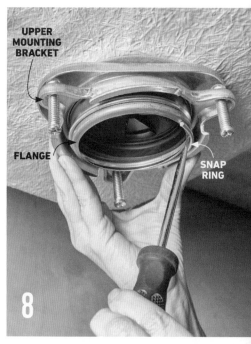

UPPER MOUNTING BRACKET

FLANGE

SNAP RING

7 PREPARE FOR A NEW DISCHARGE TUBE

Your old discharge tube probably won't be the right length for your new disposal. If it's too long, simply connect it to the disposal, mark it and cut it with a hacksaw. (Loosen the other pipe connections, if necessary, to insert the tube back into the tee.) If the old discharge tube is too short, you may have to make a time-wasting trip to the store. To avoid this, make sure the new disposal includes a tube or buy one separately at the same time.

8 DON'T STRUGGLE WITH THE SNAP RING

The snap ring fits into a groove on the lower end of the sink flange. When you're working under the sink, it prevents the upper mounting ring from falling off. Removing an old snap ring can be frustrating—unless you know this trick: Starting at the break in the snap ring, insert a thin-blade screwdriver between the ring and the flange. Pull down on the ring with the screwdriver's blade and walk the blade around the ring. The ring will pop right off.

9 WEIGHT DOWN THE FLANGE

After you install the new sink flange, you don't want it shifting around when you're assembling the parts underneath. Movement of the flange could break the seal between the flange and the sink, inviting a leak.

Your best bet is to ask a helper to press down on the sink flange, or if you're working alone, find something to weight it down, such as the old disposal. Place an old towel under the weight so you don't scratch the sink. If the bottom of your sink is quite concave, the old disposal might not contact the flange. In that case, place a can on the flange, and then weight down the can.

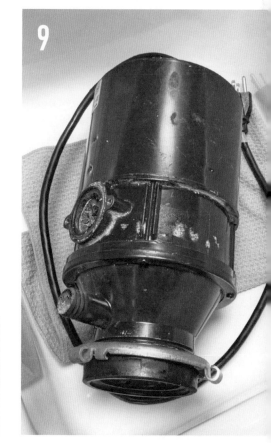

PRO TIP
If your old sink flange is undamaged and tight, with no signs of leakage, you can probably leave it in place. Chances are good that the mounting brackets on the new unit will fit just fine. To find out, remove the old disposal and install the new flange on it. If it fits, you can install the new disposal using the old flange.

10 TIGHTEN WITH PLIERS

When you hang the new disposal, rotating the lower mounting ring tightens the seal between the disposal and the sink flange. The lower ring rides up a set of ramps on the upper ring—pretty neat! But the final inch or so of rotation requires a fair amount of force.

The easiest way to apply that force is to squeeze them together using tongue-and-groove pliers, such as Channellocks. You'll need medium or large pliers to do this. Unlike prying on the lower ring with a screwdriver or hex wrench—the method recommended in most instruction sheets—squeezing can't disturb the position of the sink flange and cause it to leak. Plus, it's easier on the wrists.

11 COMPARE OUTLET HEIGHTS

A disposal's discharge tube must slant about 1/4 in. downhill in order to drain properly (see **Photo 3**). Creating that drop may be a small problem if the outlet on your new disposal is lower than the outlet on your old one (as shown in **Photo 11**). To be prepared, measure the distance from the outlet to the top of each disposal before you remove the old unit. If the new unit's outlet is lower, you must also lower the tee that the discharge pipe connects to. Loosen the two nuts that connect the tee to the tailpiece above and the trap below. Try lowering the tee to see if the tailpiece is long enough. If it's not, you'll have to replace it with one that's slightly longer.

12 SILICONE SEALS BEST

Plumber's putty is typically recommended for sealing the sink flange to the sink itself, but silicone will provide a more reliable seal. With silicone, there's almost no chance—now or later—that the flange will leak.

However, when it's time to replace the disposal and the sink flange again, you should know that old silicone is much harder to remove than old plumber's putty. But that's why it works better!

13 INSPECT THE PLUMBING FIRST

Look over all the pipes under your sink for any sign of leakage before heading to the store to buy a new garbage disposal. You may want to replace more than just the disposal itself, so you might as well make a list and be prepared!

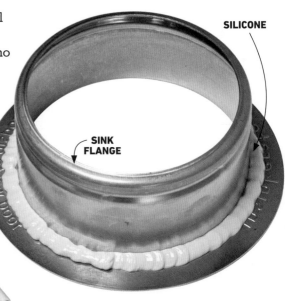

SILICONE

SINK FLANGE

A

FLIP-FLOP
STEP STOOL

RIDICULOUSLY SIMPLE STOOLS

THESE THREE STOOLS ARE INSPIRED BY THE CONCEPT "SIMPLER IS BETTER."

We love projects that allow us to walk into a workshop with a few boards under one arm and then walk out a few hours later with something sturdy, useful and attractive—in other words, simple projects. Here are three stool projects inspired by that "simpler is better" concept, and all are doable in less than half a day.

WHAT IT TAKES

TIME	SKILL LEVEL
2 hours	Beginner

TOOLS
Basic hand tools, drill, jigsaw, router, 1/4-in. round-over bit

The projects have a few things in common: They're all stools, they're all made with dimensional lumber or plywood, and they're all better looking because they've been "dressed up" with the use of a round-over router bit.

How often do we use that bit? Often enough that we have it in a dedicated router so it's always ready to go. Round-over bits have a way of making jigsaw cuts look smoother, straight cuts look straighter, cheap wood look classier and paint jobs look better. Round-over bits also make wood furniture more comfortable to sit on and touch.

A. FLIP-FLOP STEP STOOL

With the back swung up, it's a perfect chair for little kids to plunk down on. With the back swung down, it's a perfect step stool for reaching slightly out-of-reach faucets, shelves and cabinets—for kids of all ages.

Begin by cutting the two sides to length and laying out the boards **(Photo 1** and **Figure A)**. Note that the sides will be mirror images.

To mark the curved sides, hook your tape over the lower corners and then swing 15-in.-radius curves on each side. Use a pint can to create the rounded inner edges of the legs. The positions of the pivot and dowel holes are critical, so measure carefully. The pivot holes go all the way through the board, but the dowel hole is only 1/2 in. deep. Drill the holes, and then use a jigsaw to cut out the parts. Use a 1/4-in. round-over bit or sandpaper to soften all the edges.

Connect the 1x10 bottom shelf and 1x4 back brace to create an L shape. Secure this assembly to the sides so the top edge of the 1x4 is flush with the upper back corner of the sides. Use 2x4 blocks to ensure

1 MARK THE TWO SIDE PIECES
Use a tape measure to swing and mark arcs for the edges as shown in **Figure A**, then mark the holes for the pivot screws and the back dowel stop.

TEMPORARY 2x4 PROP BLOCKS

2 ASSEMBLE THE STOOL WITH 2-IN. SCREWS
First screw the back brace to the bottom shelf to create an L shape, then secure this assembly to the sides. Drill the holes for the pivot screws and the back dowel stop.

1x6 BACK

BACK DOWEL STOP

1x4 BACK BRACE

2" BOLTS WITH LOCKNUTS

WASHERS

3 INSTALL THE BACK
Screw the back to the pivot arms to create a U-shape. Drill the holes in the pivot arms, then secure the back using 2-in. bolts, washers and nuts. Don't permanently fasten the top until you've "test swiveled" the back to make sure you have enough clearance.

Figure A Flip-Flop Step Stool

OVERALL DIMENSIONS: 16-3/8" W x 15" D x 16" H (IN CHAIR MODE)

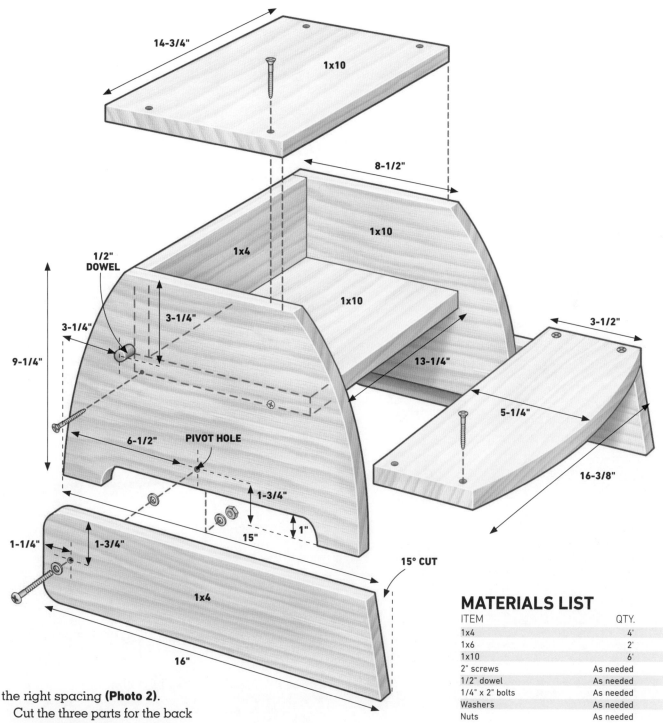

MATERIALS LIST

ITEM	QTY.
1x4	4'
1x6	2'
1x10	6'
2" screws	As needed
1/2" dowel	As needed
1/4" x 2" bolts	As needed
Washers	As needed
Nuts	As needed

the right spacing **(Photo 2)**.

Cut the three parts for the back assembly **(Figure A)**. To create the curved back, drive a pair of finish nails 3-1/2 in. from the edge of a 1x6, and flex a thin piece of wood upward between the nails to create an arc. Mark the arc with a pencil, and then cut it out with a jigsaw. Secure the back to the two 1x4 sides to create a U-shape. Use 2-in. bolts **(Photo 3)** to secure the back assembly to the sides of the stool. (Tip: To install the washer between the back assembly and the stool, tape the washer over the hole in the side before installing the assembly.) Finally, position the top about 1/2 in. from the front of the sides so that the back doesn't hit the front lip as it pivots.

WHAT IT TAKES

TIME
2 hours

SKILL LEVEL
Beginner

TOOLS
Basic hand tools, circular saw (or miter saw), drill, router, 1/4-in. round-over bit

WORKSHOP
STOOL

B

B. WORKSHOP STOOL

Flip the top down and you have a stool for sitting or working; flip it up and you have a small stepladder for reaching. Build two of them and you have sawhorses for supporting sheets of plywood or long boards when working.

Begin by building the two side ladders using the spacing shown in **Figure A**. Use a square to ensure each "rung" is square to the leg, then secure each using glue and 1-1/4-in. screws **(Photo 1)**. Use a 1/4-in. round-over bit to soften the outer edges of each leg. Stand the two ladder sides facing each other, and install the two steps and the back brace. Predrill the holes to prevent splitting.

Cut the two top boards to length and round over the top edges. Secure the two top edges to each other using 2-1/2-in. no-mortise hinges; regular hinges will also work but will leave a slightly wider gap. Position the hinged-together top boards so they overhang the sides of the legs by about 3/4 in. and the front and back by about 3/8 in. Attach one of the top boards to the top "rungs" of the ladder using 2-in. screws.

Figure A Workshop Stool
OVERALL DIMENSIONS: 19" W x 14" D x 25-3/4" H

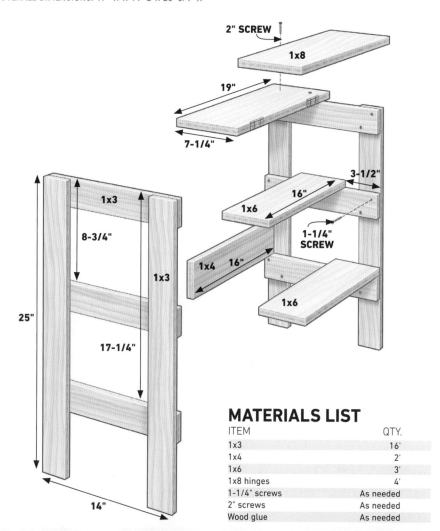

MATERIALS LIST

ITEM	QTY.
1x3	16'
1x4	2'
1x6	3'
1x8 hinges	4'
1-1/4" screws	As needed
2" screws	As needed
Wood glue	As needed

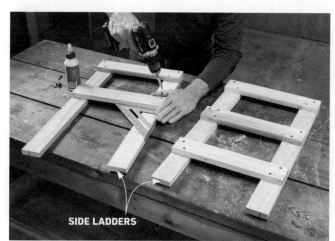

1 BUILD THE TWO SIDE LADDERS
Cut the pieces to length, then glue and screw the crosspieces to the legs. Use a square to ensure the assemblies are square.

SIDE LADDERS

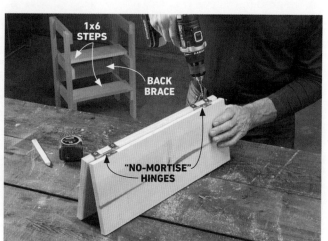

2 PUT IT ALL TOGETHER
Attach the steps and back brace to the ladder sides. Use hinges to join the two top pieces, then secure one of the boards to the top "rungs."

1x6 STEPS
BACK BRACE
"NO-MORTISE" HINGES

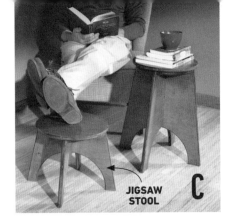

JIGSAW STOOL C

C. JIGSAW STOOL

This stool is designed so you can create eight short ones or four tall ones (or combinations of the two heights) from a single sheet of plywood. We'll show you how to build the short version; building the taller stool employs the very same concepts.

Rip a 24 x 24-in. piece of plywood into 18- and 6-in. strips, then draw "crosshairs" **(Photo 1)** to locate the center of the larger board. Drive a drywall screw in the center; use that as a pivot point for swinging a 7-in.-radius circle **(Figure A)**. Draw lines 3/8 in. from the crosshairs on each side to create 3/4-in.-thick layout marks for cutting the interlocking notches and installing the leg brace blocks.

Drill a 1/2-in. pilot hole in the lower notch **(Figure A)**, then insert a fine-tooth jigsaw blade and cut out the round top. Use a jigsaw to cut out the legs and the 3/4 x 2-1/2-in. notches for interlocking them. Use a router with a 1/4-in. round-over bit to soften the sides of both the top and legs but not the edges along the tops of the two legs **(Photo 2)**. If you don't have a router, ease the sharp edges with sandpaper. Cut the triangular blocks from the 6-in.-wide cutoff **(Photo 1)**; secure two of them to the underside of the top disc with glue and 1-1/4-in. all-purpose screws. Slip the legs into place as shown in **Photo 3**, then secure them to the blocks using 2-in. screws. Add the other two triangular blocks and apply a finish.

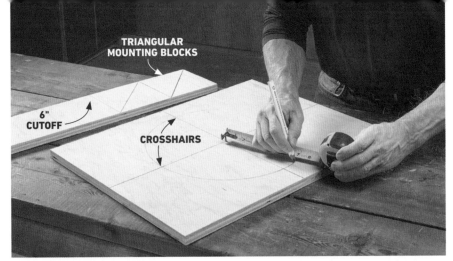

TRIANGULAR MOUNTING BLOCKS

6" CUTOFF

CROSSHAIRS

1 LAY OUT THE LEGS AND TOP
Rip the plywood into 18- and 6-in. strips. Draw "crosshairs" on the larger piece, drive a screw in the center, hook your tape over it, then with a pencil snugged against the 7-in. mark, draw a circle. Cut four triangular mounting blocks from the narrow piece.

LEG WITH TOP NOTCH

TOP

ROUTER WITH ROUND-OVER BIT

2 CUT OUT THE PARTS AND ROUT THE EDGES
Use a jigsaw to cut out the parts (see **Figure A**), then use a router with a 1/4-in. round-over bit to ease the edges as shown.

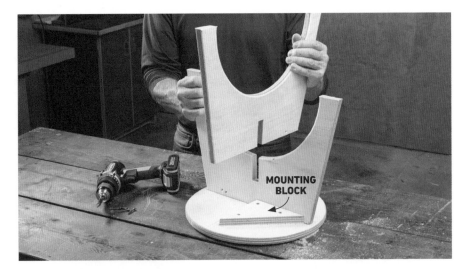

MOUNTING BLOCK

3 ASSEMBLE THE STOOL
Screw two triangular blocks where the top layout marks intersect (kitty-corner from each other), then secure the legs using 2-in. screws. Install the other two blocks, then apply a finish.

Figure A Jigsaw Stool plywood layout (short version)

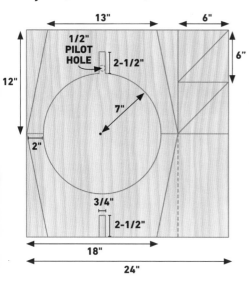

13"
6"
12"
1/2" PILOT HOLE
2-1/2"
6"
7"
2"
3/4"
2-1/2"
18"
24"

Figure B Jigsaw Stool plywood layout (tall version)

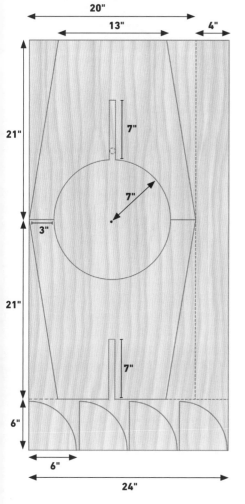

20"
13"
4"
21"
7"
3"
7"
21"
7"
6"
6"
24"

Figure C Jigsaw Stool assembly (tall version)

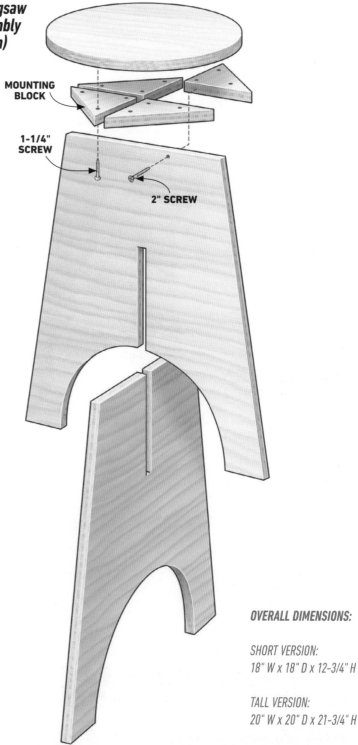

MOUNTING BLOCK

1-1/4" SCREW

2" SCREW

OVERALL DIMENSIONS:

SHORT VERSION:
18" W x 18" D x 12-3/4" H

TALL VERSION:
20" W x 20" D x 21-3/4" H

MATERIALS LIST

ITEM	QTY.
SHORT STOOL	
3/4" x 24" x 24" plywood	1
TALL STOOL	
3/4" x 24" x 48" plywood	1
1-1/4" screws	As needed
2" screws	As needed
Wood glue	As needed

WHAT IT TAKES

TIME	SKILL LEVEL
2 hours/stool	Beginner

TOOLS
Basic hand tools, drill, jigsaw, router and round-over bit

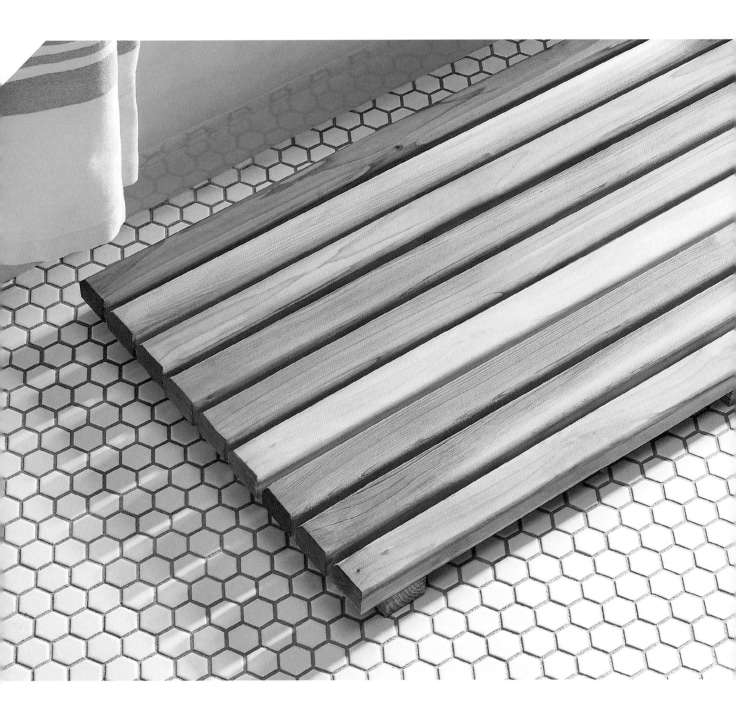

CEDAR BATH MAT

IT'S ALSO JUST RIGHT FOR AN ENTRYWAY OR A CLOSET.

This project is super simple, practical and versatile: It can be a bath mat, an entry mat for a patio or a drip-dry platform for wet shoes. Here are some planning and building tips:

- We chose cedar for its looks and rot resistance. But any wood would be fine.

- This mat is 14-1/2 x 30 in., but you can make yours any size. Just be sure the slats are supported by runners no more than 15 in. apart.
- Large knots create weak spots, so you may need to buy some extra lumber to ensure you have enough sections that are free of knots.

MATERIALS LIST

ITEM

1x2 or 1x6 lumber
1-1/4" brads or nails
Paint stir stick
Sandpaper
Anti-skid pads
Finishing supplies

WHAT IT TAKES

TIME	SKILL LEVEL
1 hour	Beginner

TOOLS
Basic hand tools, circular saw, nail gun (optional), router

- Although the nail holes won't show, we patched them with wood filler before sanding and finishing the mat. If they are left exposed, the nail heads could rust and then stain the floor.
- We finished our mat with tung oil, a water-resistant finish that doesn't mold or darken. Although oil finishes aren't as durable as some other finish options, they're very easy to renew when the finish starts to wear off—all you have to do is simply wipe on a fresh coat.
- Be sure to apply anti-skid pads on the bottom to keep the mat from sliding on hard floors and creating a safety hazard.

1 CUT THE SLATS
If your local home center doesn't have good-quality 1x2 stock for the slats, buy a 1x6 and cut 1-1/2-in. strips. An 8-ft. 1x6 provided all the slats we needed.

2 ROUND THE EDGES
We rounded the slat edges with a 1/4-in. round-over bit. If you don't have a router, ease the edges with 100-grit sandpaper.

3 ASSEMBLE THE MAT
Clamp wood scraps to your workbench to form a square. Lay out the slats against the guide using spacers cut from a paint stir stick. Then cut three runners 1 in. shorter than the width of the mat. Fasten the runners to the slats with 1-1/4-in. brads or nails.

STRIP FURNITURE

REMOVE THE FINISH TO MAKE OLD FURNITURE LOOK NEW AGAIN IN A WEEKEND!

Have you ever thought about stripping and refinishing an old piece of furniture? Maybe you inherited a worn-out dresser from a loved one or just rescued a wooden chair from a dumpster. Or maybe your dining room table has taken a beating over the years. Here you'll find all the tips you need to do the refinishing job right.

Furniture refinishing is an easy and very satisfying DIY project. It's also a great way to furnish your house on the cheap. With just a little elbow grease and not too much money, you can easily remove paint or other finishes and give an old piece of furniture a new lease on life and a special place in your home.

WHAT IT TAKES	
TIME 1 weekend	**SKILL LEVEL** Beginner
TOOLS Brass brushes, dental picks, scrapers	

MATERIALS LIST
ITEM

Furniture stripper
Disposable paintbrushes
Disposable metal pans
Protective gear including goggles, gloves and a respirator
Plastic trash bag or drop cloth

SAFER STRIPPERS

In 2019, the Environmental Protection Agency (EPA) banned the manufacture and sale of methylene chloride paint removers. Several paint and varnish stripper products contained methylene chloride, and they worked well, albeit dangerously. Removing that chemical, and others including n-methylpyrrolidone (NMP), was a good thing.

While safer to use, stripper products that no longer contain methylene chloride or NMP can work well but require more time to do their work. Depending on the type and quantity of paint or finish you're trying to remove, some stripper products require up to 24 hours of contact time to be effective.

CITRISTRIP:

This popular finish remover has been on the market for years and was reformulated to remove NMP when the EPA banned that chemical. Citristrip can remove multiple layers of paint and varnish in one application, working on wood, masonry and metal surfaces. Brush or roll on the gel, and let it sit on the surface. With a scraper, test its effectiveness after 30 minutes or so.

As with any household solvent, when using a paint stripper, read the label on the product package and follow the manufacturer's recommendations. Because there may still be products containing methylene chloride floating around on store shelves, be sure to check the ingredients list before buying the product to avoid the serious health risks associated with the use of methylene chloride. The manufacturers of such products produce a Safety Data Sheet (SDS) that outlines the product's contents and any associated hazards. You can find SDS documents on the websites of manufacturers and retailers.

When using any furniture stripper products, work in only well-ventilated areas. Follow our guidelines for stripping safely in "Work Safely."

3M'S SAFEST STRIPPER:

This product has no strong fumes and won't burn your skin. The bad news is that it can take up to 24 hours to work. It can also be hard to find in stores, so call around before you shop, or search for it online. Strippers like this containing water can raise the grain of wood, so some light sanding may be needed after using it.

IF YOU'RE JUST REMOVING CLEAR FINISH

Just about any stripping product will remove clear finishes, but products labeled "refinisher" do it faster and they are less likely to remove stain. Refinishers contain a mixture of solvents like methanol, acetone and toluene, and they dissolve clear finishes like lacquer and shellac in minutes. But you can't use them for stripping paint. When using a refinisher, follow the manufacturer's directions for application and removal, and take the recommended safety precautions.

CHOOSE THE RIGHT PRODUCT

Most stripping products work well on just about any type of finish. When you're shopping for a product, it comes down to two factors: speed and safety. Don't blindly accept marketing claims on the front of the container about how safe it is. Some "safe" strippers contain chemicals that are dangerous if you touch them with bare hands or inhale the fumes. Read the back of the bottle where you'll find information about what chemicals the product contains and how quickly the stripper works.

WORK SAFELY

Stripping products require the use of eye, skin and lung protection. Wear splash-proof goggles, long sleeves and pants, chemical-resistant gloves and a respirator with new organic vapor cartridges. Keep a bucket of water with rags handy to wipe off stripper that gets on your skin. Work outside if possible. If you must work indoors, open as many windows and doors as you can.

1

2

3

4

5

1 CARPET YOUR WORKBENCH

A piece of used carpeting or a new carpet remnant placed on a table or workbench makes a great surface for stripping finish off of furniture. The soft carpet protects wood from nicks and scratches, and it absorbs drips. You also have the option to use a tarp, a plastic drop cloth or even old newspapers.

2 BRUSH IT ON THICK

Many strippers go on like a gel, so don't be afraid to apply a thick coat—1/8 to 1/4 in. Add a second coat if the first one dries before you have time to scrape it off or if all the finish doesn't come off the first time.

3 STRIP IN ZONES

When stripping a really large piece of furniture, do it in "zones." Apply stripper to only part of the piece and scrape it off before the stripper dries.

4 KEEP IT WET

Stripping products work only while wet. To help keep your stripper from evaporating too quickly while you give it time to work, brush it on, then cover it with a plastic trash bag or drop cloth.

5 USE A BOX

A small cardboard box works great for cleaning off your putty knife. Let the stripper residue in the box dry completely before disposing of it in the trash.

METAL CONTAINER

Because some stripping products eat plastic, manufacturers recommend pouring their products into a metal container, even though some are sold in plastic containers. Use a foil pan, a paint can or an old coffee can.

FURNITURE-FRIENDLY SCRAPERS

Use a wide putty knife to scoop the finish off once the stripper has softened it. Be sure to round off the corners of the putty knife with a file or electric grinder to prevent gouging the wood. A 3 x 3-in. piece of 1/4-in. plywood with the corners rounded off also makes a good scraping tool.

BRASS BRUSH

A brass brush has soft bristles and is less likely than a steel brush to damage wood. Use it to remove finish from deep wood pores and turned parts like chair legs. Also use it (or fine-grit sandpaper) to gently score the surface of hard finishes so the product will penetrate.

DISPOSABLE BRUSH

Use a disposable chip brush or an old paintbrush. When finished, allow the brush to dry completely and throw it away.

ABRASIVE PAD

Use plastic scouring pads to gently remove leftover stripper and residue after scraping. Avoid using steel wool, especially with water-based strippers, because it can leave rust marks behind.

DENTAL PICKS

Dental picks are ideal for removing finish from small cracks and crevices. Slightly dull ones work even better because they're less likely to damage the wood.

ROUND SCRAPERS

A piece of dowel with a drywall screw or wood screw embedded works well for getting into rounded areas where a flat putty knife won't reach. A pair of locking pliers with a round fender washer also works great.

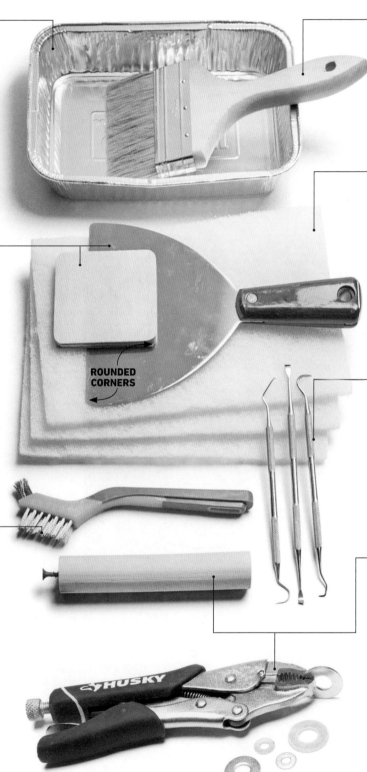

ROUNDED CORNERS

HUSKY

PRO TIP Using an abrasive pad (not steel wool) and lacquer thinner, clean off any remaining stain or finish, and wipe up with paper towels.

The paint should practically fall off the next day. If it doesn't, gently scrub it off with a stiff plastic brush.

6 IS IT REALLY WORTH STRIPPING?

Sometimes a piece of painted furniture is painted because somebody tried to hide a repair, ugly wood or finger-jointed boards. Try stripping a small area to see what's under the paint before committing to the full job.

7 DON'T BOTHER STRIPPING FURNITURE YOU PLAN TO PAINT

If you're going to paint (or repaint) a piece of furniture, you probably don't need to strip it.

Wash it with TSP substitute mixed with water. Then, using medium- or fine-grit sandpaper, smooth out bumps or flaking paint and scuff-sand other areas so the new paint will adhere. This also applies to painting over clear finishes.

8 LEARN TO STRIP HARDWARE THE EASY WAY

Got a lot of old hardware with paint on it? Fill an old slow cooker with water and a couple of drops of dish soap. Then turn it on low and let the hardware "cook" overnight.

9 GET RID OF STAIN (OR NOT)

Strippers do a very good job of removing clear finishes, but they won't always remove stain. If your goal is to get down to raw wood, you should make it a goal to remove as much stain as possible using lacquer thinner and an abrasive scrubbing pad. You might be able to remove the remaining stain with sandpaper. If that doesn't work, you could apply a new stain that's about the same color or darker than the old stain. Or you should consider painting the piece.

WHAT IT TAKES

TIME	SKILL LEVEL
1 hour	Beginner

TOOLS

Basic hand tools, drill driver, jigsaw or circular saw, 18-gauge nailer (*A miter saw and a table saw will speed things up and give you better results.*)

UNDER-CABINET DRAWER

EXTRA STORAGE WILL BE RIGHT WHERE YOU NEED IT.

Coffee pods, knives, utensils, spices—there are so many different ways you could utilize an extra drawer or two tucked under your upper cabinets. And you can put a drawer under almost any upper cabinet as long as there's enough space underneath to accommodate your countertop appliances. So take a look at what's currently cluttering your countertop, and make a nice, neat home above for all of it!

BOARDS AND PLYWOOD

You'll need 1/4-in. plywood for each drawer bottom (see **Figure A**), 1x3s for the drawer frame and 1x4s for the drawer supports, drawer front and trim board. (You'll need two trim boards if the drawer is visible from both sides.) We used poplar because the exposed parts will be painted. If you have natural wood cabinets, choose a wood and finish to match. Finish the drawer front and trim boards before installing.

SIDE-MOUNT DRAWER SLIDES MADE EASY

Ordinarily, installing drawers with side-mount slides is very challenging. But with the technique shown in **Photos 4–6**, everything is built around the drawer, making it very easy.

Most upper cabinets are 12 in. deep. If that's the case with yours, you'll need a pair of 10-in. side-mount drawer slides for each drawer. You won't find these at home centers; you'll have to buy them online or at a woodworking store. If you have unusually deep cabinets, you can create deeper drawers and use 12-in. slides, which are sold at home centers.

THE DRAWER SIZES

Peek under your cabinets and you'll see the cavities **(Photo 1)**. You can put several drawers under a row of cabinets if you wish, but each cabinet needs a separate drawer.

If you're putting in adjoining drawers, don't cut the drawer fronts until all the drawers are installed so you can cut them to fit with even gaps between them. For a single cabinet drawer, cut the front the same length as the cabinet face.

You won't need drawer pulls. The drawer front drops about an inch below the drawer, so you'll have a built-in lip on the underside that creates a finger pull.

1 SIZE THE DRAWER
Carefully measure the cavity under the cabinet. Then cut a piece of 1/4-in. plywood 2-1/2 in. narrower and 1/4 in. shallower than those dimensions.

DRAWER FRONT AND BACK

DRAWER SIDE

2 BUILD THE DRAWER FRAME
Cut 1x3 frame parts to match the plywood dimensions, then glue and nail them together with 1-1/2-in. 18-gauge brads.

1/4" PLYWOOD DRAWER BOTTOM

DRAWER FRAME

3 ADD THE DRAWER BOTTOM
Glue and nail the plywood to the frame using the plywood to square up the frame as you fasten it.

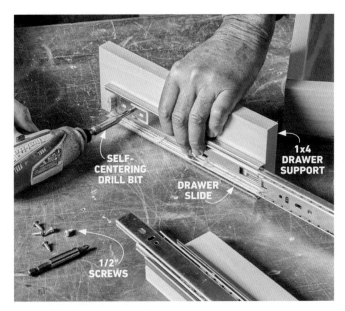

4 ATTACH THE DRAWER SLIDE

Cut 1x4s the same length as the drawer sides. Attach the slides to the drawer supports flush with the bottom and end. Use a self-centering drill bit in the round mounting holes, then screw in.

5 JOIN THE SLIDE TO THE DRAWER

Pull out the slide on each drawer support a few inches to expose the mounting holes, then predrill and screw the slides to the drawer sides flush with the front.

Figure A Under-Cabinet Drawer

Before you adhere and screw the assembly onto the cabinet, have someone help you hold it in place to make sure the drawer clears the cabinet face frame. If it doesn't, rip 3/4-in. strips of 1/4-in. plywood for spacers (as many as needed) and nail them to the drawer support before mounting the assembly.

MATERIALS LIST

ITEM
1/4" plywood
1x3 lumber
1x4 lumber
Side-mount drawer slides
1-1/2" brads
Wood glue
Double-face tape
1-1/4" brads
1-5/8" brads
1" brads

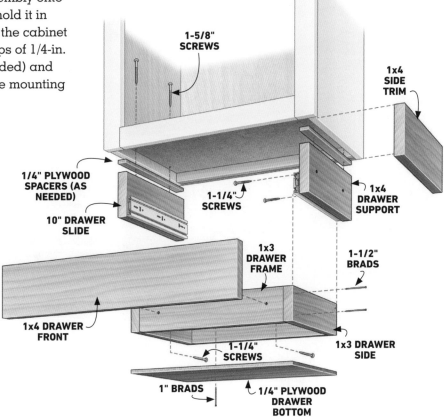

6 FINISH ATTACHING THE DRAWER SLIDE
Pull out the slide the rest of the way so that you can mount the slide to the back end of the drawer side.

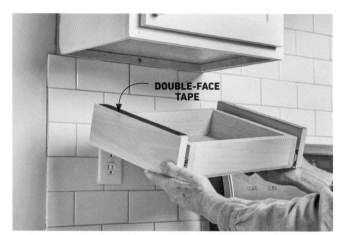

DOUBLE-FACE TAPE

7 STICK THE ASSEMBLY TO THE CABINET
Use double-face tape to temporarily stick the assembly to the underside of the cabinet. (Center it in the opening.)

DRAWER SUPPORT

8 SCREW DRAWER SUPPORTS TO CABINET BOTTOM
Drill two 1/8-in. pilot holes through the cabinet bottom, and then screw the bottom to the drawer supports.

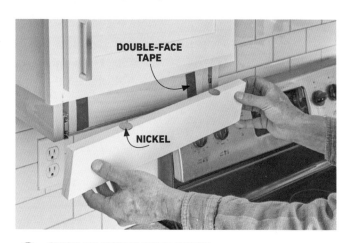

DOUBLE-FACE TAPE

NICKEL

9 STICK ON THE DRAWER FRONT
Cut the drawer front the length of the cabinet face frame. Space it from the cabinet frame with two nickels; attach with double-face tape.

DRAWER FRONT

10 ATTACH THE DRAWER FRONT
Drill, then permanently attach the drawer front to the drawer frame from the inside with 1-1/4-in. screws.

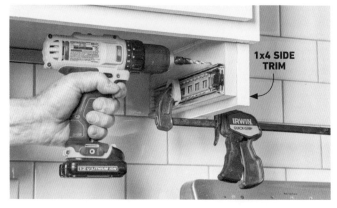

1x4 SIDE TRIM

11 CLAMP AND SCREW THE SIDE TRIM INTO PLACE
Drill pilot holes above the drawer slide and attach the 1x4 side trim piece using 1-1/4-in. screws.

CLEVER CLOSET SYSTEM

THIS SIMPLE SHELF–AND–ROD SYSTEM WILL BRING ORDER TO YOUR CLUTTERED CLOSET AND DOUBLE THE STORAGE SPACE.

Annoyed by an overstuffed closet packed so tightly that you can't find your favorite shirt or shoes? Does the closet rod bend under the weight of all of the clothing that you have hanging from it?

The simple closet organizing system shown here is a great solution. It utilizes closet space much more efficiently by dividing your closet into zones that give your slacks, dresses, shirts, shoes and other items their own home. As a result, your clothing is better organized and you can find your party shirt or power skirt quickly and easily. Overall, you'll get double the useful space of a traditional single pole and shelf closet.

We'll show you how to build this simple organizer step-by-step and how to customize it to fit closets of different sizes. We designed it for simplicity—you can build it in one weekend, even if you're a novice.

WHAT IT TAKES	
TIME	**SKILL LEVEL**
1 weekend	Beginner

TOOLS
Basic hand tools, brad nailer (optional), circular saw, drill driver, miter saw (optional)

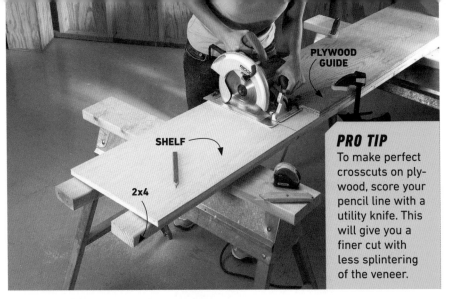

PLYWOOD GUIDE

SHELF

2x4

PRO TIP
To make perfect crosscuts on plywood, score your pencil line with a utility knife. This will give you a finer cut with less splintering of the veneer.

1 MEASURE AND MAKE ACCURATE CUTS
Measure your closet dimensions, and cut the plywood vertical dividers and shelves to size **(Figure A)**. Use a guide to make crosscuts perfectly square.

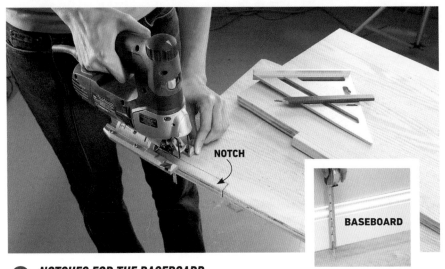

NOTCH

BASEBOARD

2 NOTCHES FOR THE BASEBOARD
Measure the baseboard height and thickness. With a jigsaw, cut notches on the vertical dividers to fit over the baseboard.

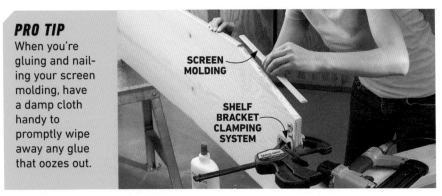

PRO TIP
When you're gluing and nailing your screen molding, have a damp cloth handy to promptly wipe away any glue that oozes out.

SCREEN MOLDING

SHELF BRACKET CLAMPING SYSTEM

3 ATTACH SCREEN MOLDING
Smooth the cut plywood edges with 80-grit sandpaper and a block, then glue and tack 3/4-in. screen molding onto the edges that will show. Apply a stain or finish, and let it dry.

DON'T BUY AN ORGANIZER—BUILD IT!
While you may be tempted to buy a prefabricated organizer, it'll be surprisingly expensive when you tally up the cost of all the pieces. The materials for our organizer cost only a couple hundred dollars. We used oak veneer plywood, 1-1/2 sheets, plus several types of standard oak trim that you'll find at most home centers and lumberyards. (See the Materials List). Keep in mind that if you use other wood species, you may have trouble finding matching trim and you'll have to custom cut it from solid boards on a table saw. If you choose to paint your organizer, you can use less expensive plywood and trim, cutting your expenses.

Begin by measuring the width of your closet. The system we show works best in a 6-ft. closet. If your closet only measures 5 ft., consider using a single vertical divider rather than the two in **Figure A**.

ASSEMBLE THE CENTER UNIT
After referring to the Cutting List and your closet dimensions, rip the plywood into two 13-3/4-in. pieces for the vertical dividers. If you plan to rip plywood with a circular saw, be sure to use a straightedge to get perfectly straight cuts. We'll be using hook strips to attach the center unit and shelves to the closet walls, as well as to space the uprights **(Figure A)**. If you want to save a bit of cash, you can rip these strips from the leftover plywood (and enjoy the gratification that comes from using the entire sheet). Cut the plywood to length using a factory plywood edge as a guide **(Photo 1)**. Always check for accuracy by just nicking the plywood with the blade to make sure you're hitting your

Figure A Closet Organizer
OVERALL DIMENSIONS: VARIES

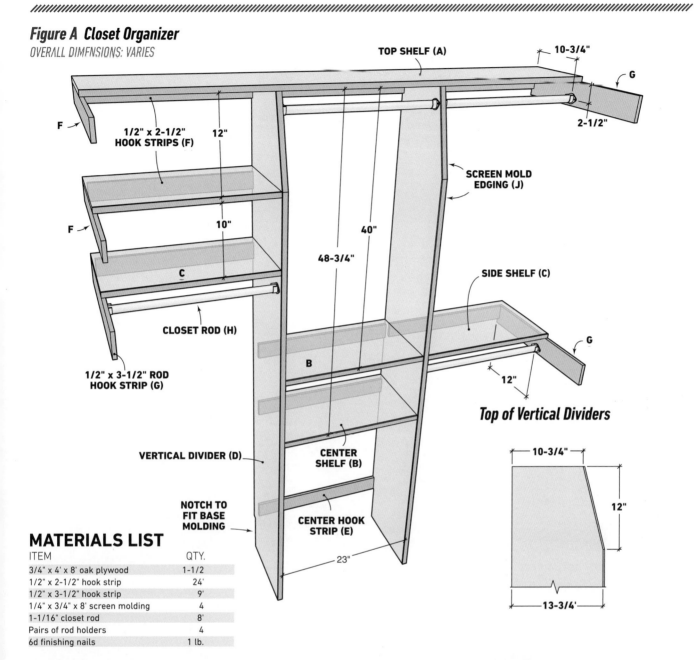

TOP SHELF (A)

10-3/4"

G

2-1/2"

F

1/2" x 2-1/2"
HOOK STRIPS (F)

12"

10"

F

C

CLOSET ROD (H)

1/2" x 3-1/2" ROD
HOOK STRIP (G)

SCREEN MOLD
EDGING (J)

40"

48-3/4"

SIDE SHELF (C)

G

12"

B

VERTICAL DIVIDER (D)

CENTER
SHELF (B)

NOTCH TO
FIT BASE
MOLDING

CENTER HOOK
STRIP (E)

23"

Top of Vertical Dividers

10-3/4"

12"

13-3/4'

MATERIALS LIST

ITEM	QTY.
3/4" x 4' x 8' oak plywood	1-1/2
1/2" x 2-1/2" hook strip	24'
1/2" x 3-1/2" hook strip	9'
1/4" x 3/4" x 8' screen molding	4
1-1/16" closet rod	8'
Pairs of rod holders	4
6d finishing nails	1 lb.

mark. Fully support your project with 2x4s so the cutoff doesn't fall and splinter. Also, for smoother cuts, use a sharp blade with at least 40 teeth.

You don't have to cut out the baseboard in the closet or even trim the back side of the dividers to fit the baseboard's exact profile. The back of the unit will be mostly out of sight, so square notches will do **(Photo 2)**.

You'll have to trim the tops of the dividers back to 10-3/4 in. to make

it easier to slide stuff onto the top shelf (unless you have an extra-deep closet). We angled this cut to the first shelf point **(Figure A)**.

Apply the screen molding to hide the raw plywood edges on the dividers and shelves. You'll have to cut a 7-degree angle on the molding with a circular saw, jigsaw or miter saw to get a perfect fit on the dividers. Cut this angle first, and when you get a nice fit, cut the other ends to length. You could also apply edge veneer

CUTTING LIST

KEY	QTY.	PART
A	1	3/4" x 10-3/4" x closet length, plywood (top shelf)
B	2	3/4" x 13-1/2" x 23" plywood (center shelves)
C	3	3/4" x 13-1/2" x measured length, plywood (side shelves)
D	2	3/4" x 13-3/4" x 82" plywood (vertical dividers)
E	4	1/2" x 2-1/2" x 23" (center hook strips)
F	7	1/2" x 2-1/2" x measured lengths (hook strips)
G	3	1/2" x 3-1/2" x closet depth (hook strips for rods)
H	4	1-1/16" x measured lengths (closet rods)
J		1/4" x 3/4" x measured lengths (screen molding)

4 GLUE AND NAIL THE SHELVES

Lay out the intermediate shelf positions with a square, spread glue on the shelf edges and nail each shelf to the dividers with 6d finish nails. Nail the 1/2-in. hook strips to the dividers as well.

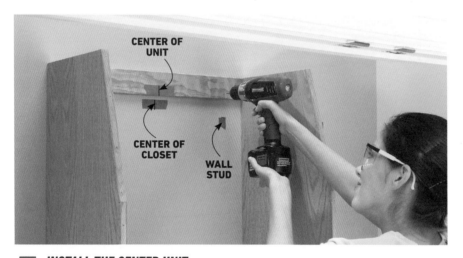

5 INSTALL THE CENTER UNIT

Set the center unit in the closet, level it with shims, predrill and tack the hook strips to the wall studs with 6d finish nails.

6 INSTALL THE REMAINING HOOK STRIPS

Level the hook strips with the tops of the dividers, then predrill and nail them to the studs. Continue the strip around closet sides.

(iron-on) or any other 3/4-in. wood strips to cover the edges.

Now sand all the parts to prepare them for finishing. A random orbital sander with 120-grit sandpaper will make quick work of this, but a few squares of sandpaper and a wood block will also do the trick. After sanding, wipe the surface of the wood with a clean cloth to remove dust.

It's easiest to apply your finish before assembling the closet system. We chose a warm fruitwood-tone Danish Finishing Oil. This type of finish brings out the natural grain of the wood, looks velvety smooth, and is easy to renew when you scratch or scuff it. Use a small cloth to rub a generous amount of oil into the surface until the plywood and

PROTECT PRIME SPACE

Your bedroom closet is valuable real estate, and the only way to protect it is to store off-season or rare-occasion clothing elsewhere.

Many of us use garment bags, plastic bins (stored off the floor in a humidity-controlled basement) or a freestanding wardrobe. However, many mid-century homes have closets on the main level that are 4-1/2 ft. deep or better, and they're perfect candidates for off-season use.

Deep closets can fit double rods mounted parallel to each other in the front and the back. It's an ideal setup for stashing off-season outfits. Add a rolling bin on the closet floor to store accessories, beachwear or ski gloves in Ziploc Big Bags. This will keep your bedroom closet clear and your active gear at hand.

Every clothing item should be handled annually, and those not worn in a given season should be cast off. Passing along unused attire creates the luxury of space and ease in any closet.

hook strips have an even sheen, and allow it to dry overnight.

After the oil dries, assemble the center unit. Lightly mark the vertical dividers where the interior shelves and hook strips will be positioned, and drill 1/8-in. pilot holes to simplify the nailing. Then spread a thin bead of glue onto the shelf ends and clamp the unit together. Use four 6d finish nails to pin the shelves securely **(Photo 4)**, and then countersink the nail heads with a nail set. Nails and glue are strong enough for holding garments and other light items, but if you plan to store something heavy on a closet shelf, put a cleat under the shelf to bear the weight.

Position one of the center unit's interior hook strips at the very top of the dividers, one above the bottom notches, and one under each shelf. The strips will shore up the unit and keep the plywood from bowing when you install it.

IN THE CLOSET

If you have a thin carpet and pad, you can place the center unit directly on top of it. However, if you have a plush rug with a soft padding, stability is a concern. After determining the exact placement of your unit (by centering the unit on the midpoint of the closet; **Photo 5**), mark and cut out two 3/4-in.-wide slots in the carpet and pad so the dividers rest on the solid floor below.

Find the studs with a stud finder; mark them with masking tape. Also measure and mark the center of the wall on tape. This way you'll avoid marking up your walls. Set the unit in position against the wall. Level and shim as necessary **(Photo 5).**

Predrill the hook strips using a 1/8-in. bit, and then nail the unit to the studs. Next, level and nail on the remaining hook strips **(Photo 6)**, starting with wider

TOP SHELF

ROD HOLDER

7 INSTALL THE TOP SHELF
Trim the top shelf ends to fit the side walls, drop the shelf into place, and nail it to the tops of the vertical dividers and to the hook strip with 6d nails.

hook strips along the side walls to accommodate the hanging rod hardware **(Figure A** and **Photo 8)**.

The inside walls of the closet will never be perfectly square because of the mudding and taping of the drywall corners. Measure your closet width and cut your shelf to the widest dimension, then tilt the shelf into position. At the corners, mark a trim line along each end to achieve a snug fit **(Photo 7).**

Getting the top shelf over the central unit and onto the hook strips may take some finagling. Once the shelf is resting squarely, drill pilot holes. Nail it to the dividers and hook strips **(Photo 7)**.

RODS AND HARDWARE

To avoid having to put yourself in awkward positions as you work around the shelves, you should install all of your closet rod hardware before you put in the side shelves. The hardware for the closet rods should be positioned about 1-1/2 to 2 in. down from the shelf above and about 10 to 12 in.

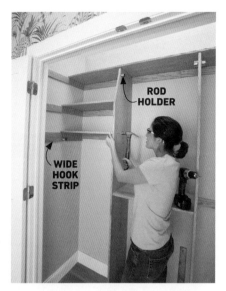

ROD HOLDER

WIDE HOOK STRIP

8 INSTALL THE SIDE SHELVES
Sand the cut edges of the side shelves. Determine the exact shelf placement; drill pilot holes. Spread glue on each shelf end and secure it with 6d nails.

from the back wall. In our closet, we chose to hang our top rods 10 in. from the back, which is good for pants, and our bottom rods 12 in. away, for shirts and blouses. Alternatively, if you want your top rod placed 12 in. out, make the top shelf 12 in. wide and trim less off the top of the vertical dividers.

INSTALL SIDE SHELVES

To firmly secure the side shelves, sand the cut edge that will be in contact with the center unit with 100-grit sandpaper. This provides a cleaner surface for the glue.

Lay out the remaining shelves on their side wall hook strips. Use a level to determine their exact position on the center unit.

Mark and drill the pilot holes through the center unit, then lift out each shelf and apply a thin bead of glue. To prevent smearing, put the center unit side in first while tipping up the wall side of the shelf. Keep a cloth handy to wipe up glue smudges. Attach the shelves and you're done!

INTERMEDIATE PROJECTS

WHAT IT TAKES

TIME
1/2 day staining, 1-1/2 days to build

SKILL LEVEL
Intermediate

TOOLS
Basic hand tools, circular saw, compressor, drill, handsaw, 4-ft. level, masonry bit, miter saw, sawhorses, 6- and 8-ft. stepladders, table saw, tin/aviation snips, 18-gauge trim gun

GRILLZEBO

///

BUILD THE PERFECT PLACE TO COOK THE PERFECT STEAK, RAIN OR SHINE.

Entertain and feed your guests outdoors without ever having to leave your burgers unattended. This "grill-zebo" is big enough to accommodate most standard grills but small enough that it might just fit on your existing patio. Customize it with lighting, grill accessory storage, wine glass racks or built-in coolers.

With a helper, you can build it in a weekend. All the building materials are available at home centers. We built ours from western red cedar because it's resistant to rot and insects, and it looks great. But you could save money by using pressure-treated wood instead. The cedar will require some upkeep over the years, but the metal roof is maintenance free. This beefy project is built to last a lifetime—a lifetime of grilling bliss.

GETTING STARTED

We poured a prestained slab that was 8 x 14 ft., which left about a foot of space on the two open ends and plenty of room for chairs on the others. For information on how to create a concrete slab, search "pour concrete" at familyhandyman.com.

Order the roofing components for this project at the lumber desk in your home center. You'll be able to get the roof panels at the exact length you need, which is 78 inches.

It is much easier to finish all the lumber with a good-quality outdoor stain before you assemble the grillzebo. After the stain has dried, set aside the three most twisted and bowed 8-ft. 4x4s. They will be used for smaller truss webs and angle braces (**D** and **E**). We made most of the cuts with a miter saw.

LAY OUT THE POST LOCATIONS

Cut the bottom chords (**A**) to size, and line them up next to each other on a pair of sawhorses. Take a couple of 12-ft. 2x4s and line them up on the horses as well. The 2x4s will be used to build a temporary template to help locate the post bases.

Measure 28-1/2 in. from each end of the bottom chords, and mark a pencil line using a framing square as a guide (**Photo 1**). Measure from that line to mark three more lines, all of them spaced 3-1/2 in. apart.

MATERIALS LIST

ITEM	QTY.
4x4 x 12' cedar	2
4x4 x 8' cedar	23
1x4 x 8' cedar	3
2x4 x 12' cedar	6
1x6 x 12' cedar deck boards	10
2x4 x 12' pine bracing	2
2x4 x 8' pine bracing and roofing stop	8
1x3 x 8' pine stakes	2
4x4 adjustable post bases	8
1-1/4" 12d galvanized joist hanger nails (1-lb. box)	1
1/2" x 3" concrete anchor (10-pack)	1
6" heavy-duty wood/structural screws (50-pack)	2
3" exterior-grade wood screws (1-lb. box)	1
2" exterior-grade trim-head screws (100-pack)	2
18-gauge galvanized brad nails (small box)	1
Construction adhesive (tube)	1
42" x 78" roofing panels	6
7/8" x 10-1/2' J-channel	4
14" x 10-1/2' ridge cap	1
1-1/2" metal roof/pole barn screws (250-pack)	1

BUILD THE ENDS

Cut the posts **(B)** to length. Line them up with the marks on the bottom side of a bottom chord; fasten the posts and the chord together **(Photo 2)**. Build one end, including the truss (the next three steps), before moving the assembly to make room for the other end.

CUT THE TOP CHORDS

The slope of the roof is 4/12, meaning the angle rises 4 in. for every 12 in. it runs horizontally. To mark the proper bottom angle on the top chord **(C)**, line up the outside edge of your framing square at the 4-in. and 12-in. marks **(Photo 3)**.

Cutting the long angle is a bit tricky, so make this cut first **(Photo 4)**. If you make a mistake, move over a bit and try again. Once all the cuts are done, line up all the top chords at the cut end and make sure every angle was cut the same. Cut the tops with a miter saw set to a 20-degree angle. Once the top chords are cut to length, lay them next to each other and mark the purlin **(F)** locations on the top side of each top chord.

1 MARK POST LOCATIONS

Align the two bottom chords next to each other in order to mark the post locations. Mark two 12-ft. 2x4s at the same time; you'll use them later to make a template that will position the posts perfectly on the slab.

2 SCREW THE POSTS TO THE BOTTOM CHORDS

The slab is the perfect surface to assemble the ends of the grillzebo. Secure each post to a chord with two 6-in. structural wood screws.

3 MARK THE TOP CHORDS

Use a framing square to mark the long angle cuts at the bottom of each top chord. Stair gauges placed at 4 in. and 12 in. guarantee correct marking on all four chords.

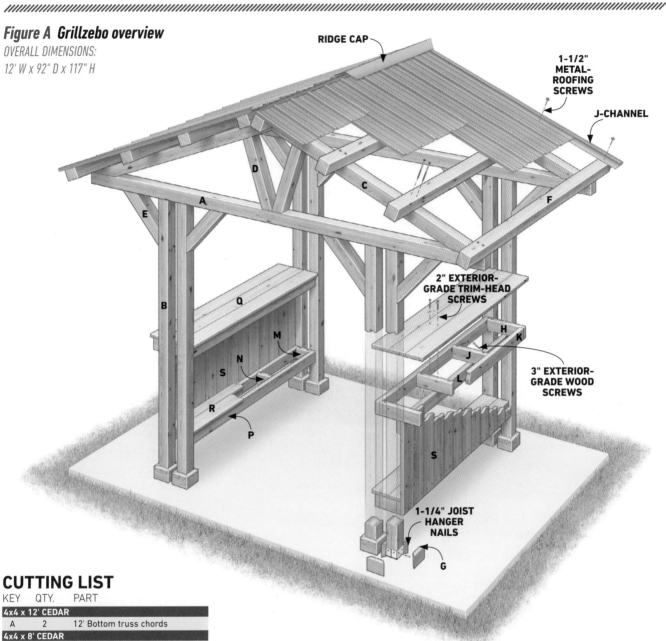

Figure A *Grillzebo overview*

OVERALL DIMENSIONS:
12' W x 92" D x 117" H

RIDGE CAP

1-1/2"
METAL-
ROOFING
SCREWS

J-CHANNEL

2" EXTERIOR-
GRADE TRIM-HEAD
SCREWS

3" EXTERIOR-
GRADE WOOD
SCREWS

1-1/4" JOIST
HANGER
NAILS

CUTTING LIST

KEY	QTY.	PART
4x4 x 12' CEDAR		
A	2	12' Bottom truss chords
4x4 x 8' CEDAR		
B	8	7' Posts
C	4	76" (top side) Top chords
D	4	Truss webs (Cut length to fit)
E	8	20" Angle braces
F	8	92" (or cut length to fit) Purlins
1x4 x 8' CEDAR		
G	32	Post trim (Cut length to fit)
2x4 x 12' CEDAR		
H	4	13" Table frame ends
J	4	Table frame center braces (Cut length to fit)
K	4	Table frame sides (Cut length to fit)
L	2	Skirt nailer (Cut length to fit)
M	4	5-1/2" Shelf frame ends
N	4	Shelf frame centers (Cut length to fit)
P	4	Shelf frame sides (Cut length to fit)
1x6 x 12' CEDAR (DECK BOARDS)		
Q	3	Tabletop boards (Cut length to fit)
R	2	Shelf boards (Cut length to fit; rip two at 4 in.)
S	24	26" Skirt boards

There should be a gap about
20-5/8 in. between all the purlins.

BUILD THE TRUSSES

Fasten each top chord to a bottom
chord with two 6-in. screws. Cut
the truss webs **(D)** a bit long with a
20-degree angle on one end. Hold
the truss webs to the center of a
bottom chord; mark a cutting line
on the other end using a top chord
as a guide **(Photo 5)**. Fasten them
with one 6-in. screw in each end.

LAY OUT THE POST
LOCATIONS AND
INSTALL THE BASES

Cut two 2x4s (pine lumber) at
72 inches. Align them with the
outside post location lines you
made on the two 2x4s you marked
along with the bottom chords.
Fasten the 2x4s together with 3-in.
wood screws. The inside perimeter

4 FINISH CUTS WITH A HANDSAW

Cut the long angles with a circular saw first. But a standard circular saw with a 7-1/4-in. blade won't cut all the way through, so you'll have to finish the cut with a handsaw.

20° ANGLE

CENTERLINE

TRUSS WEB

5 MARK THE TRUSS WEBBING

Cut each truss web a little long. Line up the truss webs with the center of the bottom chord, and mark the tops with a pencil.

ANGLE BRACE

TEMPLATE

6 POSITION POSTS WITH A TEMPLATE

Center the template on the slab. Square it up by measuring diagonally from inside corner to inside corner in both directions. Attach angle braces on two corners to keep the template square. Use a 4x4 scrap to mark the post base locations on the concrete.

of the frame should be 72 x 87 in. Square and center the frame, and mark the post locations **(Photo 6)**.

Metal bases not only keep the posts secure but also keep them off the concrete so the wood doesn't wick up water and prematurely rot. Drill the holes for the bases and slide them into position. Tap the anchors into the holes and tighten the nuts **(Photo 7)**.

RAISE THE ENDS AND BRACE THEM

Raise one end and slip the posts into the bases. Brace the end upright temporarily with 2x4s run from the posts to stakes in the ground. Fasten the posts to the bases with joist hanger screws. After the posts are secured to the bases, plumb all the posts both ways with a 4-ft. level, adjusting the temporary braces to keep them from moving **(Photo 8)**.

Once one end is secure, raise the other end and keep it upright and plumb by running 2x4s from the bottom chord of the first end over to the bottom chord of the second. Fasten two 2x4s straight across and a third at an angle.

CUT AND INSTALL THE ANGLE BRACES

Cut the angle braces **(E)** to size, with 45-degree angles on each end. Make sure the angles sit flush on the post and bottom chord. Then fasten the braces on each end with two 3-in. exterior-grade screws **(Photo 9)**.

CUT AND INSTALL THE PURLINS

Ripping down metal roofing is no fun, so we cut the purlins **(F)** to fit the roofing panels. The panels we used were 3 ft. wide, but we increased the overlaps, so the total width of the three panels was as close to 8 ft. as possible (in our case, 92 in.). Then we cut the purlins to that size **(Photo 10)**.

The top and bottom purlins line up with the top and bottom edges of each top chord, and the center two purlins will line up with the marks you made earlier. Install the top and bottom purlins first and check to see that all four overhangs are the same **(Photo 11)**.

INSTALL THE ROOFING

Attach a scrap 2x4 with a couple of screws to the outside edge of the bottom purlin. Fasten another 2x4 to the first, except hold it up an inch **(Photo 12)**. This will create a stop that you can slide your roof panels down to, resulting in a perfect 1-1/2-in. overhang.

Install all the J-channels before the roofing panels. Line them up flush with the outside edges of the purlins. Cut them to length with snips so they meet at the peak and butt into the temporary stop. Secure them with 1-1/2-in. metal-roofing screws.

Slide the first panel into the J-channel, down to the 2x4 stop. Fasten it with 1-1/2-in. metal-roofing screws. Follow the screw pattern recommended by the manufacturer. Slide the next two panels into place before fastening so you know they fit nicely in the J-channel on the other end.

Let the ridge cap overhang by 4 in. at each end. Center the cap and fasten it with metal-roofing screws into the top purlins. Space the screws according to the manufacturer's recommendation. Trim back each side of the ridge to the J-channel.

TRIM THE BOTTOMS OF THE POSTS

The metal post bases will prevent the 1x4 trim boards from fitting

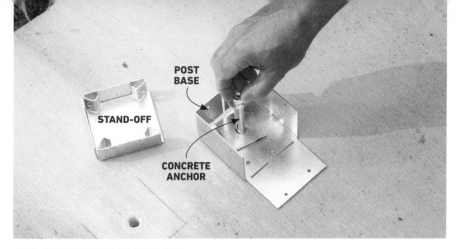

7 INSTALL THE POST BASES
Drill holes for the concrete anchors and fasten the post bases. (Check the anchor requirements for your particular base.)

8 PLUMB AND BRACE THE POSTS
Stand up one side of the grillzebo. Fasten the posts to the bases. Make sure all the posts are plumb as you add temporary braces.

9 INSTALL THE ANGLE BRACES
Fasten the braces with two 3-in. exterior-grade screws angled in at both the top and bottom of the brace.

THREE ROOF PANELS

PURLIN

10 FIND THE LENGTH OF THE PURLINS

To avoid cutting the roof panels to width, overlap them. You want them to cover about 8 ft. A little less is fine. Use your roof panel layout to mark the length of the purlins.

PURLIN

11 INSTALL THE PURLINS

It's important that the purlins all overhang by the same amount. Secure each purlin to the top chords with two 6-in. structural screws in each end.

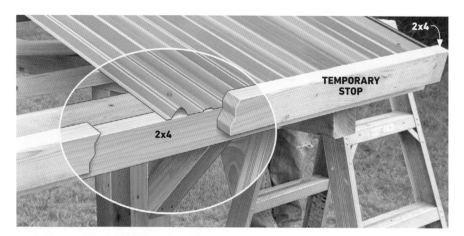

2x4

TEMPORARY STOP

2x4

12 INSTALL THE ROOF PANELS

Screw two 2x4s to the bottom purlin. The 2x4s will act as a stop, making it easy to install the panels with a perfect 1-1/2-in. overhang.

snugly against the posts. Before cutting the trim boards (**G**), run the full-length cedar 1x4s vertically through a table saw a couple of times until about 3/16 in. of material has been removed.

Fasten the trim boards to the posts with an 18-gauge trim gun fitted with 2-in. galvanized brad nails (**Photo 13**). Strengthen the joint by applying construction adhesive before nailing. Secure the trim boards with brad nails at the top and through the miters. To keep them dry, shim them up off the concrete with a pencil.

ASSEMBLE THE TABLE FRAMES AND SHELF FRAMES

Cut the table frame ends and center braces (**H** and **J**) to size. Use a square to mark a line on both posts 41 in. up from the slab. That will be the top of the frame. Install the ends 1 in. away from the outside edge of the inside post, and secure them with 3-in. exterior wood screws, two in each post.

Measure and cut the table frame sides (**K**) to size. Install the board with screws angled into the post. This keeps them from being visible after the top is installed.

Measure the distance between the posts and cut the cedar 2x4 that will serve as the skirt nailer (**L**). Center it on the outside post, leaving 1 in. on each side. This makes the skirt boards flush with the outside edges of the posts.

Install the center braces (**J**) so they're 20 in. in from each post. Secure them by angling two screws into the side boards (so they're not visible) and one down into the skirt nailer (**Photo 14**). Cut the shelf frame ends and centers to size (**M** and **N**). Use a square to mark a line on both posts up 15 in. from the slab. That will be the top of the shelf frame.

Install the end pieces so they overlap onto each post 1 inch. Cut the shelf frame sides **(P)**. Secure them to the end boards with screws. No need to angle these screws because the outside screws will be covered with the skirt boards and the inside ones are too low to notice. Install the shelf frame centers in from both posts by 20 inches.

INSTALL THE TABLETOPS, SHELVES AND SKIRT BOARDS

Cut the deck boards for the tabletops **(Q)** to fit between the posts at each end. Secure with two 2-in. exterior-grade trim-head screws through each deck board. Keep the screws about 1 in. from the edges of the deck boards. Start with the tabletop board closest to the inside, and line it up with the edge of the inside posts **(Photo 15)**. There's no need for a gap between the boards.

Measure and cut the shelf boards **(R)** to length. Rip two boards down to 4 inches. Install the cut ends flush with the outside edges of the shelf frame so they're hidden by the skirt board.

Cut the skirt boards **(S)** to length. Center the first one between the posts, and attach it to the skirt nailer and shelf frame using two trim-head screws. Work your way in each direction, and trim down the last skirt boards so they fit flush with the posts.

FINISH UP

Remove the temporary braces and touch up the cut ends of the boards with stain. Then all that's left is for you to slide your grill into place and invite the neighbors over for a party.

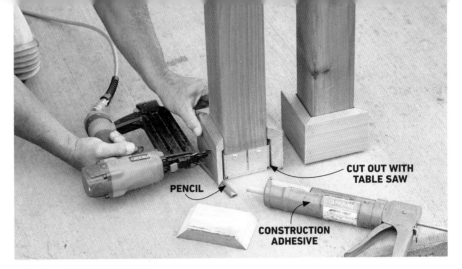

CUT OUT WITH TABLE SAW

PENCIL

CONSTRUCTION ADHESIVE

13 TRIM THE POSTS
To keep the trim boards off the damp concrete, rest them on a pencil while you install them with nails and adhesive. Cutouts on the backs of the trim pieces allow them to fit over the post bases.

SKIRT NAILER

ANGLED SCREWS

NO SCREWS

14 BUILD THE TABLE FRAMES
Assemble each table frame by driving screws at an angle from inside the frame so screw heads will not be visible. Install a skirt nailer under each frame to support the skirt boards.

15 ADD THE TOP BOARDS
Fasten the deck boards with trim-head screws since they're less conspicuous than standard deck screws. Fasten each deck board with two 2-in. screws, one 1 in. from each end.

WHAT IT TAKES

TIME	SKILL LEVEL
8 hours	Intermediate

TOOLS
Basic hand tools, brad nailer (optional), circular saw or table saw, drill driver

CONCRETE TABLE

GET NATURAL STONE'S LOOK AND DURABILITY, BUT CONCRETE'S COST AND SIMPLICITY.

If you want a tabletop that's elegant enough for any indoor setting and tough enough to withstand outdoor weather, you've found it. Tables similar to this one sell for hundreds at garden centers and furniture stores. But you can make one yourself for much less.

Your cost will depend mostly on the wood you choose for the base and the cement mix you use (see "Choosing a Mix," p. 95). You don't need special skills or tools, although a table saw and a brad nailer will speed up the build. Give yourself half a day to build the form and pour the concrete, and an hour to build the table base. A few days after casting the top, you'll spend a couple of hours removing the form, chipping the concrete edges and applying a sealer.

ENDLESS POSSIBILITIES

Most of us think of concrete as a practical material, but it's also one of the most versatile decorative materials around. It can take on just about any color or shape. And surface treatment options are endless: You can cast "fossil" imprints using leaves, ferns or seashells. Or, for a completely different look, you can cast inlays like glass or tile permanently in the surface. To find out how, see "Easy inlays" on page 93.

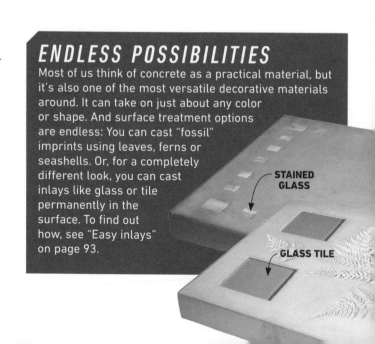

STAINED GLASS

GLASS TILE

Figure A Concrete Table cutting diagram for the concrete form

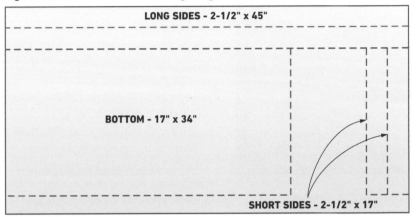

LONG SIDES – 2-1/2" x 45"

BOTTOM – 17" x 34"

SHORT SIDES – 2-1/2" x 17"

MATERIALS LIST

ITEM	QTY.
2' x 4' sheet of 3/4"-thick melamine	1
4x4 x 8'	1
2x4 x 8'	1
Plastic furniture feet	4
Silicone caulk	As needed
Spray adhesive	As needed
Cement colorant	As needed
1-1/4" screws	As needed
Metal brackets (we used Simpson GA2 gusset angle brackets, which measure 1-1/4" x 3-1/4")	8
Acrylic grout and tile sealer	As needed
Countertop mix	As needed

EASY INLAYS

It's easy to embed small decorative objects in the concrete top. Unlike the casts of ferns and leaves, which leave only the imprint behind, an inlay stays in place permanently. You can inlay anything that's durable and has crisp edges. Tiles and colored glass are the most common inlays, but you can also use coins or other metal objects. Simply spread a thin coat of silicone caulk over the face you want exposed and press it down on the melamine base. After the concrete mix hardens, carefully scrape away the silicone film left on the inlay with a razor blade.

Glue inlays facedown to the form with silicone caulk. Be sure to remove excess caulk that squeezes out around the inlay.

Figure B Concrete Table base

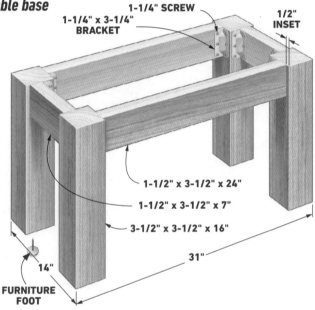

1-1/4" SCREW

1-1/4" x 3-1/4" BRACKET

1/2" INSET

1-1/2" x 3-1/2" x 24"

1-1/2" x 3-1/2" x 7"

3-1/2" x 3-1/2" x 16"

14"

31"

FURNITURE FOOT

OVERALL DIMENSIONS, INCLUDING THE TOP: 17" W x 34" L x 17-1/2" H

PRO TIP

Cut the parts to the dimensions shown and join them with metal brackets. We used cedar lumber, but any rot-resistant wood in 2x4 and 4x4 dimensions is a good choice. Pressure-treated lumber is less expensive. Fasten the top to the base with a few dabs of hot-melt glue.

BUILD THE FORM

Melamine-coated particleboard is the perfect form material for this project because it's smooth, water-resistant and inexpensive. Cut the form parts as shown in **Figure A**. The two long sides overhang the form for easier removal later. A brad nailer is the fastest way to assemble the form **(Photo 1)**. If you use screws or drive nails by hand, be sure that you drill pilot holes to avoid splitting the particleboard. Whatever fastening method you

use, space fasteners about 6 in. apart and make sure that they don't create humps inside the form.

Next, caulk the inside corners to seal the form and create rounded edges on the tabletop **(Photo 2)**. Do this even if you plan to chip off the edges later. Use colored silicone caulk, which will show up well against white melamine. That way, you can spot and clean off any smudges. Keep in mind that every imperfection on the form will show up on the finished tabletop.

1 BUILD THE FORM
Use melamine-coated particleboard to give the concrete form a smooth finish and to make the form easy to remove.

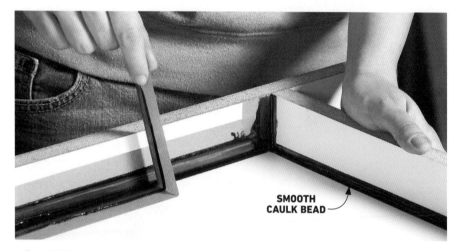

SMOOTH CAULK BEAD

2 CAULK THE CORNERS OF THE FORM
Any imperfections in the caulk will show up on the tabletop, so use masking tape to create neat, even edges.

3 ADD OBJECTS FOR IMPRINTS
Glue down leaves (or other items) with spray adhesive to cast "fossils" in the tabletop. Press the leaves completely flat so concrete can't seep under them.

For neat caulk lines, run masking tape about 3/16 in. from the corners. Apply the caulk one side at a time, smooth it with your finger and remove the tape quickly before the caulk skins over (**Photo 2**). The tape ridges along the caulk lines will show on the finished top, making a perfect chisel guide for chipping the edges later (**Photo 8**).

If you want to cast leaf or fern "fossils" in the top, first press them for a day or two in a book or between scraps of cardboard. Then lay them out on newspaper and coat them with spray adhesive (such as 3M General Purpose 45). Press them onto the form so they lie perfectly flat (**Photo 3**). Thick stems may not lie flat and can leave imprints that are too deep. To avoid this, shave down some of the fern stems with a razor blade.

MIX AND POUR
You can mix the cement in a bucket using a drill and a large paint mixer attachment. This method is fast, but it requires a powerful 1/2-in. drill and won't work well with thicker mixes. Another option is to use a garden hoe and a plastic cement tub. Be patient and mix the cement thoroughly so you completely wet all the powdered ingredients. Pay attention to the product's mixing instructions, especially the recommended amount of water. Adding an extra cup of water can make the mix too thin.

Set your form on a solid surface; level it both front to back and side to side. If you don't do this, one side of your top will be thicker than the other. Then pour the mix around the edges to get an even distribution of material (**Photo 4**). Pouring the entire mix in the middle might concentrate the heavier particles there, weakening the edges. Be sure to wear plastic gloves as you work the material into all corners and edges **(Photo 5)**. Use a gentle touch if you have fragile objects glued to the bottom. If the mix requires wire reinforcement, pour and work in about two-thirds of the mix. Then add the wire and the remaining mix.

All concrete pours contain trapped air bubbles that will leave holes in the finished top unless you take time to work them out. To drive out air bubbles, tap the sides and the bottom of the form with a hammer, and continue rapping until you don't see any more bubbles coming up. However, if you have pea gravel or other aggregate in your mix, you should limit your tapping. Otherwise, the aggregate will settle to the bottom and weaken or perhaps even ruin the appearance of your table. Also keep this in mind: The tabletop doesn't have to be perfectly smooth. Having a few holes or imperfections in the surface may simply add more natural character and charm to the table's appearance.

4 ADD THE CONCRETE
The form must be level—set a level across it and slip shims under the low end. Pour the mix evenly around the perimeter of the form.

CHOOSING A MIX

The best cement mix for this project is a countertop mix, which pros use to cast concrete countertops. Ask for countertop mix at a local concrete products dealer. You'll need about 50 lbs. of mix to make the 17 x 34 x 1-1/2-in. top in this project. The brands share one key factor—special additives called "super-plasticizers" that allow you to add less water. Less water means a denser, stronger top. Some mixes contain fibers to help prevent cracking. Others require wire reinforcement.

You can buy color additives when you buy the mix, or buy concrete color from a more limited selection at a home center. To get the gray, slate-like color shown here, we added 5 oz. of Quikrete Liquid Cement Color ("Charcoal") to a 50-lb. sack of mix.

Here are a few mixes worth considering:

■ LIFETIME FLOORS QUICKTOPS ONE MIX
We chose this product for our project because it is easy to mix, doesn't need reinforcement and hardens in just four hours. It's white, so it can take on any color. The fine consistency allows for detailed imprints, and the edges chip neatly. The version used here contains white aggregate that you can expose if you chip the edges or grind the surface.

■ QUIKRETE NON-SHRINK PRECISION GROUT MIX
Although it's not designed for tops, you can get good results using this inexpensive mix. It takes imprints well, chips neatly and is available at some home centers. It does require reinforcement, however. Quikrete also makes a countertop mix.

■ BUDDY RHODES CONCRETE COUNTERTOP MIX
This countertop mix takes color well, hardens in about 12 hours and requires reinforcement.

■ CX ALL-WEATHER CONCRETE COUNTERTOP PRO-FORMULA MIX
This is a package of plasticizers, reinforcing fiber and colorants that you mix into standard high-strength cement mix. These products are designed for surface grinding, which exposes the aggregate.

5 SPREAD THE MIX

Work it into corners and around any objects cast into the tabletop. Then lightly tap the sides of the form with a hammer to drive out air bubbles.

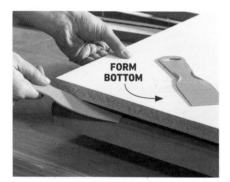

FORM BOTTOM

6 REMOVE THE FORM

Start with the long sides, then remove the short sides. Next, flip the tabletop over and pry off the bottom panel with a plastic putty knife.

When you're finished removing the air bubbles in the mix, cover the top of the mix with plastic and let the concrete harden and cure anywhere from four hours to two days, depending on the brand of mix you're using.

RELEASE THE FORM AND FINISH

To remove the form, pry off the long sides and then the short sides, prying against the form base rather than the concrete. To pry off the form bottom, use a plastic putty knife (Photo 6); metal will mar the surface. If your top has imprints with fine detail, cover the top with plastic and let it harden for an extra day. Then scrub the top with water (Photo 7). Use a plastic putty knife to scrape

7 CLEAN THE TABLETOP SURFACE

Scrub the leaves out of their imprints with a stiff plastic brush. Scour the whole surface to remove excess colorant and melamine residue.

off melamine residue that won't simply scrub off.

The mix we used chipped off neatly for a rough-edge look (Photo 8). Be sure to set the top on plywood on a solid surface. Shown here is a 3/4-in.-wide cold chisel, but you can use whatever width best produces the effect you want. For safety, hone down any sharp edges with a file or sandpaper.

Your top will withstand outdoor weather, but it's susceptible to stains. To prevent them and to bring out more color, seal the top with an acrylic sealer (found in the tile aisle at home centers). The first coat will sink in and the surface will remain dull. After it dries, apply a second coat, and perhaps even a third one, until the surface retains a shine.

8 CHIP THE EDGES

Create a natural stone look by chipping the edges with a cold chisel. Chip around all four edges, then flip the top over and chip from the other side.

ARCHED PLANTER

BEND WOOD TO CREATE THIS GRACEFUL PLANT STAND. YOU CAN MAKE IT WITH ONLY TWO BOARDS!

With this elegant curved deck planter, you can have a splash of garden anywhere you'd like. Add flowerpots to accent your patio, deck or front entrance. We'll show you how to build the whole project in a weekend. Bending wood strips into laminated arches may seem challenging, but we'll walk you through the process step by step. The key, as you'll see, is a simple plywood "bending" jig that you can use over and over again. After you build your first planter, you'll have the hang of it and making the next one will be a cinch.

You can complete this project if you're handy with basic carpentry tools. However, you'll need a table saw equipped with a thin-kerf blade for ripping the strips and other parts—a circular saw just won't do the job no matter how steady you are. But you'll still need a circular saw, as well as a belt sander and at least four 3-ft. pipe or bar clamps **(Photo 4)**.

WHAT IT TAKES	
TIME 1 weekend	**SKILL LEVEL** Intermediate
TOOLS	
Basic hand tools, belt sander, circular saw, 3-ft. bar or pipe clamps, drill driver, nailer, paint scraper, random orbital sander, table saw	

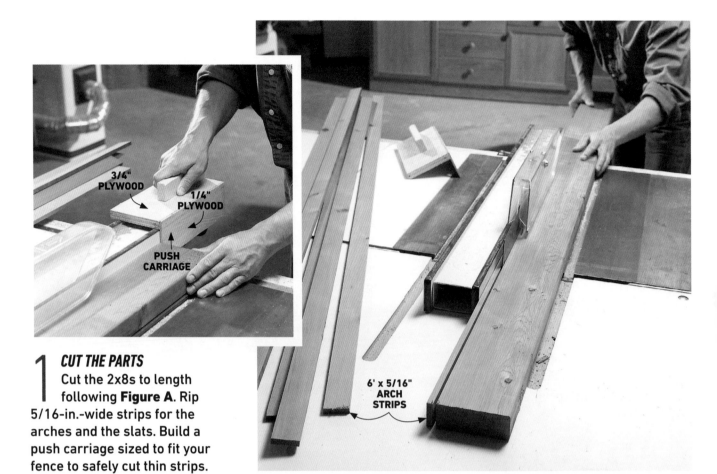

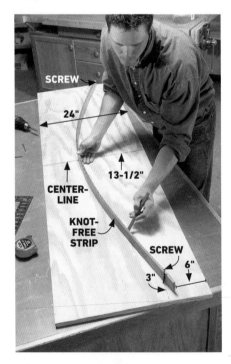

1 CUT THE PARTS
Cut the 2x8s to length following **Figure A**. Rip 5/16-in.-wide strips for the arches and the slats. Build a push carriage sized to fit your fence to safely cut thin strips.

SELECT WOOD WITH SMALL, TIGHT KNOTS

You need only two 8-ft.-long 2x8s for the entire project. Our planter is made from western red cedar, chosen for its beauty and natural decay resistance, but any wood you choose will be fine as long as you select straight boards with small, tight knots. The long thin strips will break at large knots during the bending process. Also, you'll be using nearly every inch of each board, so pick ones without splits or cracks at the ends. It may take some sorting at the home center, but the effort's worth it.

MATERIALS LIST

ITEM	QTY.
2x8 x 8'	2
4x8 sheet of plywood	1
10' x 20' roll of painter's plastic (3 mil)	1
Quart exterior woodworking glue	2
Mini paint roller	1
Galvanized 1" brads	As needed

CUT THE PARTS

Cut each 2x8 to the lengths called for in **Figure A** and then start the ripping process. Ripping 5/16-in.-wide strips can be hazardous, so be sure to use a push carriage **(Photo 1)**. Make your carriage from 1/4- and 3/4-in. plywood, custom-sized to match the height of the table saw fence. We were able to cut 15 strips from each board, but you may get fewer depending on the thickness of your blade. Don't worry if you wind up with fewer or unusable ones; you can build each arch with as few as 13 strips. Just make sure to use the same quantity for each arch so they'll match. If any of the strips break at knots, keep the pieces together because you can still use them (more on this later).

Rip the platform slats next and then the 1/2 x 3/4-in. platform cleats. Rip the pieces first to 3/4 in.

2 MARK THE ARCH
Draw the arch on the bending jig plywood using one of the knot-free strips of wood and a pair of 3-in. screws.

Figure A Arched Planter built from two 8-ft.-long 2x8s
OVERALL DIMENSIONS: 14-1/2" W x 68" D x 13" H

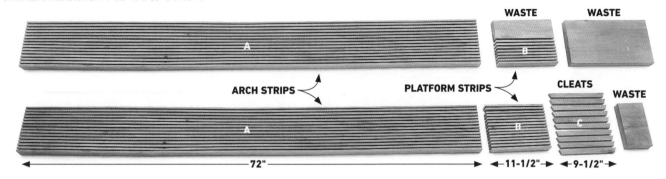

ARCH STRIPS — A — A

PLATFORM STRIPS — B — WASTE — WASTE

CLEATS — C — WASTE

72" — 11-1/2" — 9-1/2"

wide from a chunk of 2x8, then turn the 1-1/2-in. strips on their sides and rip them into 1/2-in. strips. Cut the cleats to length with decorative 22-degree angles on the ends.

MAKE THE BENDING JIG

Cut the plywood for the bending jig to size **(Photo 2)** and use one of the knot-free strips to form the curve. Use 3-in. screws partially driven into the plywood at the locations shown and push the center of the strip 13-1/2 in. out from the edge while you scribe the curve. Don't beat yourself up striving for a perfect curve; small variations

won't be noticeable. It may seem odd to make this curved cut with a circular saw **(Photo 3)**, but it's surprisingly easy and safe on a gentle curve like this, and the curve will be smoother than any you can achieve with a jigsaw. Just make sure to set your blade depth at 7/8 in. Any deeper and the blade may bind and kick back.

The two curves on the two sections of the jig are slightly different, and you'll have to recut the top part of the jig to match the bottom. To find this difference, lay 15 strips in the jig and tighten the clamps until the arch is completely

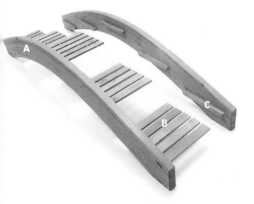

CUT 7/8" DEEP

GAP

3/4" SPACER

3 CUT THE PLYWOOD CURVE
Clamp the plywood to the workbench; set the blade to cut 7/8 in. deep. Hold the saw with both hands; cut the curve.

4 RECUT THE CURVE
Clamp 15 strips in the bending jig and re-mark the top curve of the jig with a 3/4-in. spacer block. Then remove the strips and recut that curve only.

CAUL BLOCKING

2x4

EXTERIOR WOOD GLUE

MINI ROLLER

CENTER-LINE MARK

PAINTER'S PLASTIC

5 MAKE CLAMPING CAULS

Screw together three clamping cauls, adding blocks as needed so they'll be even with the top of the laminating strips (see **Photo 7**).

formed (**Photo 4**). You'll have to tighten the clamps in turns as the strips gradually bend. That is, tighten two clamps until they run out of threads, then leave them in place while you completely unscrew the other two. Slide those jaws tight to the jig and continue tightening those two.

Work in pairs, tightening the outer two, then the inner two. You'll get the feel for the clamping process on this glue-less dry run, and it'll make the actual glue-up easier. When the clamps are tight, the strips will be tight to the jig at the bottom and there'll be a gap between the arch and the jig at the top. Trace around the top with a 3/4-in. spacer to re-mark the top curve (**Photo 4**). Then unclamp everything and recut that portion of the jig.

BLOCK UP THE CAULS AND GLUE UP THE ARCHES

During glue-up, the strips have a tendency to lift away from the clamps while the glue is wet and slippery because of the stresses in the curves. "Cauls" are simply blocks of wood that hold the strips flat and prevent this. Make the

6 GLUE UP THE STRIPS

Using a mini roller, apply glue to both sides of each strip (but to only one side of the top and bottom strips). Position the strips, keeping the jig and strip centerlines aligned.

CAUL

7 SCREW DOWN THE CAULS AND TIGHTEN THE CLAMPS

Push the jig together as far as possible and snug up the clamps. Then screw the cauls down and finish tightening the clamps.

cauls from six 2x4s (three on both the bottom and the top) and space them evenly with blocking sized so the cauls will be flush with the top of the arch (**Photo 7**). Have these ready to go before the glue-up—you won't have time to spare later.

Mark a centerline on the strips and keep it aligned with the bending jig centerline when you start gluing (**Photo 6**). Lay painter's plastic directly below the jig to keep your workbench and clamps clean, then start gluing the strips. A mini paint roller greatly speeds up the process, and time is of the essence.

Glue both sides of each strip and push the glued surfaces lightly together to delay glue setup. Slip in any broken strips near the middle of the arch, matching up the breaks after they're coated with glue. Use flawless strips for the first and last strips of each arch. After you spread the glue, pull the jig together, bending the strips as far as you can while a helper slides the clamps closed (this will speed up the clamping process). Then lay plastic over the caul locations, screw the cauls into place, screw the top 2x4s into place and tighten

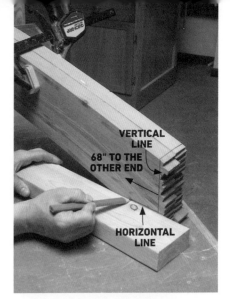

8 SCRAPE OFF THE GLUE

Remove the cauls after one hour and scrape off the excess glue from that side. Remove the clamps after three hours and scrape the glue from the other side.

9 SAND THE ARCH

Belt-sand both sides of the arch flat with 60-grit sandpaper, then 80-grit sandpaper. Smooth the surface with a random-orbital sander with 100-grit sandpaper.

10 CUT OFF THE ENDS

Clamp the arches together; draw vertical lines just short of the ends. Then scribe the bottom horizontal lines with a 2x4 spacer. Cut the ends with a circular saw.

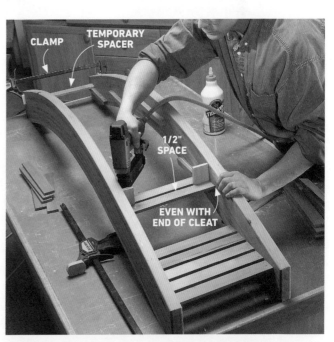

11 GLUE AND NAIL THE CLEATS

Lay the cleat-mounting template **(Figure B)** flush with the arch bottoms. Then glue and nail the end cleats. Rest the template over the first set of cleats and mount the next two cleats, then move it again to mount the top cleat.

12 GLUE AND NAIL THE PLATFORM STRIPS

Space and clamp the arches. Then glue and nail the platform strips on the cleats, keeping them even with the cleat ends and spacing them 1/2 in. apart on the cleats.

the clamps. Again, work in pairs, progressively tightening them. Work quickly. If you still see gaps between any strips, close them by driving a wedge between the jig

and the arch or by adding more bar clamps from above. Ignore the clamping instructions on the glue bottle—leave the clamps in place for at least three hours.

You don't have to wait until you've removed the clamps to start cleaning up excess glue and flattening the arch. As the glue starts to "gel" (become dry to the touch but

Figure B Arched Planter cleat template

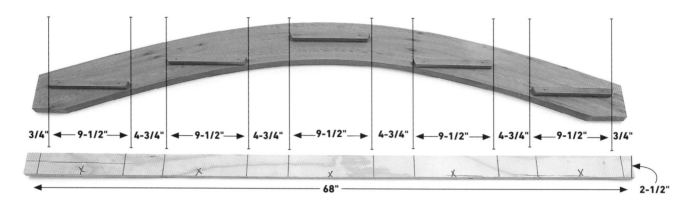

3/4" ← 9-1/2" → 4-3/4" ← 9-1/2" → 4-3/4" ← 9-1/2" → 4-3/4" ← 9-1/2" → 4-3/4" ← 9-1/2" → 3/4"

← 68" →

2-1/2"

gooey beneath the surface, about one hour into clamping), remove the cauls (leave the clamps tightened) and start scraping away the glue from the top side of the arch **(Photo 8)**. A paint scraper works great for most of it; use a small chisel or screwdriver to get into the crevices. The key is to remove as much glue as possible. Whenglue is hardened, it's nearly impossible to remove, and any leftover glue will clog and ruin sanding belts in no time.

After scraping off the glue, wipe off any other glue smears with a damp (not wet!) rag. Don't worry about the bottom side; you can get it after the clamping period. The glue there will stay softer longer because of the plastic.

FLATTEN THE ARCHES AND CUT THE ENDS

Start belt-sanding diagonally with 60-grit belts to knock off the high spots **(Photo 9)**. After the surface is flat, remove cross-grain sanding marks by sanding following the curve. Next, belt-sand with 80- and then 100-grit belts. Finish up with 100-grit paper in a random-orbital sander. Remove the arch from the jig, scrape off the glue, and flatten and sand the opposite side. Then repeat the whole process for the other arch.

If you have a benchtop planer, use it for the whole flattening process. Feed in one end and you'll be able to gently push the arch sideways and follow the curve as it goes through the

machine. Make sure all of the glue on the surface is removed. Hardened glue will dull the cutting knives of the tool.

Mark and cut off the bottoms and ends as shown in **Photo 10**. Cut one end first, then measure over 68 in. and cut the other end. Ease the sharp edges of each arch with a round-over router bit or sandpaper.

MOUNT THE CLEATS AND THE PLATFORMS

In **Photo 11** we show you an easy way to mount the cleats on both arches using a mounting template made from plywood **(Figure B)**. Cut the plywood to 68 in. and lay out the cleat positions as shown. Then position, glue and nail the cleats.

Separate the arches with temporary platform strips and lightly clamp the arches together **(Photo 12)**. Make sure the arch ends are even, then glue and nail the platforms to the cleats.

If you'd like a finish on your planter, use any stain designed for exterior siding. To further protect your planter against rot, spread exterior wood glue on the feet of each arch.

COBBLESTONE PATH

BUILD THIS HANDSOME FEATURE AND ENHANCE YOUR BACKYARD.

You don't need heavy equipment and a week of work to lay an attractive and durable path. This one is designed for simplicity and ease of construction.

The path is made from old street pavers and granite cobbles set on a sand bed. But you can substitute just about any pavers or types of stone that are available and fit your landscape. These stone-setting techniques will even accommodate stones of varying thicknesses. You can build this path using a shovel, a wheelbarrow and a few inexpensive hand tools.

Here you'll learn all the path-building details, from breaking ground to breaking the cobbles to fit in tight spots. Usually the main stumbling block is making

the path smooth and flat. To solve that problem, you'll learn a simple leveling technique using ordinary plastic landscape edging. With this method, you can lay a top-notch path, even if you're a novice.

WHAT IT TAKES	
TIME 2 weekends	**SKILL LEVEL** Intermediate
TOOLS Basic hand tools, 3-lb. hammer, deadblow hammer or rubber mallet, hand tamper, 3-in. mason's chisel, shovel, wheelbarrow	

Figure A Cobblestone Path details
OVERALL DIMENSIONS: 21-1/2" W x VARIABLE LENGTH

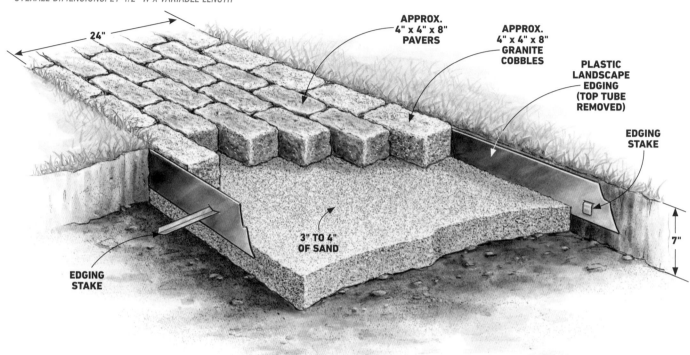

24"

APPROX.
4" x 4" x 8"
PAVERS

APPROX.
4" x 4" x 8"
GRANITE
COBBLES

PLASTIC
LANDSCAPE
EDGING
(TOP TUBE
REMOVED)

EDGING
STAKE

3" TO 4"
OF SAND

7"

EDGING
STAKE

Keep in mind that this path is designed for foot traffic and other light use. Don't try to drive on it. Because the path is set on only sand, it won't stay as flat and smooth as a traditional paver walk that's set on a compacted gravel bed. It's ideal for narrower secondary walks in a garden or backyard, where slight imperfections and undulations add to its character. And if an edge stone gets loose from a wheelbarrow bouncing over it, you can reset it in minutes. Expect to pull an occasional weed growing up in the joints. Or if you prefer an English cottage look, encourage moss or other ground covers to grow in the joints.

SELECT THE PATH MATERIALS FIRST

To achieve the aged, timeless look, you'll have to track down old street pavers. If you're lucky, you may be able to salvage material from a local project where a street is being torn up. Otherwise look for older materials at a landscape supplier or an architectural salvage store. You can also check online resale market sites. Sizes vary, but it usually takes about 4-1/2 pavers to cover a square foot. The granite cobblestone isn't antique; the stones were run through a rock tumbler to make them look worn. Figure on three cobbles per linear foot of path. Use ordinary washed concrete sand for the setting bed. Figure on 1 cu. yd. per 80 sq. ft. of path. You can have the pavers,

Figure B Measure the path width

21-1/2"

> **CAUTION:**
> Call 811 or visit call811.com to locate underground lines before you dig.

1 MARK THE PATH AND SITTING AREA

Lay out the path with stakes and marking paint. Define the sitting area first, and the starting and ending points next. Then connect them.

2 EXCAVATE THE PATH

Dig the path about 7 in. deep between the lines. Then cut the edge vertically along the painted line on one side. Scrape the bottom flat.

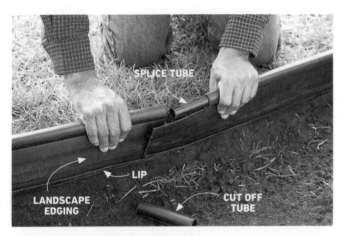

3 INSTALL LANDSCAPE EDGING

Set the edging along the vertical cut edge. To splice sections, cut away 7 in. of the top tube, insert a splice tube and then overlap the sections.

4 DRIVE SPIKES THROUGH EDGING

Hold the top of the tube about an inch above the sod and drive spikes every 5 ft. through the edging into the side of the excavation.

cobbles and sand delivered. Use "contractor's grade" landscape edging for the border (**Photo 3**). Buy it from a landscape supplier in 20-ft. strips that are stored flat. They usually come with stakes, but buy a few extra packs of stakes to better hold down the edging. Don't buy edging that's coiled up; it's often difficult to set smoothly.

MATERIALS LIST

ITEM

Pavers

Granite cobbles

Washed concrete sand

Landscape edging

PATH LAYOUT

You can use a garden hose to help you lay out your path, but **Photo 1** shows another technique. First dot the starting, end and center points, then connect the dots with a smooth line. Stakes work well to mark a curve, then simply connect the stakes with paint (**Photo 1**). Don't worry about making mistakes with the paint; your next mowing will erase them. Gradual curves work best; curves with a radius tighter than 5 ft. result in unsightly wide gaps between the pavers. Plan your path width to the

full brick (**Figure B**), and then add a few inches to the width of your excavation for wiggle room for the slightly wider spacing needed on a curve. Limit the size of your path to anywhere from 2 to 3 ft. wide. Anything wider will look out of scale in a garden setting.

ROLL UP YOUR SLEEVES AND DIG!

When you're digging through sod, it's always easiest to drive the shovel through the grass and push it into the area you've already dug out (**Photo 2**). When you're on a

LEVEL

SCREED
BOARD

HAND
TAMPER

DAMP
SAND

5 SPACE THE OTHER SIDE
Notch a 32-in. 1x6 board to the desired path width. Use it as a guide to space the other side. Set landscape edging along the second side.

6 ADD THE SAND
Fill the excavation with damp sand to a level about 4 in. below the top of the tube. Compact the sand firmly with a hand tamper.

SCREED
BOARD

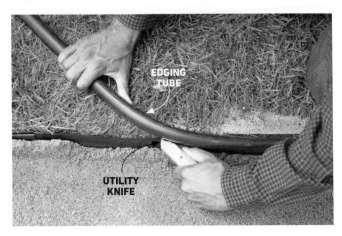

EDGING
TUBE

UTILITY
KNIFE

7 LEVEL THE SAND
Pull the screed board along the edging to level and smooth the sand 4 in. below the top of the tube. Fill and tamp any low spots.

8 REMOVE THE TUBE
Cut the tube off the top of the edging with a sharp utility knife. Keep the cut at or slightly below the soil level to keep it out of sight.

slope, use gravity in your favor. Start at the bottom and back your way up the hill. Use the blade of a round-nose shovel as a rough depth gauge. Stepping the shovel almost all the way into the ground gives you about a 7-in. depth.

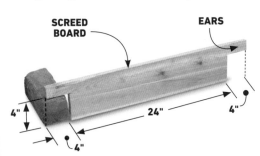

SCREED
BOARD

EARS

4"

24"

4"

4"

Roughly dig out the entire path, and then dig out one of the sides back to the paint line with an edging spade that you hold vertically. Finally, level the bottom flat with a shovel. You'll be amazed at how much dirt will come out of that narrow little path. If possible, find a place for it onsite by building a berm or adding soil around the house to improve drainage. Otherwise, roughly calculate the volume of the soil you have to remove and rent a roll-off container to dispose of the soil.

SETTING THE EDGE
The top of the plastic landscape edging will be the finished height of your path. Set it a little higher than the surrounding lawn or garden so water will drain off the path, but set the top of the tube flush where the path meets a patio or driveway. The heavy-grade plastic edging will form a smooth, flat surface without telegraphing the minor dips or bumps in your lawn. Most edging has a little lip on the bottom to keep it from creeping up **(Photo 3)**—set this to the inside of the path. With one side spiked in place

GRANITE
COBBLES

DEADBLOW
HAMMER

STREET
PAVERS

HALF
PAVER

EXISTING
PATIO

9 SET THE FIRST PAVERS

Begin setting the pavers at the most visible end. Stagger the joints by one-half paver. Set each with a few whacks of a deadblow hammer.

10 KEEP THE TOP OF THE PATH FLAT

Remove or add sand as needed to accommodate the uneven thickness of the granite cobbles and to keep the top of the path flat.

11 MARK PAVERS FOR CUTTING

Measure cuts by holding the paver in place and marking one edge. Use a speed square to extend the mark completely around the paver.

3-LB.
HAMMER

3" MASON'S
CHISEL

3"
MASON'S
CHISEL

12 BREAK PAVERS WITH A CHISEL

Set the chisel on the mark; rap several times with a 3-lb. hammer on all sides until the paver breaks. Be sure to wear safety glasses.

(Photo 4), cut your screed board to the path width and use it to space the edging on the other side **(Photo 5)**. Set this edging about 1/2 in. higher or lower to encourage drainage from the path. At the 4-ft.-wide seating area, allow a 1-in. height difference across the entire width.

ADD SAND

Now add sand to the excavation and compact it **(Photo 6)**. Although a motorized plate compactor works best, a hand tamper works just fine for a small path like this one. The sand should be slightly damp when you tamp it to help it pack down.

To flatten it, place the ears of the screed board on the edging and pull a ridge of sand down the path, filling in any depressions as you go **(Photo 7)**. Work from the top of the slope downhill. Whether you remove the edging tube is purely a matter of aesthetics **(Photo 8)**. If you don't mind the appearance of the tube, leave it on.

SETTING THE PAVERS

Laying the pavers will move quickly, especially if you have a helper handing them to you.

Start where you want the best fit, which is usually where the path meets a patio, walk or driveway **(Photo 9)**. Set one side of the cobbles first and follow along with the pavers, staggering each row by half a paver.

As you work your way through a curve, the stagger will change because of the wider radius at the outside of the curve. If the joints from row to row come within 1 in., simply insert a half paver to increase the separation. The pavers will set in pretty uniformly, but you'll probably have to adjust

EDGING GARDEN BEDS

Add a garden edging with extra cobbles to create flowerbeds and to blend the path and garden into the yard. Leave the cobble tops slightly above ground level to create a nice edge for easy lawn mowing.

Cut a clean 5 x 5-in. trench with an edging spade. Then add a few inches of sand.

Push each cobblestone into the sand, leaving the top about 1/2 in. above the adjacent ground. Set the cobblestones with a whack of a deadblow hammer.

SEATING AREA

Figure out the dimensions for a seating area by roughly laying out the pattern on your driveway. Then set the sand base in the same manner as the path, placing edging on two sides to serve as screed guides. (Use a longer screed board.) Because you'll be setting a bench or chairs on it, make the surface relatively level. Only allow a 1-in. height difference from one side to the other. Lay the pavers in staggered rows (a running bond pattern) that will wrap around the sides. Start at the outside and work your way around to the middle. It'll take a bit of fiddling to get the pavers to fit. You'll have to space some pavers up to 1/4 in. apart and cut a few as well. The informal design allows for looser spacing. Sand will fill the gaps.

LARGE GAP

SPLIT COBBLE

13 DEAL WITH GAPS

Hide large gaps up to 1-1/2 in. by shifting adjacent pavers up to 1/4 in. apart. Avoid using paver pieces less than about 1-1/2 in. wide.

14 FINISH THE SIDE OF THE PATH

Fill in along the side of the path with topsoil and tamp firmly with your foot.

15 PUT SAND IN THE JOINTS

Sweep sand over the path, working it in until all the joints are full. Save some sand to sweep into the joints after the first rain.

the height of the cobbles a little so their tops remain flush with the pavers (**Photo 10**).

The best way to cut a paver is to split it (**Photo 12**). The resulting ragged edge is in keeping with the worn and tumbled look, but splitting is a little tricky because pavers are extremely hard. Work on a soft surface like the lawn or a pile of sand. With the chisel, strike the paver sharply on all sides, turning it from top to bottom, then side to side. Hold the chisel perpendicular to the paver's face. Don't try to split off anything smaller than 1-1/2 in. It just won't break cleanly. Instead, to deal with gaps up to 1-1/2 in. wide, space six or eight pavers slightly farther apart (**Photo 13**). And save the cutoff pieces. Chances are you can work them in somewhere.

After filling along the sides of the path with topsoil (**Photo 14**), the last step is to fill the joints with sand. Sweep the sand into the joints, leaving a thin layer on top. Let it dry and sweep it in again, working the broom back and forth until the joints are full (**Photo 15**). Your path will need little or no maintenance; it will just continue to look better and better as it ages.

WHAT IT TAKES

TIME
1 weekend

SKILL LEVEL
Intermediate

TOOLS
Basic hand tools, circular saw, drill

EASY TO LOAD

ONBOARD TOOL STORAGE

HUGE LOAD? NO PROBLEM

WONDER CART

IT'S EASY TO BUILD, AND IT'S BETTER THAN A WHEELBARROW.

Wheelbarrows are great for hauling stuff around the yard—unless you're working on a hill, trying to negotiate steps and rough terrain, moving a lot of bulky material like leaves and branch trimmings, or trying to load something big into them.

Since we added this garden cart to our outdoor arsenal of tools, life has gotten way easier. Two wheels means it doesn't tip; large pneumatic tires mean it's easy to push; a big box lets us haul 10 bags of mulch in one load; and because the front tilts down for loading, our aching backs don't ache as much. We'll still use our trusty wheelbarrow for mixing concrete and hauling the super-heavy stuff, but these days we "cart" nearly everything else.

We designed this cart to be as rugged and durable as any cart you can buy at any price. It's one of the wisest landscaping investments you can make.

ROUND UP MATERIALS

You'll need a straight-cutting jig to cut the plywood. To learn how to make one, go to familyhandyman.com. Search for "straight cuts" or "cutting guides." We used exterior plywood and standard pine boards for the structure. You can use treated plywood and lumber, but it may be hard to find treated material that's both dry and flat.

We bought wheels online at northerntool.com. The threaded rod, washers and nuts are available at home centers and hardware stores.

ASSEMBLE THE BOX

Lay out the plywood as shown in **Figure B**. Start by cutting the sheet lengthwise into 14-in., 30-in. and 3-1/2-in. strips (**Photo 1**). After positioning the jig for each cut, clamp or screw it into place. Cut the angled sides (**A**) from the 14-in. strip and the bottom braces (**E**) from the 3-1/2-in. strip. Cut the front (**C**), bottom (**D**) and back (**B**) from the 30-in. strip.

If you use your straight-cutting jig as is for cutting the 45-degree bevels, you'll cut a bevel on the jig itself, making it unusable for future square cuts. Temporarily modify your jig by screwing a 3/4-in. strip

1 CUT THE PLYWOOD PARTS
A homemade straight-cutting jig turns your circular saw into a precision plywood slicer. To see how to make this jig, go to familyhandyman.com and search for "straight cuts."

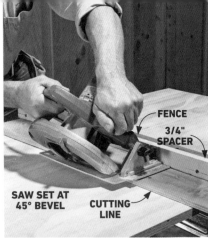

2 CUT THE BEVELED EDGES
Screw a spacer to the fence of your jig, and line up the edge with your cutting line just as you would for a standard cut. Then you can make the long 45-degree cuts.

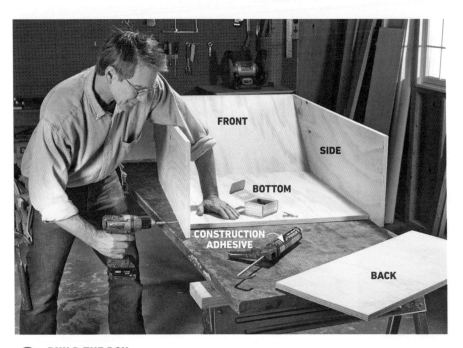

3 BUILD THE BOX
Secure the panels to one another using construction adhesive and 2-in. screws. Drill pilot holes to avoid splintering the edges of the plywood. Flip the cart upside down and then install the three bottom braces (E).

4 INSTALL THE WHEEL ASSEMBLY
Install a washer, a wheel, another washer and a locknut on one end of the threaded rod. Measure the overhang required by the wheel assembly, add that length to the other end and then cut the rod to length. Install the axle braces and cover.

of wood to the jig's fence **(Photo 2)**, positioning the edge of the guide on the cutting line (as you would for a square cut), then make your 45-degree cut.

Drill 1/8-in. holes about 3/8 in. away from the edges of the sides **(A)**, spaced about 4 in. apart. Then secure the front with 2-in. exterior screws through the predrilled holes in the sides.

NOTE: To ensure maximum sturdiness, use construction adhesive for all the connections— even for the metal corners.

Install the bottom **(Photo 3)** flush with the edges of the sides **(A)**. Make sure the front beveled edge of the bottom makes solid contact with the bottom edge of the front **(C)**. To complete the box, add the back **(B)**. If you've cut and assembled everything correctly, there will be a 3-1/2-in. cavity at the back of the box to accommodate the tool rack. If it's a little larger or smaller, no big deal.

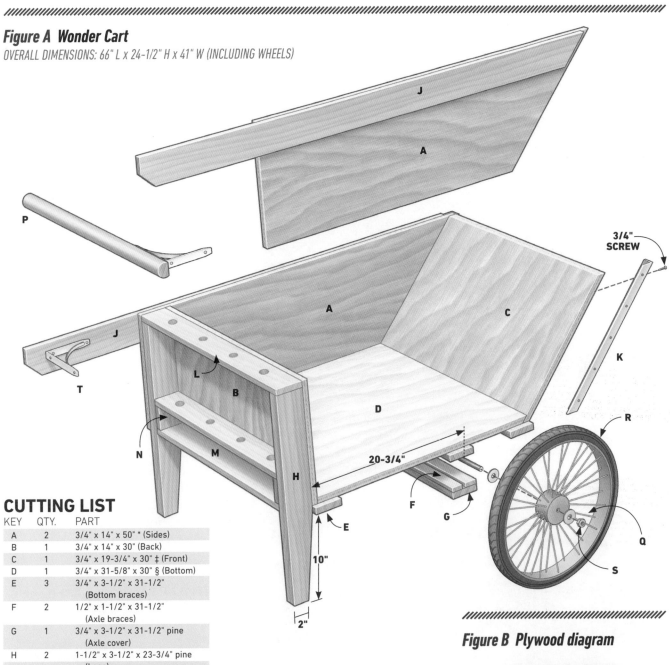

Figure A Wonder Cart
OVERALL DIMENSIONS: 66" L x 24-1/2" H x 41" W (INCLUDING WHEELS)

3/4"
SCREW

20-3/4"

10"

2"

CUTTING LIST

KEY	QTY.	PART
A	2	3/4" x 14" x 50" * (Sides)
B	1	3/4" x 14" x 30" (Back)
C	1	3/4" x 19-3/4" x 30" ‡ (Front)
D	1	3/4" x 31-5/8" x 30" § (Bottom)
E	3	3/4" x 3-1/2" x 31-1/2" (Bottom braces)
F	2	1/2" x 1-1/2" x 31-1/2" (Axle braces)
G	1	3/4" x 3-1/2" x 31-1/2" pine (Axle cover)
H	2	1-1/2" x 3-1/2" x 23-3/4" pine (Legs)
J	2	3/4" x 3-1/2" x 64-1/2" pine # (Handles)
K	2	Cut to fit # (Corner braces)
L	1	3/4" x 3-1/2" x 30" (Long tool rack slat)
M	2	3/4" x 3-1/2" x 27" (Short tool rack slats)
N	2	3/4" x 3-1/2" x 3" (Tool rack blocks)
P	1	1-1/4" handrail (Handlebar)
Q	4	1/2" fender washer (Washers)
R	2	20" w/pneumatic tire (Wheels)
S	2	1/2" locknut (Locknut)
T	2	6" shelf brackets (or similar) (L-brackets)

NOTES:
* Angled cut
‡ 45-degree bevel cut, both ends
§ 45-degree bevel cut, one end
# 45-degree cuts, both ends

MATERIALS LIST

ITEM	QTY.
4' x 8' x 3/4" exterior plywood	1
2x4 x 48" pine	1
1x4 x 96" pine	3
1-1/4" x 30" handrail	1
1/2" x 3" x 31-1/2" plywood or solid wood	1
20"-dia. wheels	2
1/2" x 48" threaded rod	1
1/2" washers	4
1/2" locknuts	2
6" L-shaped shelf brackets	2
1" x 1" x 2' aluminum angle	2
3/4" exterior screws	20
1-1/4" exterior screws	1 lb.
2" exterior screws	2 lbs.
Heavy-duty construction adhesive (pint tubes)	2

Figure B Plywood diagram

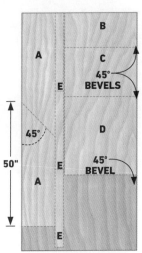

B

A

C

45°
BEVELS

E

45°

D

50"

E

45°
BEVEL

A

E

LEG (H)

3/4" SPACER BLOCK

5 INSTALL THE LEGS
Apply two beads of construction adhesive, clamp the legs into place and secure them with screws. The spacer block positions each leg, leaving room for the tool rack.

HANDLE (J)

3/4" SCREW

CORNER BRACE (K)

6 STRENGTHEN THE CORNERS
Cut aluminum angle stock to length, then drill holes and countersink "dimples" for the screw heads. Install the corner braces using construction adhesive and screws.

INSTALL THE WHEELS

Turn the cart box upside down. Secure the bottom braces (**E**). Secure the middle bottom brace so its center is exactly 20-3/4 in. away from the back of the back bottom brace (**E**). If you don't get this positioned right, it will affect the balance of the cart.

Position the assembly in **Photo 4** snugly against one side of the cart and measure the amount of space it takes up. Transfer that measurement to the other end of the rod; mark the rod. Cut the rod and install the other wheel assembly. Tip: Before cutting the rod to length, twist a regular nut onto it past the cut mark. After making the cut, twist the nut off; this will "recut" any damaged thread so a locknut goes on easily.

Apply glue to the axle braces (**F**), snug them tightly against the axle, then secure them to the middle bottom brace (**E**) with 2-in. screws. Finally, install the axle cover (**G**). **NOTE:** If you want to strengthen the wheel assembly for hauling heavier loads, use oak for the middle bottom brace, two axle braces and cover.

INSTALL THE LEGS, THE HANDLES AND THE TOOL RACK

Cut the legs and screw them to the protruding sides (**Photo 5**). Use the spacer block as shown so the legs can accommodate the upper tool rack slat. Cut and install the handles (**J**), leaving space at the front for the aluminum angle.

Cut two lengths of aluminum angle stock for corner braces. Don't try to measure them; just hold them in place and mark them for cutting. Drill holes and countersink "dimples" for the screw heads to nest into. Then install the braces using adhesive and 3/4-in. screws (**Photo 6**).

Position the handlebar **(P)** and add the L-brackets **(Photo 7)** to reinforce the handle. Finally, install the three tool rack slats **(Photo 8)**.

Remove the wheels and apply a coat of high-quality exterior primer followed by two coats of exterior paint. To keep your cart in good condition, you should store it inside; if it will be outside, make sure you flip it upside down on a couple of scrap 4x4s.

HANDLE-BAR (P)   L-BRACKET (T)

7 INSTALL THE HANDLEBAR
Secure the handlebar by driving screws through each handle into the end of the rail. Add the L-brackets to beef up the connection.

LONG SLAT (L)

SHORT SLATS (M)

8 ADD A TOOL RACK
Cut three tool rack slats and drill holes for tool handles. Adjust the sizes and spacing of the holes to suit your tools. Use adhesive and screws to install the slats.

WHAT IT TAKES

TIME
1-2 days

SKILL LEVEL
Intermediate

TOOLS
Basic hand tools, circular saw, drill, shovel, string and string level

ISLAND DECK

//

CREATE A COMFORTABLE RETREAT ANYWHERE IN YOUR YARD.

Most decks are attached to houses, but there's no reason they have to be. Sometimes the best spot to set up a deck chair and relax is at the other end of the yard, tucked into a shady corner near the garden. And if you don't attach the deck to the house, you don't need to dig deep frost footings—which can save hours of backbreaking labor, especially in wooded or rocky areas where digging footings is difficult.

We designed this deck with simple construction in mind. If you can cut boards and drive screws, you can build it. The only power tools you'll need are a circular saw and a drill. We used a premium grade low-maintenance composite decking with hidden fasteners, but using standard treated decking and screws would lower the cost. You may need to special-order composite decking and hidden fasteners if you use the same types we did, but everything else is stocked at home centers or lumberyards.

A few cautions: If all or part of the deck is higher than 30 in. off the ground, you'll need a building permit and

A DECK YOU CAN BUILD IN A DAY

The simplicity of this deck makes it fast to build. With a helper and all the materials ready to go first thing in the morning, you can have a completed deck by sundown. But if you add a step to your deck and use hidden deck fasteners as we did, you might need a few more hours to finish the job.

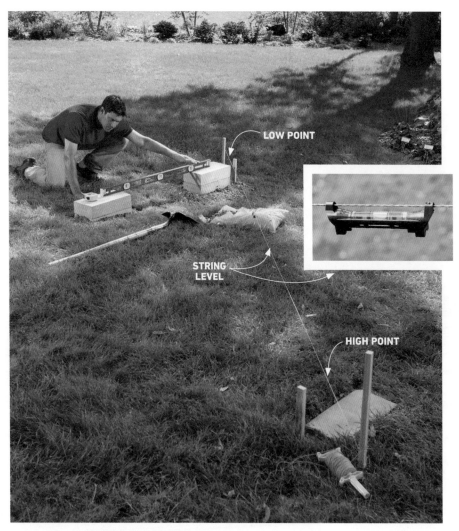

1 BUILD THE FOUNDATION
Lay a quick foundation with minimal digging by setting concrete blocks on gravel. Level from high to low spots with a string level.

railings. If you intend to build any kind of structure on top of the deck or attach the deck to the house, you'll also need a permit. If you dig footings, call 811 first to check for underground utilities. Also, keep the deck at least 4 ft. back from the property line.

PLACE THE FOOTINGS AND BEAMS

Lay out the two beams **(A)** parallel to each other and 9 ft. apart. Screw on temporary 1x4 stretchers across the ends of the beams, overhanging them each the same distance. Then measure diagonally to make sure the beams are square to each other. Mark the locations of the gravel bases (see **Figure A)** by cutting the grass with a shovel, then move the beams away and cut out the sod where the gravel will go.

Establish the highest and lowest points with a string and string level to get a rough idea of how deep to dig and how much gravel to put in to make the blocks level **(Photo 1)**. Tamp the dirt with a block to make a firm base, then spread the gravel. Place the blocks, and level them against

2 SQUARE THE BEAMS
Take diagonal measurements, and tap one beam forward or back to square the beams. Temporary stretchers hold the beams parallel.

3 USE ANGLE BRACKETS
Screw on angle brackets at each joist location instead of toenailing, which can split and weaken the joists and knock the beam out of square.

Figure A Island Deck

OVERALL DIMENSIONS:
11' 8" SQUARE
(NOT INCLUDING STAIRS)

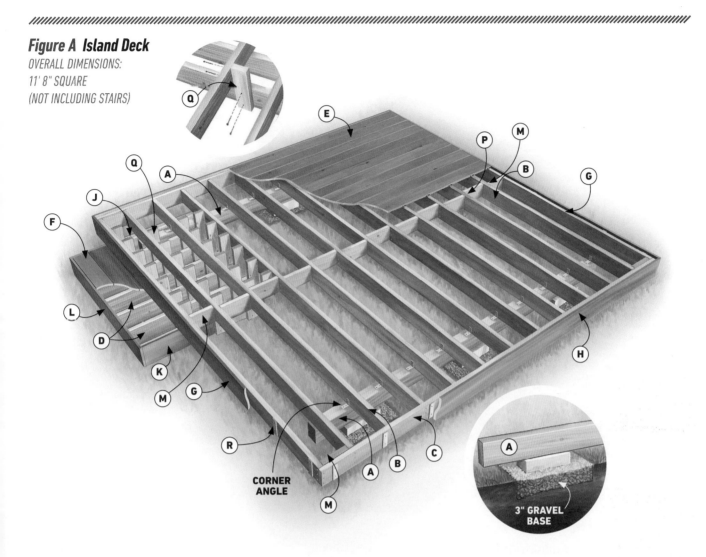

CORNER
ANGLE

3" GRAVEL
BASE

CUTTING LIST

KEY	QTY.	PART
A	2	3-1/2" x 5-1/2" x 120" beams
B	13	1-1/2" x 5-1/2" x 135" joists
C	2	1-1/2" x 5-1/2" x 138" rim joists
D	7	1-1/2" x 5-1/2" x 48" stair stringers
E	24	1" x 5-1/2" x 138" deck boards (cut in place)
F	2	1" x 5-1/2" x 55-1/2" stair treads
G	2	3/4" x 7-1/2" x 140" skirt board
H	2	3/4" x 7-1/2" x 138-1/2" skirt board
J	1	3/4" x 7-1/2" x 48" skirt board
K	1	3/4" x 7-1/2" x 24" skirt board
L	1	3/4" x 7-1/2" x 57-1/2" riser
M	6	1-1/2" x 5-1/2" x 7-1/2" blocking
P	10	1-1/2" x 5-1/2" x 10-1/2" blocking
Q	25	1-1/2" x 3-1/2" x 11" joist supports (can be used instead of metal reinforcing angles)
R	40	1/4" x 5-1/2" spacers

each other and in both directions, adding or scraping out gravel as needed. Use construction adhesive between 4-in.-thick blocks if you stack them, or use 8-in. blocks. If

your site slopes so much that one side will be more than 2 ft. off the ground, support it on a 4x4 post on a frost footing instead—it'll look better and be safer.

Set the beams across the blocks and square them to each other, using the same 1x4 stretchers to hold them parallel and square **(Photo 2)**. If the beams are not perfectly level, shim them to make them level using composite or pressure-treated wood shims (sold in home centers).

Mark the joist locations on the beams, starting with a joist on the end of each beam. We used 11 joists spaced 12 in. on center to keep the composite decking we used from sagging over time, but

wood decking can be spaced 16 in. on center.

Instead of toenailing, which often splits the wood, use metal angle brackets to hold down the joists. This also makes it easy to place the joists. Attach one alongside each joist location **(Photo 3)**.

CANTILEVER THE JOISTS ON ALL SIDES

Set the two outer joists and the center joist on the beams against the metal angles. Extend the joists by 10-1/2 in. over the beam on one side, but let them run long over the opposite beam. Trim them to exact length when the deck is almost done so you can avoid ripping the last deck board.

END JOIST

RIM JOIST

4 ATTACH THE JOISTS

Install the middle and end joists, then screw on the rim joists, using clamps (or a helper) to hold them in place.

FASTEN FROM BOTH SIDES

5 STRENGTHEN THE CORNERS

For strong connections at the corners, set corner blocking between the last two joists, then nail the rim joist from both directions.

STRINGER

6 HANG THE STAIR STRINGERS

Frame the steps next. You can avoid additional footings by hanging stringers from the deck joists with metal angles or 2x4s.

Fasten the joists to the angle brackets with deck screws. Screw on both rim joists—you'll have to take the second rim joist off when the joists are trimmed and then reattach it, but it's needed to hold the joists straight and the outside joists up **(Photo 4)**. The decking will hold up the outside joists when the rim joist is removed later on.

Set the other joists on the beams, and fasten them to the beams and rim joists. Reinforce the outside corners with additional blocking **(Photo 5)**. Finally, mark the center of the joists and run blocking between each pair of joists. Set the blocking 1/2 in. to the side of the center mark, alternating from side to side, so that the blocking doesn't end up in the gap between the deck boards.

ADD A STEP

The deck surface should be no more than 8 in. above the ground where you step up. If it's close, just build up the ground or add concrete pavers. If it's not, add a step.

To cantilever the stairs, extend the stair stringers underneath four deck joists, then join the floor joists and stair stringers with reinforcing angles (as we did) or wood 2x4s, which are less expensive **(Photo 6)**. Use a screw first to hold the angles or 2x4 blocks in place, then finish fastening them with nails, which have greater shear strength.

The 5/4 (nominal) decking we used (Trex; trex.com) called for a maximum spacing between stair stringers of 9 in. on center, but you can space stringers 16 in. on center if you use solid wood.

HIDDEN FASTENERS CREATE A CLEAN LOOK

We attached deck boards with hidden fasteners (see Materials List and **Photo 7**). Other types of hidden fasteners are available—

or you can use deck screws, which create lots of holes but save time and money.

Start with a full board at one side, aligning it with the edge of the rim joist. Leave the boards long at both ends, then later cut them back all at once so the edges are straight. Use four 1/4-in. spacers between each pair of boards as you fasten them, but check the distance to the rim joist after every four boards and adjust spacing if necessary.

At the next to the last board, remove the rim joist. Mark and cut the ends off the joists so the last deck board lines up with the edge of the rim joist. Reinstall the rim joist and attach the last boards.

Nail 1/4-in. spacers (**R**, ripped from treated wood) to the rim joist every 16 in. so water won't get trapped against the rim joist (**Figure A**). Screw on skirt boards with two screws at each spacer (**Photo 8**). Attach the decking to the steps after the skirt boards are fastened. Finally, finish the steps (**Photo 9**).

MATERIALS LIST

ITEM	QTY.
4" x 8" x 12" solid concrete block	6 (min.)
Class V (5) crushed gravel	6 bags
4x6 x 10' pressure-treated timbers	2
2x6 x 12' (12" o.c. joist spacing)	19
1-1/2" corner angles	22
7" reinforcing angles (or 2x4 x 11" blocks)	25
5/4x6 x 12' decking (Trex Brasilia Cayenne)	25
1x8 x 12' matching skirt board	5
Joist hanger nails	2 lb. box
1-5/8" deck screws	5 lb. box
3" deck screws	2 lb. box
2" stainless steel trim-head screws	2 lb. box
Fastenmaster IQ deck fasteners (fastenmaster.com), (100 s.f. boxes)	2
1x4 x 10' temporary stretchers (for layout)	2

7 ATTACH THE DECK BOARDS
Decks look best when you use hidden fasteners, but they make installation slower. Trim the deck boards flush with the rim joist when you're done.

HIDDEN FASTENER

RIM JOIST

SKIRT BOARD

8 INSTALL THE SKIRT BOARDS
Wrap the deck with skirt boards that match the decking, driving trim-head screws just below the surface at the spacer locations (see **Figure A**).

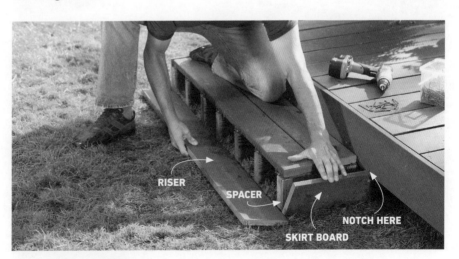

RISER

SPACER

NOTCH HERE

SKIRT BOARD

9 FINISH THE STEPS
Screw skirt boards to the sides of the steps for a finished look, then measure, cut and attach a riser board to the face of the steps.

WHAT IT TAKES

TIME
2 weekends

SKILL LEVEL
Intermediate

TOOLS
Basic hand tools, circular saw, clamps, drill/driver, furniture dolly, jigsaw (optional), table saw (optional)

GRAB-AND-GO GARDEN TOOL CABINET

///

GIVE YOUR GARDEN TOOLS THEIR OWN HOME SO THEY'RE EASY TO FIND.

Imagine this: You drive home with a carload of new plants and flowers. You open your new outdoor garden tool cabinet and grab your shovel, bulb planter, trimmer or whatever you need—and everything is there in plain view! This scenario doesn't have to be a dream. You can build our cabinet in one weekend, and paint and organize it the next.

This cabinet is compact, but it can store all of your garden hand tools plus still have room for boots, fertilizers and accessories. Most gardeners set aside a tiny spot in the garage for their tools, but the tools often end up tangled in a corner. Now they can have a home of their own outside the garage. This design is flexible, so you can customize the interior to suit your needs and add a lock if you wish.

We'll show you how to assemble the cabinet in your garage, and then you can wheel it out and mount

it on your garage wall. And you don't have to be a crackerjack carpenter or own special tools to build it.

Besides being good-looking, this project is designed to last. The shingled roof will keep the rain out. And if moisture does get in, the slatted bottom and 4-in.-dia. vents near the top allow enough air circulation to dry everything out. We mounted this storage cabinet on the outside of a garage, but you can easily mount it to the back of your house or to a shed.

The 4-ft. by nearly 8-ft. cabinet is made from exterior plywood with pine trim. All the materials are available at home centers and lumberyards. At hardware stores you can find a huge variety of tool-mounting clips and retainers for hanging rakes, shovels, clippers and everything else. Just let your imagination solve your needs. Get the needed materials, review the step-by-step photos, examine the detailed drawings and text instructions, and get started.

ASSEMBLE THE MAIN BOX

Exterior-grade plywood is the basic building material for this project. Unfortunately, you'll never find absolutely flat pieces of plywood at a home center or lumberyard, but the flatter you can find them, the better this project will turn out. Choose a BC grade of plywood. This will ensure you have one good side, "B," that'll look good on the outside, and the "C" side can go on the inside.

Once you get the plywood home, keep it out of the sun or your flat panel will turn into a tortilla chip in no time. It's best to cut the pieces in the shade or in your garage. A long straightedge cutting guide for your circular saw will help you get nice straight cuts if you don't have a full-size table saw. Look at the Cutting List and cut all the parts to size except the door stiles, rails and trim pieces, which are best cut to fit once you have constructed the main plywood box.

Choose the flattest sheet of 3/4-in. plywood for the door cores. As you lay out all the pieces, use the best-looking side of the plywood for the painted parts. The sides of the cabinet form a 30-degree slope for

1 ASSEMBLE THE SIDES
Cut the plywood sides and 2x10 shelf, prop up the shelf with 2x4 blocks and fasten the sides into the shelf with 2-in. deck screws.

2 ATTACH THE BACK
Turn the assembly over and screw the back to the sides and center shelf. Use a level or straightedge to mark the shelf location on the back side of the plywood.

3 ATTACH THE SUBRAILS AND ROOF SUPPORTS
Cut the subrails (D) and the roof supports (H), and then screw them into place. Use 2-in. screws for the subrails and 3-in. screws for the roof supports.

4 BUILD THE SLATTED FLOOR
Glue and nail the 1x2 cleats (E and F) to the sides, back and subrail (D), and then screw the 1x4 floor slats (G) to the cleats. Start with the center slat and leave 7/16-in. gaps.

the roof. Use a Speed square **(see Photo 1)** to mark the angled roof supports **(H)** and ends of the trim pieces that follow the roofline. It's easier to cut accurate slopes on the larger side pieces **(A)** by first measuring each side, marking a diagonal line from point to point and then cutting along the mark.

Next, assemble the main box of the cabinet as shown in **Figure A** and **Photos 1–5**. Drill pilot holes for all screws using a No. 8 combination countersink and

pilot bit. Use 2-in. galvanized deck screws to fasten the sides to the shelf and 1-5/8-in. screws to fasten the back to the sides.

NOTE: Cut a piece of 1/4-in. hardware cloth to fit under the floor slats of the cabinet. This wire mesh will keep furry critters from

MATERIALS LIST

ITEM	QTY.
3/4" x 4' x 8' BC plywood	2
1/2" x 4' x 8' BC plywood	1
2x10 x 4' pine	1
2x4 x 8' pine	2
1x6 x 8' pine	1
1x4 x 8' pine	12
1x2 x 8' pine	3
2x4 x 8' treated wood	1
12" x 48" hardware cloth (1/4" grid)	1

Bundle of asphalt shingles	1
3' x 5' strip of 15-lb. building paper	1
1-5/8" galv. screws	2 lbs.
2" galv. screws	2 lbs.
3" galv. screws	1 lb.
4" T-hinges	6
Shutter turn buttons	4
4" round vents	2
1-1/4" finish nails	1 lb.
1/4" x 3" galv. lag screws and washers	9
2" x 2" steel angle	1
7/8" shingle nails	1 lb.

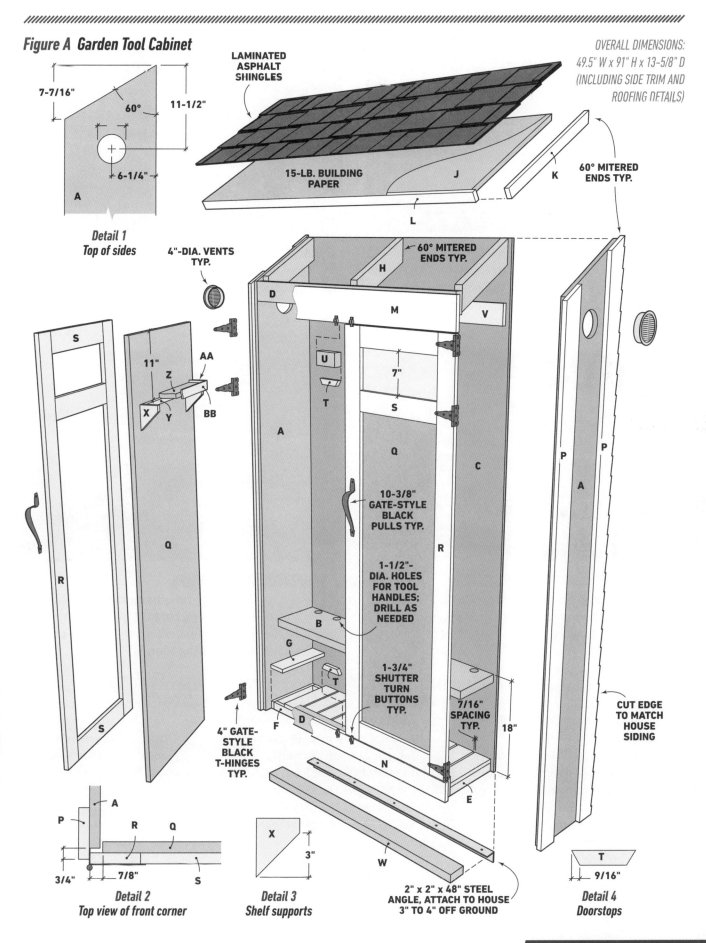

Figure A Garden Tool Cabinet

OVERALL DIMENSIONS:
49.5" W x 91" H x 13-5/8" D
(INCLUDING SIDE TRIM AND
ROOFING DETAILS)

LAMINATED ASPHALT SHINGLES

15-LB. BUILDING PAPER

60° MITERED ENDS TYP.

7-7/16"

60°

11-1/2"

6-1/4"

A

Detail 1
Top of sides

4"-DIA. VENTS TYP.

60° MITERED ENDS TYP.

11"

Z

X   Y

AA

BB

4" GATE-STYLE BLACK T-HINGES TYP.

10-3/8" GATE-STYLE BLACK PULLS TYP.

1-1/2"-DIA. HOLES FOR TOOL HANDLES; DRILL AS NEEDED

1-3/4" SHUTTER TURN BUTTONS TYP.

7/16" SPACING TYP.

18"

CUT EDGE TO MATCH HOUSE SIDING

Detail 2
Top view of front corner

3/4"   7/8"

Detail 3
Shelf supports

3"

2" x 2" x 48" STEEL ANGLE, ATTACH TO HOUSE 3" TO 4" OFF GROUND

Detail 4
Doorstops

9/16"

5 ADD THE ROOF TRIM

Mount the 1x2 roof trim to the 3/4-in. plywood roof, center it and mark the position. Then temporarily screw it to the roof supports with a pair of 2-in. screws on each side.

6 ATTACH THE SIDE TRIM

Glue and screw the 1x4 side trim to the plywood sides, keeping the trim pieces 3/4 in. proud at the front. Cut the 4-in.-dia. side vents.

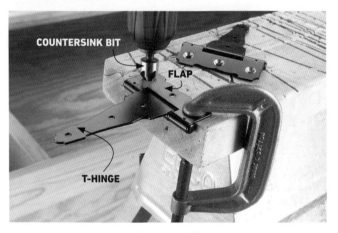

7 PREDRILL HOLES FOR THE HINGE FLAP

Countersink the holes in the inside of the hinge flaps to accept the tapered heads of the mounting screws.

8 ATTACH THE HINGE FLAPS

Position the flaps of the hinges against the plywood sides at the centers of the door rail locations. Drill pilot holes and drive the screws into the side trim to secure the hinges.

making your tool cabinet into a cozy winter home.

Cut the roof panel (J) and trim pieces (K and L), then glue and nail the trim to the front and side edges of the roof panel. Center the panel (Photo 5) and temporarily screw it to the roof supports so you can install the side trim (P) and the upper rail (M).

NOTE: You'll need to remove the roof and the doors after assembly to make the project light enough to move to your site.

ADD TRIM AND ASSEMBLE THE DOORS

Make sure to extend the front edge of each side. Set the trim (P) 3/4 in. beyond the front edge of the plywood side (Photo 6). Next, cut and nail the front upper rail (M) and the lower rail (N) to the subrails. Both ends should butt tightly to the side trim.

Even though the doors are made mainly from plywood, the rail and stile trim boards glued and screwed to the front side give

the doors a handsome frame-and-panel look. Be sure to lay out the doors on a flat surface, and then glue and nail the rails (long vertical pieces) and stiles (short horizontal pieces) to the plywood surface. The stile on each hinge side must hang 3/4 in. past the plywood (see Photo 10 inset).

You'll need to alter the factory T-hinge for the inset design of the doors. The hinge flap is screwed to the side trim (P) as shown in Photo 8. If you were to use the

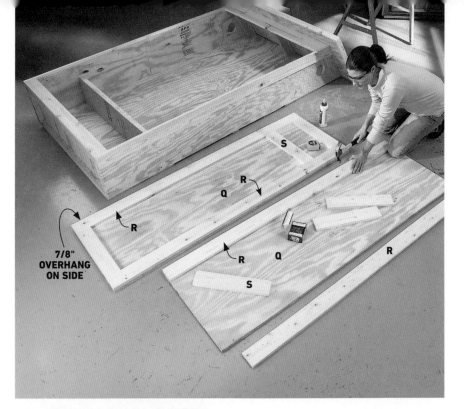

7/8"
OVERHANG
ON SIDE

9 ADD THE RAIL AND STILE TRIM

Glue and nail the door rail and stile trim to the 3/4-in. plywood doors. Overhang the stile on the hinge side of each door 7/8 in. See **Figure A** for the exact placement.

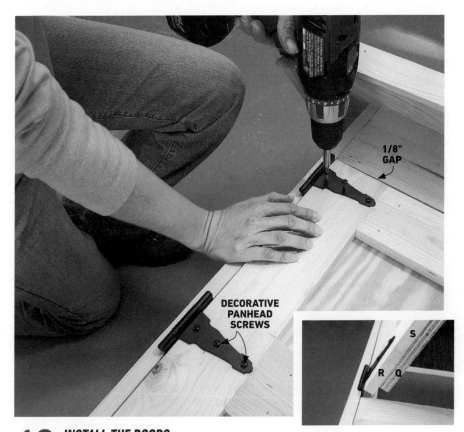

1/8"
GAP

DECORATIVE
PANHEAD
SCREWS

10 INSTALL THE DOORS

Install the doorstops **(Figure A)**, then set each door into its opening. Use the decorative panhead screws provided by the manufacturer for the long decorative flap on the door surface.

factory-supplied panhead screws, the door would bind on the screw heads. To solve this problem, taper the edges of the existing holes using a countersink bit. Remove just enough steel **(see Photo 7)** so the head of the tapered No. 8 x 3/4-in. screw fits flush with the hinge flap surface.

Cut the small doorstops with a handsaw, and then glue and nail them to the edges of the subrails. With the doorstops in place, set the doors into the opening. Make sure you leave a 1/8-in. gap at the top and bottom and a 3/16-in. gap between the doors. You may need to plane or belt-sand the door edges to get a good fit.

NOTE: Because the flaps of the hinge that fasten to the side trim are about 7/8 in. wide instead of 3/4 in., your doors will sit approximately 1/8 in. proud of the side trim.

MOUNT THE CABINET TO THE WALL

Fasten a 4-ft. 2x4 to the top flange of a 4-ft.-long piece of steel angle **(Figure A)**. You can usually find steel angle that measures 1-1/2 x 1-1/2 in. with holes drilled every 3 in. at a hardware store, but any steel angle that's 1/8 in. thick or larger will do.

Locate the precise position of your cabinet on the outside wall at least 3 in. above grade, and then fasten the angle to the wall with 1/4-in. galvanized lag screws. It must be level. You may need to cut a course or two of siding to get the angle to lie flat. Our garage slab was several inches off the ground, so we drilled holes into the side of the slab, installed lag shields and fastened the angle. If your slab is too close to the ground, you can fasten the angle farther up into the wood studs of the garage. The weight of your cabinet rests

2x4 x 8'
BRACE

2x4 x 4'
MOUNTING
BOARD

2" x 2"
STEEL
ANGLE

11 POSITION THE CABINET

Fasten a steel angle to the foundation with a 2x4 attached to its top (**Figure A**). Lift the cabinet into place and stabilize it with an 8-ft. 2x4 brace against the ground, forcing the cabinet back against the wall.

2x4 BRACE

NOTCHES FOR SIDING

P

P

12 FIT THE SIDE TRIM TO THE SIDING

Scribe the 1x4 side trim to fit the siding. Cut the notches with a jigsaw. Nail it to the cabinet side. Screw on the roof panel and shingle it.

CUTTING LIST

KEY	QTY.	PART
A	2	3/4" x 12-7/8" x 90" plywood sides
B	1	1-1/2" x 9-1/4" x 46-1/2" pine shelf
C	1	1/2" x 48" x 90" plywood back
D	2	1-1/2" x 3-1/2" x 46-1/2" pine subrails
E	2	3/4" x 1-1/2" x 11-3/8" pine bottom cleats
F	2	3/4" x 1-1/2" x 45" pine bottom cleats
G	12	3/4" x 3-1/2" x 11-3/8" pine bottom slat
H	3	1-1/2" x 3-1/2" x 15-1/8" pine roof supports
J	1	3/4" x 21-7/8" x 60" plywood roof
K	2	3/4" x 1-1/2" x 21-7/8" pine roof trim
L	1	3/4" x 1-1/2" x 61-1/2" pine roof trim
M	1	3/4" x 5-1/2" x 48" pine upper rail
N	1	3/4" x 3-1/2" x 48" pine lower rail
P	4	3/4" x 3-1/2" x 91" pine side trim
Q	2	3/4" x 23" x 72-3/4" plywood doors
R	4	3/4" x 3-1/2" x 72-3/4" pine door stile
S	6	3/4" x 3-1/2" x 16-7/8" pine door rail trim
T	2	3/4" x 1" x 4-1/2" pine doorstop
U	1	1-1/2" x 2-7/16" x 4-1/2" pine door stop support
V	1	3/4" x 3-1/2" x 46-1/2" pine hang rail
W	1	1-1/2" x 3-1/2" x 48" treated mounting board
X	1	3/4" x 3" x 4" pine shelf supports
Y	1	3/4" x 3/4" x 16-1/2" pine shelf-mounting cleat
Z	1	3/4" x 3" x 20" pine shelf
AA	2	1/4" x 1-1/2" x 3" pine shelf edging
BB	1	1/4" x 1-1/2" x 20-1/2" pine shelf edging

NOTE:

If you have vinyl, aluminum or steel siding, here's how to prevent the siding from deforming as you tighten the cabinet to the wall: Instead of tightening the lag screws one at a time, gently tighten them alternately to even out the pressure as you go.

entirely on this wall cleat. It's not necessary to fasten the bottom of the cabinet to it.

Measure the locations of the wall studs and transfer these to the cabinet back. Locate three 1/4-in.-dia. pilot holes in the hang rail (V) and another three holes 4 in. up from the bottom at the stud locations.

Now, strap your cabinet to a furniture dolly (with the doors and roof removed to reduce the weight) and wheel it over to the wall cleat. Set the bottom of the cabinet onto the cleat, center it and temporarily brace it against the wall. Drill 5/32-in.-dia. pilot holes into the wall studs using the existing pilot holes as a guide. Drive in the 3-in. lag screws (including washers) and snug the cabinet to the wall.

FINISHING TOUCHES

Lay the side trim (P) against the siding. You may need to trim it with your jigsaw to conform (Photo 12). Screw the roof panel to the cabinet. Staple a layer of 15-lb. building paper to the roof panel, and shingle the panel using 7/8-in. roofing nails. Avoid driving shingle nails through the overhangs where the points might show. When you get to the last course, trim the shingles to fit and run a bead of matching caulk at the siding to seal the edge.

Rehang the doors, and then mount the door handles and the catches at the tops and bottoms of the doors. Wait to add your vents until you've finished painting. We spray-painted the vents to match the color of the sides.

Take a trip to the hardware store and shop for a variety of fasteners, from angle screws to rake and broom holders. Once you finish organizing the cabinet, prime it and then paint it to match the wall where it's mounted.

WHAT IT TAKES

TIME
2 weekends

SKILL LEVEL
Intermediate

TOOLS
Basic hand and woodshop tools, drill press, jigsaw, router, table saw

WAVE BENCH

//

HERE'S A BOLD DESIGN THAT MAKES A SPLASH, INDOORS OR OUT.

It's a conversation piece with a practical purpose, a woodworking masterpiece you can build in a few afternoons. This bench hits the sweet spot as a project that's functional, beautiful and a vehicle for showing off your skills. If you're handy with a drill press, table saw, jigsaw and router, you're ready to build it.

WHAT YOU'LL NEED

We made this bench from cherry, a wood that's as resistant to rot as cedar or redwood. Remember that hardwood lumber prices vary widely. And whatever wood species you choose, beware of knots. Knots near the center of a board aren't a problem, but knots near edges may disrupt the wave pattern.

We recommend using a drill press to make the holes for the threaded rods that align all the parts. These holes must be plumb for everything to fit without any play. If you don't have a drill press, make the holes 1/16 in. oversize and nudge the pieces into alignment when you glue them. You'll also need an extra-large (3/4-in.) countersink bit.

A PATTERN MAKES IT POSSIBLE

Curves are always a woodworking challenge, and this bench is as curvy as projects get. But if you carefully craft a pattern, you can turn out perfect, identical seat slats. The pattern will guide your pen when you mark the slats and your router as you shape them.

PATTERN BIT

PATTERN

SEAT SLAT

Figure A Wave Bench

OVERALL DIMENSIONS: 72" L x 19-1/4" H x 14-1/4" D

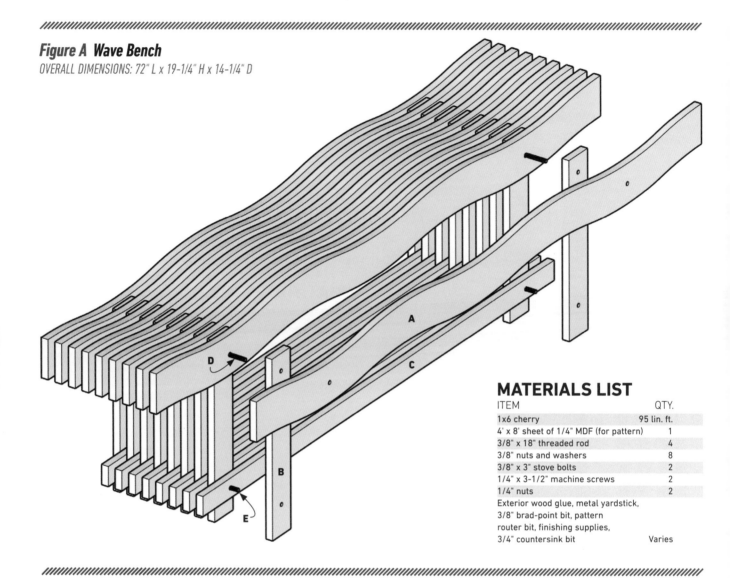

MATERIALS LIST

ITEM	QTY.
1x6 cherry	95 lin. ft.
4' x 8' sheet of 1/4" MDF (for pattern)	1
3/8" x 18" threaded rod	4
3/8" nuts and washers	8
3/8" x 3" stove bolts	2
1/4" x 3-1/2" machine screws	2
1/4" nuts	2
Exterior wood glue, metal yardstick, 3/8" brad-point bit, pattern router bit, finishing supplies, 3/4" countersink bit	Varies

Figure B Wave Bench parts

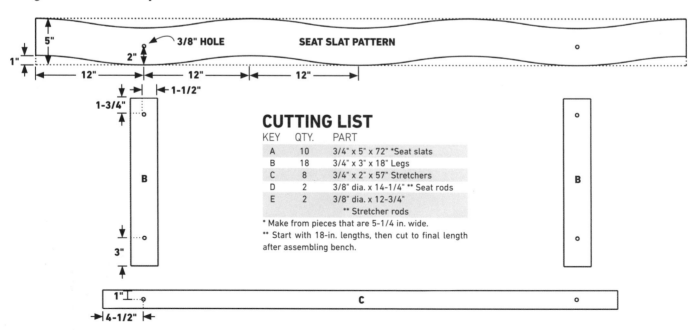

SEAT SLAT PATTERN

3/8" HOLE

CUTTING LIST

KEY	QTY.	PART
A	10	3/4" x 5" x 72" *Seat slats
B	18	3/4" x 3" x 18" Legs
C	8	3/4" x 2" x 57" Stretchers
D	2	3/8" dia. x 14-1/4" ** Seat rods
E	2	3/8" dia. x 12-3/4"
		** Stretcher rods

* Make from pieces that are 5-1/4 in. wide.

** Start with 18-in. lengths, then cut to final length after assembling bench.

To make all the waves exactly the same shape, you'll need a jigsaw and a router with a 1/2-in. collet and variable speed. For the best results, use a large-diameter top-bearing pattern bit. We used a Whiteside No. 3016 bit, which has a 1-1/8-in. cutting diameter.

START WITH A PATTERN

Make a pattern for the seat slats (A) from 1/4-in.-thick material. We used MDF, which is ideal for shaping with sandpaper. Cut the pattern 5 in. wide x 72 in. long.

Lay out the wave design on the pattern (**Figure B**). By bending an aluminum yardstick, you can easily make the perfect S-shape curve that forms each half of a wave (**Photo 1**). First, draw vertical lines 12 in. apart to mark the lengths of the waves. Next, draw marks on each line 1 in. from the top of the pattern and 1 in. from the bottom. These marks indicate the crest and trough of each wave.

Make the curve by clamping the yardstick to a stiff board. Place a 1-in. spacer block at the 24-in. mark and clamp. Tighten a second clamp near the 12-in. mark. This results in a smooth S-curve with a 1-in. rise and a 12-in. run. Use this curve to draw each 12-in. section of the wave design (**Photo 2**). We recommend using a fine-tip Sharpie to make a line that's about 1/8 in. wide.

Draw a large "X" on the right end of the pattern. Write "TOP" at one of the crests of the top wave. These marks are essential for correctly orienting each piece later on.

Lay out the centers of two 3/8-in. holes on the pattern. Drill the holes using a brad-point bit and a drill press. (It's hard to locate a standard twist bit exactly on your mark.) Place a piece of plywood under the pattern to drill

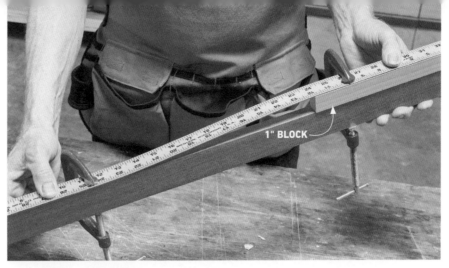

1 *BEND A YARDSTICK*
Make a perfect curve for the seat of the bench by clamping a metal yardstick and block to a stiff board.

2 *DRAW THE WAVES*
Mark out a pattern by tracing the bent yardstick on a piece of 1/4-in. material. Drill two rod holes in the pattern as well.

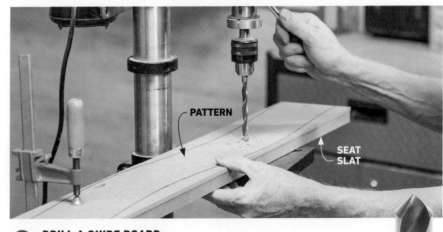

3 *DRILL A GUIDE BOARD*
Before cutting the waves in the pattern, clamp it to one of the seat slats. Drill rod holes through this slat, then use it as a guide to drill the other slats. Next, use a countersink bit to countersink the holes in the pattern from one side. Countersink both sides of the holes in the slats.

COUNTERSINK BIT

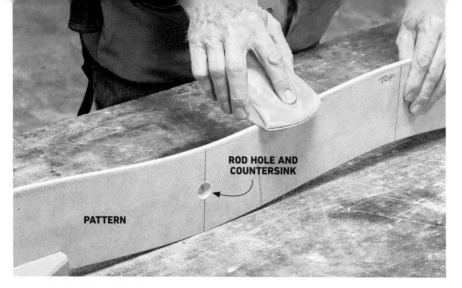

ROD HOLE AND COUNTERSINK

PATTERN

4 SHAPE THE PATTERN

Cut the pattern along the outside edge of the lines, then sand to the inside edge. Trace the pattern onto each seat slat.

5 BUILD A CUTTING PLATFORM

Fasten a 6-ft. board to a pair of sawhorses to make a sturdy platform for sawing and routing the seat slats.

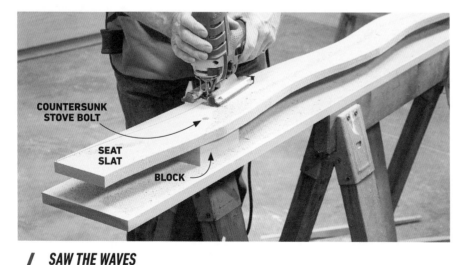

COUNTERSUNK STOVE BOLT

SEAT SLAT

BLOCK

6 SAW THE WAVES

Fasten the seat slats to the platform using bolts and the rod holes you drilled in each slat. Saw along the outside edge of the waves.

into so the bit doesn't chip out the bottom of the pattern.

Make seat slats from 5-1/4-in.-wide boards. Cut them the same length as the pattern. Mark an "X" and "TOP" on each piece.

Select one slat to use as a guide for drilling all the others. (If you'd use the pattern as a guide, its holes would become enlarged and inaccurate very quickly.) Center the pattern side-to-side on this slat, then clamp the pattern to it. With the drill press turned off, line up the bit with one hole in the pattern. Drill the hole all the way through **(Photo 3)**. Drill the second hole in the same way.

Clamp the guide to each seat slat and drill both holes in each piece. This ensures the holes will be the same distance apart even if your slats vary slightly in length.

Countersink both sides of each hole. Drill deep enough so that the depression is about 9/16 in. wide. Doing this now makes the bench much easier to assemble later on.

Next, saw along the pattern's waves using a jigsaw or band saw. Stay on the outside edge of the line. Smooth the curves to the inside edge of the line **(Photo 4)**.

Place the pattern on each seat slat and align the holes using 3/8-in. stove bolts or dowels. Be sure the "X" and "TOP" marks on the pattern are oriented the same way as the marks on each seat piece. Trace around the pattern with a marker. Once more, make a 1/8-in.-wide line.

MAKE WAVES

You'll use a jigsaw to cut each slat slightly oversize, and then use a router and a pattern bit to make each piece exactly the same shape. To make both jobs easier and safer, build a platform **(Photo 5)**: Screw a 3/4 x 8 x 72-in. board to sawhorses. Clamp one slat to the platform and use it as a guide to drill two 3/8-in. holes through the platform.

Two blocks elevate the slats above the platform so the blade doesn't hit it. We used 1-1/2 in. thick x 3 in. wide blocks. Drill 3/8-in. holes through the blocks and platform. Fasten each slat to the platform with two flat-head 1/4 x 3-1/2-in. machine screws and wing nuts. Fasten the template to the workpiece and both parts to the platform using two 3/8 x 3-in. stove bolts. Saw along the outside edge of the lines **(Photo 6)**. Cut both sides of each piece.

Before you begin routing, countersink the holes in the pattern so the heads sit slightly below the surface to avoid being hit by the router. You'll also need two 1/2-in.-thick supports with 3/8-in. holes to elevate the workpiece so the router bit won't cut into the platform. Fasten the pattern, workpiece and supports to the platform.

Rout each slat **(Photo 7)**, moving the router in the correct direction (with the pattern on your left, you push the router forward). Round the edges of each slat with a 1/8-in. round-over bit **(Photo 8)**. Smooth the waves with 100-grit sandpaper.

MAKE LEGS AND STRETCHERS

Cut the legs **(B)** to width and length. Use a stop on your miter saw or table saw to ensure they're all the same length. Mark one edge of each leg with an "X." Drill two 3/8-in. holes in the middle of each leg **(Photo 9)**. Use the "X" mark to orient each leg the same way. Countersink both sides of each hole as you did with the slats. Round over all the edges and ends of each leg using a router.

Cut the stretchers **(C)** to width and length. Mark one edge with an "X." Select one stretcher as a

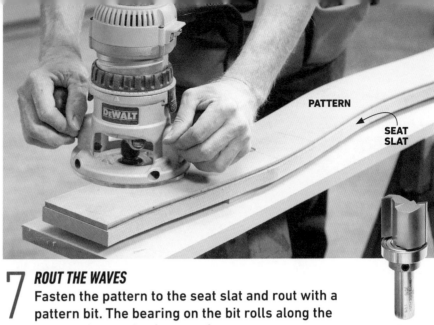

PATTERN
SEAT SLAT
PATTERN BIT

7 ROUT THE WAVES
Fasten the pattern to the seat slat and rout with a pattern bit. The bearing on the bit rolls along the pattern, creating perfectly smooth waves.

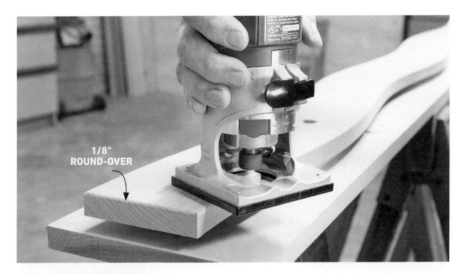

1/8" ROUND-OVER

8 ROUND THE EDGES
To make the seat comfortable, soften the edges of the slats with a 1/8-in. round-over bit.

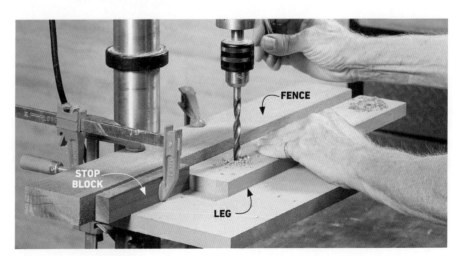

FENCE
STOP BLOCK
LEG

9 DRILL THE LEGS
Position each leg against a fence and a stop block to ensure that all the holes are at exactly the same location.

THREADED ROD

10 TEST THE FIT

Assemble the bench layer by layer to make sure all the parts fit. Keep them aligned with long sections of threaded rod.

RAW WOOD FOR GLUING

11 FINISH THE PARTS

Apply an exterior finish to all the parts. Leave the areas where parts overlap each other unfinished so glue will stick to them.

THREADED ROD

SQUARE

12 GLUE THE BENCH

Start with just a few parts and make sure they're square. Clamp the parts together with nuts on the threaded rod.

guide, then drill 3/8-in. holes in it that are exactly the same distance apart as the holes in the seat slat template. Use the guide to drill holes in all the other stretchers. Countersink both sides of each hole and round the edges.

For the seat rods **(D)** and stretcher rods **(E)**, cut four pieces of 3/8-in. rod about 18 in. long. After sawing, file the ends of the rods so that a nut will easily thread onto them.

Assemble the bench on its side, adding one part at a time **(Photo 10)**. Use the rods to keep parts aligned. Be sure the X's on each part are oriented the same way. If a part doesn't fit, widen one of its holes with a larger bit. After test-fitting, disassemble the bench.

FINISH AND ASSEMBLE

It's best to finish the bench parts before final assembly **(Photo 11)**. You'll glue the parts together afterward, using a waterproof glue like Titebond III. Glue won't stick to a finish, so mark the contact areas and keep them free of finish.

After the finish dries, glue just one set of parts together (one slat, two legs and a stretcher). Be sure the legs are square to the stretcher. Use the 3-in. stove bolts from the template-routing job along with washers and nuts to align the parts and clamp them together. Once this first set is complete, adding more parts and making sure they're square will be much easier.

Remove the stove bolts. Use the rods to align and clamp the remaining parts. Center the rods on the set of parts you glued, then add a few parts at a time on both sides **(Photo 12)**. Check for square as you go. Before you add the outermost slats and legs, cut the rods so they're flush with these parts. Clamp and glue these parts to the bench. No nuts are needed.

PREASSEMBLED
MARBLE
MEDALLION

TUMBLED
LIMESTONE
TILE

TILE AND MARBLE ENTRYWAY FLOOR

USING A PREASSEMBLED MEDALLION MAKES INSTALLATION EASIER AND FASTER.

A tumbled marble medallion adds a distinctive tile feature to any room. It's easy to install because it is preassembled and comes on a backer mat (this one came in two pieces so all we had to do is carefully slide each piece into place after placing the surrounding tiles). The medallion enhances a tile floor that's already durable and beautiful. We show you how to tile an entryway, but you can use the same techniques in a bathroom or kitchen with equally dramatic results.

MATERIALS, COST AND TIME

Your local tile showroom may have medallions on display for you to view, but we found that most have to be ordered. The 12 x 12-in. tumbled limestone tiles that surround our medallion were expensive. Order about 20 percent extra to allow waste for the diagonal cuts. You could also use one of the many other floor tiles that look like stone (and are much less expensive). Just make sure whatever floor tile you choose is about the same thickness as the medallion. Even though the medallion is preassembled, you should have some til-

ing experience to tackle this project. Plan on spending a couple of weekends to complete it. For tile to last, it must be installed on a strong, solid base.

IF YOU HAVE WOOD FLOORING

Jump on your floor to check for bounce. If it moves much, stiffen it by adding posts and beams under it or by reinforcing the floor joists (the wood framing that supports your floor).

Next, peer alongside a heat duct or drill a 3/4-in. hole in the floor to determine how many

WHAT IT TAKES	
TIME 2 weekends	**SKILL LEVEL** Intermediate
TOOLS	
Basic hand tools, angle grinder, chalk line, circular saw, drill with mixing paddle, grinder with dry-cut diamond blade, grout float, 4-ft. level, notched trowel, pry bar, safety gear, shop vac, stapler, tile saw with diamond blade (rental), tin snips	

layers of flooring there are and how thick each is. The self-leveling underlayment we're using requires a minimum of 3/4-in. thick boards or plywood under it. If you have less than that, glue and screw another layer of 1/2-in. plywood over the existing floor.

If your subfloor (the lowest layer next to the joists) is covered with any flooring material or underlayment, like particleboard, 1/4-in. plywood or even ceramic tile mortar, tear it out to make room for the tile and self-leveling underlayment **(Photo 1)**.

CAUTION: Sheet vinyl or vinyl tiles may contain asbestos. If you must tear out a vinyl floor, the Consumer Product Safety Commission (cpsc. gov) has information about testing for asbestos and guidelines for safely removing it.

IF YOU HAVE CONCRETE FLOORS

You can glue tile directly to concrete, but it has to be clean and structurally sound. Ask a knowledgeable tile salesperson for specific instructions on how to do this. If the concrete has cracks, the tile you lay over it can also crack if the concrete isn't stable. It's best to play it safe. Install a special isolation membrane between the tile and the concrete. The membrane prevents any movement in the cracked concrete from cracking the tile. Some membranes are liquids that are painted over the crack. Others are sheets of rubber that you glue down over the crack. Consult your salesperson, a tiling book or a tile installer for more information on the various types of isolation membrane and how to install them.

DEALING WITH LEVEL DIFFERENCES

New tile almost always raises the floor height. You might have to trim door bottoms and install special transition pieces at doors and openings. Rather than install a wood or plastic transition, we made our own bullnose tile by rounding the cut edges of the limestone with 80-grit sandpaper. Larger level differences may require stone, plastic, metal or wood transition pieces. A tile dealer will have a wide selection in stock and will help you plan the transitions.

MAKE A STRONG BASE

A durable tile floor requires a strong, level, tile-setting base. We used a self-leveling underlayment. It's basically mortar with latex additives that you mix with water. It can be mixed up soupy enough

3/4" PLYWOOD SUBFLOOR

OLD PARTICLEBOARD UNDERLAYMENT

MASKING TAPE ON WOODWORK

SEALED HEAT REGISTER

PRIMER

MASKING TAPE OVER SEAMS

EXPANDED WIRE LATH

TIN SNIPS

STAPLER

1/2" STAPLES 6" APART

1 TEAR OUT OLD FLOORING
Tear out old hardwood flooring, ceramic tile, or carpet and underlayment to allow extra room for the mortar bed and tile. This will minimize level changes at the openings into other rooms. Cut flooring or underlayment into smaller pieces to make them easier to remove. Make sure to leave the subfloor fully intact. Use a large pry bar for extra leverage.

2 CLEAN AND PRIME THE SUBFLOOR
Prepare the area for the self-leveling mortar bed. Protect woodwork with masking tape. Cover heat ducts with blocks of rigid foam and seal around them with duct tape. Cover the seams between sheets of plywood with masking tape. Plug all holes with tape or expanding spray foam. Prime the floor according to the instructions on the bag containing the self-leveling mortar.

3 STAPLE DOWN METAL LATH
Cut sheets of expanded metal lath with tin snips to fit around obstacles and between walls. Allow each piece to lap over the previous one about 2 in. Secure the lath to the floor with 1/2-in. staples placed about 6 in. apart. Staple from the center of the sheet to the outside to eliminate bulges.

to pour from a bucket and yet is extra strong when it hardens. You don't need any special skill to pour a perfectly smooth and level floor. You'll find 25-lb. bags of self-leveling underlayment powder at full-service tile shops and most large home centers. For our tiles, the manufacturer suggested a minimum thickness of 3/8 in., but to be safe we poured our underlayment 1/2 in. deep. For a 1/2-in. depth, you'll need one bag for every 12 sq. ft. of floor. You'll also need primer (check the underlayment bag for the exact type) to seal the wood subfloor and expanded metal lath to reinforce the mortar. Sheets of metal lath are usually 30 x 84 in. and are available where you buy your other tile supplies. Buy enough to cover the entire floor, plus about 10 percent extra to allow for waste.

Photos 1–4 show how to prepare the floor and pour the mortar underlayment. Mixing and pouring the self-leveling underlayment is easy, but there are a few things to watch out for.

The self-leveling underlayment we used starts to harden in about 10 minutes at 70 degrees, and even faster if it's hotter. (Some products are formulated to give you a little more open time; check the bag to find out the specifics

1/2" DRILL MIXING PADDLE

SELF-LEVELING UNDERLAYMENT

MATERIALS LIST

ITEM

Tumbled marble medallion
Tumbled 12-in. square limestone tile
Plywood
Primer
Self-leveling underlayment
Expanded metal lath
5-gal. buckets
Cardboard
14-gauge stranded wire
Chalk line
White multipurpose thin-set mortar adhesive
Liquid stone enhancer
Grout release sealer
Disposable foam brush
Sanded grout
Grout sealer
Sandpaper

4 POUR LEVELING UNDERLAYMENT

Pour the self-leveling mortar underlayment around the perimeter. Then quickly fill in the center, working toward your mixing area. Have a helper continue the mixing process. Use a trowel to help the mortar into corners and around obstacles. Work quickly. Reach out and spread the mortar with a trowel as you work your way out of the room. Then leave it alone as it levels out and hardens.

on yours.) The secret to success is having everything ready to go.

Before you start mixing, measure the exact amount of water into five or six 5-gal. buckets, open all the bags you'll need, and have extra water and the measuring bucket handy. Then have a helper mix while you pour. You should be able to mix and pour a bag every minute, which is plenty of time unless you have a very large floor.

TIP: For a better gauge of thickness, use a 4-ft. level to set up a grid of drywall screws with the heads level with the desired top surface. Then pour the mud even with the top of the screws; remove them after it hardens.

When you're finished, clean tools and buckets right away. Let the underlayment harden overnight. If you return the day after pouring to find some low spots in the floor, don't panic. We had this

TUMBLED
MARBLE
MEDALLION

14-GAUGE
STRANDED
WIRE

CARDBOARD
FOR TEMPLATE

REFERENCE
MARK

5 MAKE A CARDBOARD TEMPLATE

Stretch a length of 14-gauge stranded wire around the medallion and trace around it with a pencil. Carefully cut along the line with a sharp utility knife to make a cardboard template that includes a 1/8-in. grout joint (the thickness of the wire). Use thicker wire for larger grout joints. Mark the medallion and the cardboard with two reference points labeled "1" and "2." You'll use these marks later to align the medallion with the cut tile.

MARK THE MEDALLION AND TILE POSITIONS

Before you start tiling, you'll have to snap chalk lines on the floor to keep the tile in alignment. This process of laying out the tile is half mathematical and half aesthetic. The goal is to arrive at a starting point for the tile that leaves nicely sized cut pieces around the edge of the room. Unless you're really lucky, though, you'll have to make a few compromises. The trick is to position the layout so small pieces, or ones that are tapered because the room isn't square, are in the least conspicuous spots. Arranging the actual tiles on the floor, including the spaces be-

problem and fixed it by priming the underlayment and pouring another 1/8-in. layer to fill the low spots.

tween them for grout, is the most foolproof method of laying out tile. You could also make a scaled drawing on graph paper to get a preliminary idea of how the tile and medallion will fit on your floor.

Photo 6 shows how to start the layout by positioning the medallion and extending the tile out to the edges of the room. This allows you to see what size the cut border tiles will be. You may be able to shift the location of the medallion slightly to improve the look of the cut border tile. We moved the medallion 1/2 in. closer to the front door to avoid being left with a tiny triangle of tile.

Once you determine a starting point, the rest is just a matter of snapping chalk lines **(Photo 7)** to form a diagonal grid. Each square of the grid contains four tiles, and

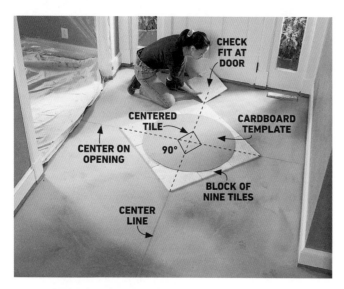

CHECK FIT AT DOOR

CENTERED TILE

CARDBOARD TEMPLATE

CENTER ON OPENING

90°

BLOCK OF NINE TILES

CENTER LINE

6 CENTER THE MEDALLION

Snap a chalk line down the center of your room, parallel with the most visible wall. Use a framing square to make a line perpendicular to the first line, centered on your proposed medallion location. Center a block of floor tile on the lines, and set the template over them to see how the cut tiles around the medallion will look and how the medallion looks in the room. Extend tiles to the edges of the room to see what size the border cuts will be. Adjust the medallion location if necessary to improve the look of the border tile.

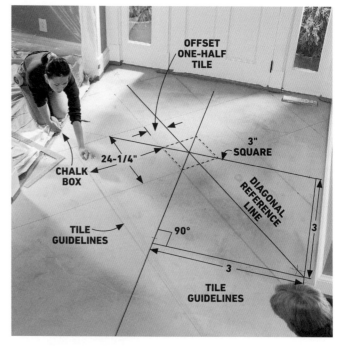

OFFSET ONE-HALF TILE

3" SQUARE

24-1/4"

CHALK BOX

DIAGONAL REFERENCE LINE

3

TILE GUIDELINES

90°

3

TILE GUIDELINES

7 MARK A SQUARE TILE GRID

Make a diagonal grid of tile guidelines. First draw a 3-ft. square and connect opposite corners to establish the diagonal reference line. Use this reference line to establish the 24-1/4 in. square grid (two 12-in. tiles plus two 1/8-in. grout lines). To avoid confusion, mark around the center tile to indicate the center of the medallion.

the distance between the lines is equal to the width of two tiles and two grout joints. It's simple to keep track of where the grout joints are if you place an "X" in the same corner of every box, and always start tiling by aligning both edges of the tile with the lines forming this corner.

PRECUT FIELD TILES ALONG THE EDGES

Photos 8–13 show how to measure, mark and cut the stone tile. Diamond blades make this process as easy as sawing wood. Most home centers and tile shops have a wet-cutting diamond saw like the one shown in **Photo 10** available for rent. Water is pumped onto the blade to keep it cool and keep dust to a minimum. You'll still want to set up the saw outside or in the garage, though, since the blade throws out a fine mist of dirty water. Ask the rental store for instructions and safety precautions to follow when you're using the saw.

With the grid marked on the floor, it's an easy matter to cut all the tiles before you spread any adhesive. Be sure to number the backs of the tiles with a pencil so you'll know where they go. Leave the cut tiles in place, and move them out of the way just before you spread the thinset on each section.

PRECUT FIELD TILES AROUND THE MEDALLION

We used a grinder equipped with a dry-cutting diamond blade to make the curved cuts **(Photo 13)**. Purchase a grinder or rent one. We bought the diamond blade at a home center.

SET THE FIELD TILE

Install all the tile and let the adhesive harden overnight before installing the medallion. Use the

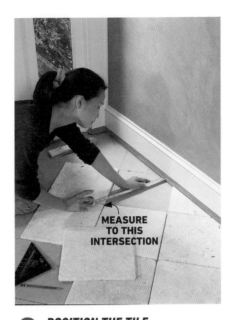

MEASURE TO THIS INTERSECTION

8 POSITION THE TILE AND MARK CUTS

Measure for the cuts on the border tiles. Align full tiles with the grid marks, and measure from these to the wall, allowing space for grout.

PENCIL

SPEED SQUARE

9 MARK THE TILES

Measure and mark the tiles. Then make a diagonal cutting line across each with a Speed square. Number the tiles on the back so you can precut and position them correctly when you're ready to install.

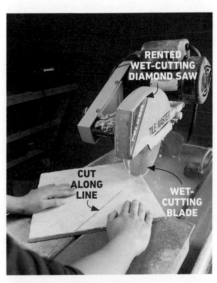

RENTED WET-CUTTING DIAMOND SAW

CUT ALONG LINE

WET-CUTTING BLADE

10 CUT THE TILES

Saw along the line with the wet-cutting diamond saw. Wear safety goggles and hearing protection. Steer the tile along the line as you slowly push it into the blade. Make very subtle adjustments to avoid binding the blade.

FINE-TOOTH SAW

LIMESTONE TILE **CARDBOARD SPACER**

11 UNDERCUT THE DOOR TRIM

Saw off the bottoms of door trims or doorjambs so the tile will slide under them. Set a floor tile on a piece of cardboard to guide the saw cut. Use a saw with sharp, fine teeth. Remove the cutoff chunk of molding with a screwdriver or small chisel.

TRACE AROUND TEMPLATE

ALIGN TILE EDGES WITH Xs ON CORNERS

CUT BORDER TILE

12 MARK THE MEDALLION PERIMETER

Align a block of floor tile with the grid lines. Include exact grout spaces. Tape the cardboard template to the tiles, making sure the space around the edges is even. Draw around the template with a pencil. Transfer the two reference marks **(Photo 5)** to the tile. Number the template for each tile and mark the back of each tile with the corresponding number.

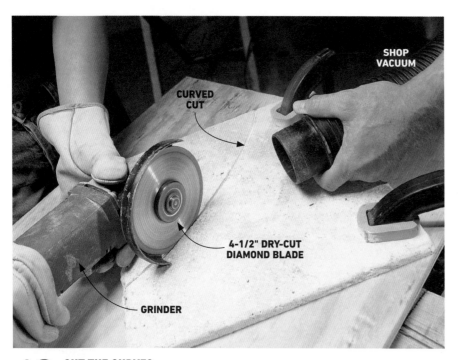

SHOP VACUUM

CURVED CUT

4-1/2" DRY-CUT DIAMOND BLADE

GRINDER

13 CUT THE CURVES

Make curved cuts using a dry-cut diamond blade mounted in a 4- or 4-1/2 in. grinder. Firmly clamp the tile to a piece of plywood laid over sawhorses. Wearing a dust mask, hearing protection and safety goggles, score along the line with the diamond blade. Use a shop vacuum to collect the dust and chips. Make three or four passes with the grinder to gradually saw through the tile. Round over the cut edge of the tile with 80-grit sandpaper.

cardboard template to precisely position the curved tiles that surround the medallion.

Follow **Photos 14** and **15**, and these tile-setting guidelines.

- Use white multipurpose thin-set mortar adhesive to glue the tile to the floor **(Photos 14** and **15)**. Standard gray thin-set will stain some light-colored stone and can show through light-colored grout.
- Mix the thin-set according to the instructions on the container.
- Mix only what you can use in about an hour. Restir it occasionally to keep it workable, but never add more water. Discard and mix a new batch if it starts to harden.
- Test to make sure you're putting enough thin-set on the floor by pressing a tile into the freshly troweled thin-set and pulling it off to inspect the backside. It should be fully covered with thin-set. If not, use a larger-notched trowel or increase the angle of the trowel when you're spreading to leave more thin-set on the floor.
- If a tile sinks below its neighbor (check with the flat edge of your trowel), lift it out with a margin trowel and "butter" the back with more thin-set, then reset it.
- Keep a bucket of water and sponge handy to clean thin-set from your hands, tools and the tile before it hardens. Clean excess thin-set from between tiles with a margin trowel or utility knife before it hardens.

SET THE MEDALLION

Scrape and sweep the floor where the medallion will go. Before you spread any thin-set, set the medallion in place to check the fit and get a feel for how much thin-set you'll need to hold it flush with the surrounding tile. If it's about 1/8 in. too low, you'll be able to use the same 1/4 x 3/8-in. notched trowel. If it's lower, use a 1/4 x 1/2-in. trowel; higher, a 1/4 x 1/4-in. The goal is to slide the medallion into the thin-set, have it sit a little higher than the surrounding tile and then press it down flush **(Photo 17)** without too much thin-set oozing out.

Remove the medallion, spread the thin-set and slide half of it into place (ours came in two halves). Then slide the other half into place and tamp it down **(Photo 17)**. Clean out excess grout **(Photo 18)** and gently reposition tiles that look out of place. If you have to reset a tile or add thin-set under it, cut through the mesh backing with a sharp utility knife before you lift it out. When you're happy with the way the tile looks, let the thin-set harden overnight.

TIP: Lock the front door, put pets in another room and erect barricades to keep "tourists" from testing your floor.

14 SPREAD THIN-SET MORTAR

Mix thin-set mortar according to the instructions on the package. Trowel a layer of it up to your layout lines, covering about 6 or 8 sq. ft. Press the thin-set onto the mortar bed to form a good bond. Go over the entire area with the notched trowel held at 45 degrees to the floor to create an even layer of ridged thin-set.

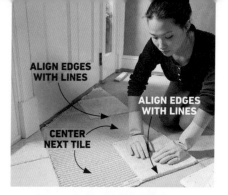

15 SET THE FIELD TILES

Wiggle and press each tile into place to ensure a good bond. Start by installing a corner tile at each position marked with an "X," aligning two edges with the corner formed by the two layout lines. Now lay the remaining tiles to fill between these corners, spacing them evenly. Complete each small section before moving on. Stand up occasionally and scan the floor for misaligned tiles. Use the round cardboard template to check the positioning of the tiles around the medallion space. Let the adhesive dry overnight.

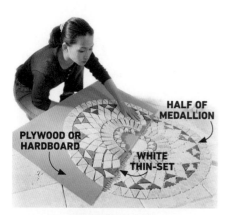

16 SLIDE THE MEDALLION INTO PLACE

Slide each half of the medallion gently onto the freshly spread thin-set, making sure the reference marks are aligned. Use a thin sheet of plywood to support the medallion as you slide it off. Carefully align the sections. The medallion should be sitting slightly above the surrounding tile.

17 FLATTEN THE MEDALLION

Press the medallion into the thin-set to embed it and bring it flush to the surrounding tile. Use a straight board or level to tamp over the entire area. If you need to raise or lower pieces or sections of the medallion, cut through the mesh backing with a utility knife before lifting them out. Then add or remove thin-set to bring the pieces to the proper level.

18 CLEAN BETWEEN TILES

Scrape the excess thin-set from between the pieces of marble with the point of a utility knife. Use a sponge to collect excess thin-set and clean the face of the tiles as you go. Then allow the thin-set to harden overnight.

19 SEAL THE STONE

Seal the porous surface of the stone with liquid stone enhancer to simplify grout cleanup and enliven the color. Spread the sealer and allow it to soak in about a half hour. Then clean up the excess with an old bath towel and allow the sealer to dry according to the instructions on the container. Read the label and follow all safety precautions.

20 SPREAD THE GROUT

Mix grout according to the instructions on the package. Press it into the spaces between the tiles with the rubber face of the grout float. Work the trowel back and forth to make sure the grout is tightly packed into every space. Complete all the grouting steps, including cleanup with a sponge, on a small section of floor (about 16 sq. ft.) before moving on to the next section.

SEAL THE TILE AND GROUT THE FLOOR

To enhance the color of the stone and make grout cleanup easier, we applied a liquid stone enhancer before grouting **(Photo 19)**. Even if you like the more subdued color of the unsealed stone, ask your salesperson to recommend a grout release-type sealer to keep the grout from sticking to the face of the porous stone. Follow the instructions and safety precautions on the label.

When the sealer is dry, you're ready to grout. Buy sanded grout for use on floors, and read the instructions to see if the powder should be mixed with plain water or latex additive. **TIP:** Glue leftover tile scraps to a piece of plywood, grout them, and let the grout dry to make sure you like the grout color.

Photos 20 and **21** show how easy grouting is, but don't be fooled. All the tile pros we know have horror stories about spreading more grout than they could clean up before it hardened. Avoid this problem by completing 4 x 4-ft. areas before moving on. Also be aware that grout sets much faster in hot, dry weather. Dampen the surface of the tile with a sponge before grouting to make cleanup easier. Use a special grout sponge, available at tile supply stores, and keep it clean and wrung out. Using too much water will weaken the grout and cause uneven grout color.

After the final cleanup **(Photo 21)**, let the grout dry overnight. Then remove the remaining haze by polishing the tile with an old bath towel. Allow the grout to dry for 48 hours. Then paint grout sealer onto grout joints with a disposable sponge applicator. This will help prevent dirt and stains from permanently discoloring the grout and make cleaning easier.

21 CLEAN THE SURFACE

Clean the grout film from the face of the tile with a special grout sponge. Allow the grout to "firm up" in the joints before cleanup. Do not allow the grout film to harden or dry on the face of the tile because it will be very difficult to remove. Start by scrubbing the face of the tile with a wrung-out sponge, rinsing the sponge in clean water when it fills with grout. Complete the cleanup process by making long overlapping swipes, using a clean face of the sponge for each pass. Polish the tile with a soft cloth to remove dried grout haze.

INSTALL KITCHEN CABINETS

///

USE THESE BASIC TECHNIQUES TO HANG THEM STRAIGHT, SOLID AND TRUE.

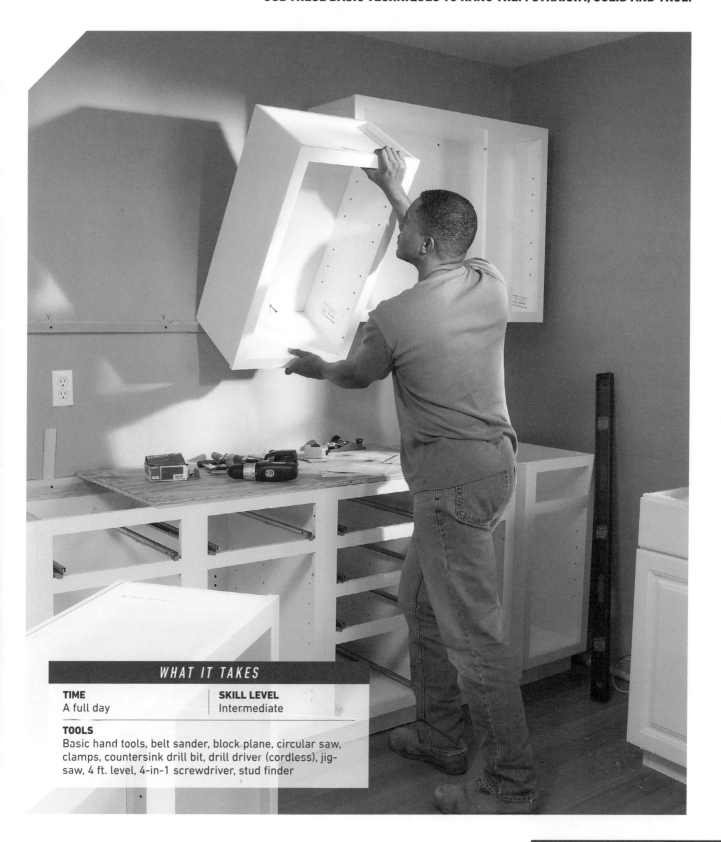

WHAT IT TAKES

TIME
A full day

SKILL LEVEL
Intermediate

TOOLS
Basic hand tools, belt sander, block plane, circular saw, clamps, countersink drill bit, drill driver (cordless), jig-saw, 4 ft. level, 4-in-1 screwdriver, stud finder

Learning how to install kitchen cabinets may seem intimidating, but the techniques are really quite simple. Think of it as screwing a series of boxes to the wall and to one another in the proper sequence. If your cabinet plan is correct, your main job is to find the best starting point and keep everything level. We'll show you how to install kitchen cabinets and master these key steps, and how to lay out the cabinet positions ahead of time to avoid missteps. Then we'll show you how to install the base cabinets so they're perfectly aligned and ready to be measured for the new countertop. Last, we'll show you a simple method for installing the upper wall cabinets.

TIME, TOOLS AND MATERIALS

The entire project typically takes less than a day. Depending on how large and elaborate your kitchen is, you'll save hundreds of dollars in installation charges.

You need only a few basic tools to do a first-class job: an accurate 4-ft. level, a screw gun powerful enough to drive 2-1/2-in. screws and a couple of good screw clamps that open to at least 8 in. Buy a 1/8-in. combination drill/countersink bit for predrilling the screw holes. You'll also need a block plane or belt sander for fine tuning the cuts to fit. A 1-lb. box of

DRILL/ COUNTERSINK BIT

SPECIAL COMBINATION DRILL BIT
This special bit saves time because it bores a pilot hole for the screw and a countersink hole for the screw head.

2-1/2-in. screws and three bundles of shims will be enough for nearly any kitchen full of cabinets.

MAKE SURE YOU HAVE THE RIGHT CABINETS

The cabinets shown are called face frame cabinets, meaning they have a 3/4-in.- thick frame surrounding the front of the cabinet box. European-style (also called frameless) cabinets are simple boxes without the face frame, and they require a few special installation steps that we won't cover here.

Just about any home center or lumberyard that sells factory-built cabinets will help you custom-design your kitchen cabinet layout. Make a drawing of your existing kitchen floor plan complete with exact appliance locations and room dimensions. Before you finalize the order, closely examine the computer screen and/or printout to make sure doors swing

in the right direction, end cabinets have finished panels on the ends, and toe-kick boards (1/4-in.-thick strips of finished wood for trimming cabinet bases) and filler strips are included. We highly recommend you order at least two extra filler strips for backup in case of miscuts. Keep a copy of the printout; you'll need it to guide your installation.

When your cabinets arrive, open the boxes and confirm that each cabinet matches one on the plan, all the parts are included, and there's no damage. A single mistake can delay the entire project. In our order, one cabinet was 6 in. undersized, the toe-kick trim boards were missing and two of the cabinets were seriously damaged. Mistakes can happen!

SET THE BASE CABINET HEIGHT
Most kitchen floors are very flat, especially in homes less than

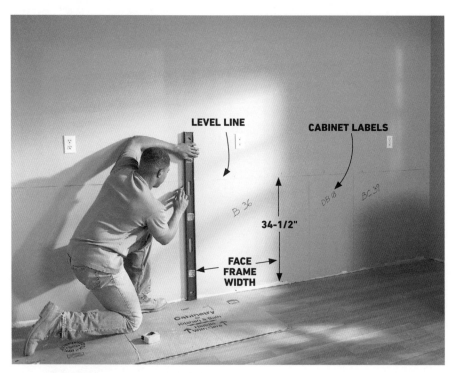

LEVEL LINE

CABINET LABELS

B 36

DB 18   BC 39

34-1/2"

FACE FRAME WIDTH

1 *MARK THE BASE CABINET HEIGHT*
Draw a level line on the wall 34-1/2 in. above the highest spot on the floor. Draw vertical lines to mark each cabinet location, label each cabinet's position on the wall, and find and mark the studs.

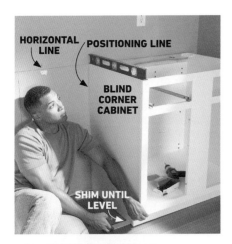

HORIZONTAL LINE POSITIONING LINE

BLIND CORNER CABINET

SHIM UNTIL LEVEL

2 POSITION THE FIRST BASE CABINET

Set the first cabinet 1/4 in. from the positioning line and shim the base until the top is even with the horizontal line, leveling it from front to back. Drive 2-1/2-in. screws through the back into the wall studs to anchor the cabinet.

40 years old. But before installing cabinets, it's best to confirm that by looking for the highest spot on the floor anywhere a cabinet will sit. You'll measure up from that spot and draw a level line to define the top of all of the base cabinets **(Photo 1)**.

Find that spot with a straight 8-ft.-long 2x4 (or shorter to fit between the end walls if needed) and a 4-ft. level. Rest the 2x4 with the level on top about 1 ft. away and parallel to the wall, and shim the 2x4 until it's level. Then mark the highest spot on the floor and repeat near any other walls that'll have cabinets. Continue until you find the highest spot. If you have two high spots, rest the board on both and find the highest one. Measure up the wall behind that spot exactly 34-1/2 in. (standard cabinet height) and mark the wall at that point. Using that mark as a starting point, draw a level line along the walls wherever base cabinets are planned **(Photo 1)**.

1" TO 2"

3 SCREW FACE FRAMES TOGETHER

Shim the next cabinet even with the horizontal line and level it. Clamp the frames together, drill 1/8-in. pilot holes, and screw the frames together with 2-1/2-in. screws. Then screw the cabinet to the wall studs.

TEST-FIT THE BASE CABINETS

In most cases, the corner cabinets determine where the rest of the cabinets go. That's especially true with lazy Susan corner cabinets, which have face frames facing two directions and have to meet adjoining cabinets perfectly. Our kitchen's blind-corner cabinets **(Photo 2)** are a bit more forgiving. Check your cabinet layout by dry-fitting all the base cabinets, starting with the corner ones, and setting all the cabinets in place as tightly together as possible. If the layout calls for filler strips, make sure to leave spaces for those, too. With the cabinets in place, check to make sure drawers and doors clear one another, appliance openings are the proper widths and sink bases center under windows above. Unless your cabinet plan is flawed, any adjustments you'll need to make are just a matter of ripping filler strips narrower or using wider ones. Next, remove

FILLER STRIP BASICS

All manufacturers offer filler strips to match the wood type and finish of their cabinets. Generally they'll offer widths about 3, 6 and 8 in. cut in the same lengths as the heights of the cabinet face frames. The filler strips fill spaces between end cabinets and walls, create additional spaces between cabinets or between cabinets and appliances for drawers and doors to clear, and close up odd gaps **(Photo 4)**.

Spaces between cabinets and walls are rarely even, so you'll have to taper many filler strips. The best strategy is to overcut slightly (1/16 in.), then plane or belt-sand the edge back. The 10-degree bevel simplifies this process **(Photos 5** and **6)**. If you have a large piece left over, protect the surface with masking tape as shown and use it elsewhere. You won't be able to clamp filler strips when they're against walls, so fit them tightly to make drilling and screwing them to the cabinet easier. Fillers that are less than 6 in. wide can float against the wall and need no support. But fillers more than 6 in. wide should be supported. Nail them to a 1x2 backer board that's glued to the drywall directly behind the filler.

MATERIALS LIST
ITEM
2-1/2-in. screws
Shims
Cabinets

the shelves, drawers and doors, and mark them and their matching cabinets with numbered masking tape to save time and confusion later. Then move the cabinets out of the room.

LEVEL AND SET THE BASE CABINETS

Starting with the corner cabinets, carefully measure, draw and label

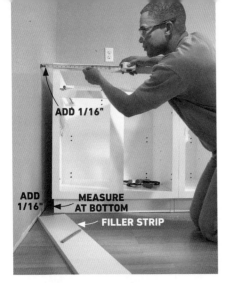

ADD 1/16"

ADD 1/16"

MEASURE AT BOTTOM

FILLER STRIP

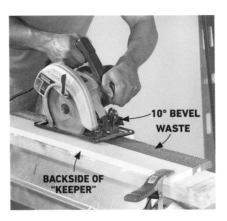

10° BEVEL WASTE

BACKSIDE OF "KEEPER"

SHARP EDGE

BLOCK PLANE

4 MEASURE THE GAP

Measure the gap between the wall and end cabinets at the top and bottom. Add 1/16 in.; draw a cutting line on the backside of a filler strip.

5 CUT THE FILLER STRIP

Clamp the filler strip and cut it at a 10-degree bevel from the backside so the wide edge of the "keeper" piece faces the front.

6 FIT AND INSTALL THE FILLER

Test-fit the filler strip and plane the sharp edge of the bevel until it fits perfectly. Set the strip in place, predrill and screw it to the cabinet frame.

until the cabinet top is even with the horizontal leveling line, and then level and shim the cabinet front to back (**Photo 2**). If there's a gap between the wall and the cabinet back (the wall isn't exactly plumb or straight), slip in shims and run screws into the studs through the cabinet back about 1 in. down from the top (see **Photo 8**). After all the base cabinets are set, score the shims with a utility knife and snap them off even with the cabinet top.

Position, level and shim the next cabinet, and clamp it to the first cabinet (**Photo 3**). Run your fingers over the joint and you'll be able to feel if it's misaligned. Loosen each clamp one at a time, and tweak the cabinet frames until they're perfectly flush, then retighten the clamp. Be fussy! Sometimes you'll have to loosen the screws holding the previous cabinet against the wall and pull it away slightly to get the frames aligned. When you're satisfied, drill pilot holes through the frames 1 to 2 in. from the top and bottom of the cabinet interior.

Make sure you're drilling straight. The most common mistake is to run the bit through the front of the cabinet frame!

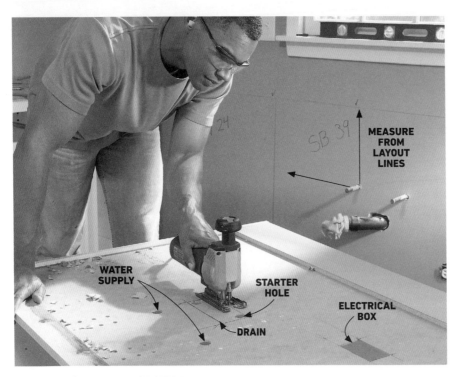

MEASURE FROM LAYOUT LINES

SB 39

WATER SUPPLY

STARTER HOLE

DRAIN

ELECTRICAL BOX

7 CUT PLUMBING OPENINGS

Lay out plumbing and electrical openings on the cabinet back, using the layout lines on the wall as reference points. Then drill and/or saw out the openings.

each base cabinet and appliance location on the wall. Use a 4-ft. level and a pencil (**Photo 1**). The marks should reflect the width of the face frame, not the cabinet back. (The cabinet back is actually 1/2 in. narrower than the front, 1/4

in. on each side.) Use a stud finder or probe with nails to find and mark the stud locations just above the horizontal leveling line.

Position the corner cabinets 1/4 in. away from the vertical positioning lines. Shim the base

With the face-frame screws in place, remove the clamps and screw the cabinet to the wall. Repeat the same process for each consecutive cabinet. Add filler strips wherever the cabinets come up short of walls, as shown in **Photos 4–6,** or wherever the plan calls for them. Leave the correct gaps for appliances. Some built-in appliances like dishwashers require very exact openings.

MAKE PLUMBING AND ELECTRICAL CUTOUTS

You'll probably have to cut openings for the drain and water supply lines and for outlets **(Photo 7)**. Lay out the openings by measuring from the layout lines at the top and side, and then transfer those numbers to the back of the cabinet. To avoid any confusion, do the layout work with the cabinet placed near its position and in the right orientation.

Drill holes for water supply lines and starter holes for square openings with a 1-in. spade bit. Stop drilling when the tip just penetrates the back, and finish the holes from the inside of the cabinet to prevent splintering the cabinet interior. Cut square openings with a jigsaw. If your drain line projects from the wall at an angle, simply cut a rectangular hole around it as we did.

SET THE PENINSULA CABINETS

Level and screw the first peninsula cabinet to the adjoining standard base cabinet. You'll probably have to fill a 1/4-in. gap with shims before screwing it to the wall studs **(Photo 8)**. If the first peninsula cabinet is only 2 ft. wide, you may have to clamp and screw filler strips to the frame so doors and drawers in the next cabinet will have operating clearance at

the inside corner. This should be marked on your plan.

After the first peninsula cabinet is in place, anchor the cabinets that follow to permanent blocks on the floor. To do that, position the next peninsula cabinet and outline its base on the floor with a pencil **(Photo 9)**. Then screw 2-by blocking to the floor after allowing for the cabinet base thickness **(Photo 10)**. Don't try to

place or cut the blocks perfectly. They can be short of the cabinet end by a couple inches and back from the inside of the cabinet 1/8 in. or so. That way you won't have to struggle to get the cabinet to fit over the blocks.

Screw the blocks into the subfloor with 2-1/2-in. screws spaced about every foot. Set the cabinet into place, level it with shims, then clamp and screw it to

SHIM GAPS AT STUDS

FIRST PENINSULA CABINET

8 SET THE FIRST PENINSULA CABINET

Orient the first peninsula cabinet at a right angle to the wall. Level and clamp it to the adjacent cabinet, and screw it to the cabinet and the wall.

9 MARK THE POSITION OF THE SECOND CABINET

Position the next cabinet in line, clamp it and draw a line around the base. Make sure it's at a right angle to the other base cabinets. Set the cabinet aside.

SPACE FOR CABINET BASE

10 INSTALL 2x2 SUPPORT

Draw a second line to mark the thickness of the cabinet base, and then screw 2x2s to the floor along the inner line.

11 SET THE CABINET

Lower the cabinet over the blocking. Shim, clamp and screw the frames together. Screw the cabinet to the blocking with two screws from each side.

the neighboring cabinet and into the blocking.

Anchor island cabinets using the same positioning and blocking techniques shown for the peninsula cabinets. However, it's best to install your upper cabinets before starting on an island to keep a clear work area in the middle of the kitchen.

INSTALL THE UPPER CABINETS

The only tricky part about installing hanging upper cabinets is supporting them in exactly the right position while you screw them to the wall and one another. That's a tough, awkward task, especially if you're working alone. The ledger method simplifies this **(Photo 12)**.

It's a fail-safe method, but you'll have to patch and retouch paint to repair the screw holes left from the ledger.

Start by making a light pencil mark 19-1/2 in. up from the lower cabinets (it'll be 18 in. after the countertop is installed), and then mark the stud locations using the ones below as a guide. Next, transfer the cabinet positioning lines from below **(Photo 12)** and screw a 1x2 ledger to the studs even with the layout lines. It's best to prestart the cabinet screws before hoisting the cabinets up onto the ledger. **Photo 13** shows an easy method to get the screws in the right place. Use the cabinet positioning lines and the stud locations on the wall, and then transfer them to the cabinet. You'll often find that a cabinet, especially a narrow one, will have only one stud behind it. Don't worry; the other cabinets will help support it too.

Start any corner cabinets first. Space the first end cabinet exactly 1/4 in. away from the layout line and screw it to the wall. Be exact with the first cabinet because it will define the locations of all the rest of the cabinets on that wall.

Start the screws and hoist the next cabinet into place, snugging its frame against the neighboring one, and screw it to the wall. Next, align the frames and clamp them together as you did with the base cabinets **(Photo 15)**. You'll probably have to back out the stud screws slightly in one or both cabinets to get the frames to line up perfectly. That's fine—leave the screws backed out while you clamp, drill and screw the frames together.

FINISH WITH DOORS AND TRIM

Finish off the cabinets by cutting, fitting and nailing the toe-kick

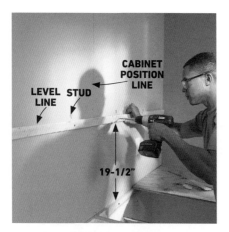

12 MARK THE UPPER CABINET POSITIONS
Draw a level line that's 19-1/2 in. above the lower cabinets; mark the upper cabinet positions. Screw a 1x2 ledger to the wall even with the level line.

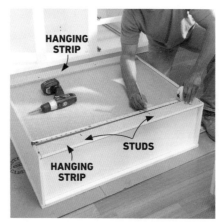

13 MARK STUD LOCATIONS
Measure from the cabinet position lines to the stud locations. Mark the stud locations on the cabinet backs and drill 1/8-in. pilot holes through the hanging strips.

14 SCREW THE CABINETS TO THE WALL
Start 2-1/2-in. screws, then rest the cabinet on the ledger. Align it with the cabinet position line and drive the screws into the wall studs.

15 HANG ADDITIONAL CABINETS
Position the next cabinet; run the top screws partially into the studs to hold it. Align the frames, clamp them and screw the cabinets together. Then screw the cabinets to the wall.

COMPLETE REPAIRS AND PAINTING BEFORE INSTALLING KITCHEN CABINETS

The perfect time to do any kitchen improvements is after your old cabinets are torn out and before you learn how to install kitchen cabinets. Here are some upgrades to consider:

■ **ELECTRICAL UPGRADES**

Older kitchens are notorious for lacking adequate lighting and outlets. Consider adding under-cabinet, task or indirect lighting, installing more outlets, and upgrading all the outlets to GFCI-protected (now demanded by code). It's easy to cut open drywall, fish new wires and install electrical boxes because you can do the work behind the cabinets. Repairs won't have to be perfect because they won't show.

■ **DRYWALL REPAIR**

Patch any holes or any other drywall damage.

■ **PAINTING**

Repaint all of the walls and the ceiling. You'll save the hassle of cutting in around the new cabinets and get a much neater job to boot. You can touch up nicks and bumps later.

■ **INSTALL NEW FINISHED FLOORING IF YOU CAN**

Most finished floor materials can be installed ahead of the cabinets. That's much easier to do because you can project the flooring under the cabinets and avoid cutting around them later. Hardwood flooring, tile, most vinyl and some laminate floors can handle cabinets resting on them with no problem. But be careful. Perimeter-glued vinyl and floating wood laminate floors need to expand and contract freely. If you rest cabinets on them, you may have problems with buckling, splitting or cracking later.

16   INSTALL CABINET DOORS

Replace the drawers, then rehang the doors and adjust the hinges to align the doors with one another.

boards to the bases. They'll be 4 in. wide, but on irregular floors, you may need to rip them narrower to get them to fit. If you have bad gaps between the floor and the toe-kicks, add base shoe contoured to fit the floor. Wherever cabinets have finished ends, run the toe-kick boards 1/4 in. past the cabinet for a nice appearance. Finish up by slipping the drawers into their slides and reattaching the doors **(Photo 16)**. Adjust the hinges until the doors line up perfectly, and move on to installing the door and drawer pulls.

TIME
3 days

SKILL LEVEL
Intermediate

TOOLS
Basic hand tools, angle grinder, awl, knot cup brush, 3/8-in. rabbeting bit, router

RUSTIC BARN DOOR

THIS DOOR IS HIGH STYLE WITH LOW-COST LUMBER—AND A FEW TRICKS.

If you've investigated rustic barn doors, you've probably gotten sticker shock. They can be very expensive. But we can help. We'll show you how to build and hang a simple barn door, including how to distress new pine boards for a weathered look.

TIME, TOOLS AND MATERIALS

The 1x6 No. 2 pine boards we used for this door are inexpensive, so be sure to buy several extras so you can experiment with the distressing and staining techniques before you start on the boards you'll use. Preparing the boards is the most time-consuming part of this project. Expect to spend several hours cutting the rabbets on the edges of the 1x6s. We used a router with a rabbeting bit to cut the rabbets; a table saw with a dado blade set would be quicker.

The grinder and knot cup brush we used make quick work of the initial distressing. It took us about 10 minutes per board. Grinders can be expensive but a cheap one will work fine for this project. You could also use a knot cup wire brush mounted in a corded drill, but it would take you more time to achieve the same results.

Staining the boards goes quickly, but set aside a day or two to get the parts cut and finished. Some companies have ready-to-ship options for barn door hardware, but you should plan ahead if you need something else since it usually requires more time.

MEASURE THE OPENING

Whether you're building a rustic barn door or ordering one, here's what you need to know about door size: Sliding doors should extend at least an inch beyond the sides of the opening that don't have trim, or an inch beyond the moldings of openings with trim. You can add more overlap for extra privacy, if you'd like. To determine the door width, add at least 2 in. to the width of the opening or to the outside dimensions of the door trim.

Before determining the door height, you should choose your hardware. Then check the measuring instructions for using it or ask the manufacturer for help in determining the proper door height. In most cases, measuring to the top of an opening with no trim, or to the top of the trim, and subtracting 1/2 in. from your measurement will give you the minimum door height required.

Finally, you have to make sure you allow enough clearance above the opening to lift the door onto the track. This distance varies depending on your hardware, so again, check with the manufacturer.

BEFORE: STANDARD PINE BOARD

AFTER: HOMEMADE BARN WOOD

FOOLED BY A FORGERY

We've harvested loads of lumber from abandoned farmsteads. But the fake barn wood technique used on this door fooled us. We really thought it was genuine barn wood until we took a closer look. Even then, we were impressed with the quality of the counterfeit. And in some ways, fake barn wood is better than the real thing: There are no rotten and splintered boards, lead paint or musty odors filling the air. In fact, the forgery made us wonder: Was collecting real barn wood—with all the sweat and splinters—a waste of our time?

THREE SLIDING OPTIONS

Before you start shopping for hardware, take a careful look at the area where you would like to install the door and figure out what door setup works best. If you want to cover the opening with one door, you'll need an area on one side of the opening that's wide enough for the door. Make sure there aren't any obstructions like light switches, sconce lights or heat registers that would be covered by or interfere with the door. If there's not enough wall space on one side of the opening, you can install a pair of doors that slide to opposite sides or buy special bypass hardware that allows the doors to stack.

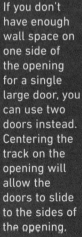

■ **SINGLE DOOR** This is the most popular choice, but you'll need enough wall space. Order a track that's at least twice as wide as the door.

■ **DOUBLE DOORS** If you don't have enough wall space on one side of the opening for a single large door, you can use two doors instead. Centering the track on the opening will allow the doors to slide to the sides of the opening.

■ **BYPASS DOORS** If you want to install barn doors on a closet opening or on an opening that goes wall to wall, you can order bypass hardware that allows you to stack the doors on one side of the opening.

1 MAKE SHIPLAP BOARDS

Mount a 3/8-in. rabbeting bit in your router. Set the cutting depth to 3/8 in. Cut rabbets on two scraps and check the fit. Adjust the depth until the joint is flush. Cut rabbets on the door boards: Rabbet one edge, then flip over the board and do the other.

2 DISTRESS THE BOARDS WITH A GRINDER

Mount a knot cup wheel in a grinder. Put on safety gear, including goggles. Nail a board to sawhorses and use the edge of the wire cup to grind out soft wood and create a weathered texture.

THREE WAYS TO SUPPORT THE BARN DOOR TRACK

To support a door, the track needs to be solidly mounted to wall framing. There are three options. First, you could install continuous wood backing between the wall studs at the track height. This allows you the freedom to install track-mounting screws at any location. But this method isn't practical in a room that's finished because you would have to remove the drywall or plaster to install the blocking.

The second option is to mount a header board to the wall surface, making sure it's securely screwed to the studs, and then screw the track to the header board. One manufacturer recommends a max door weight of 75 lbs. if you're using this method because the support screws will be engaged in only 3/4-in.-thick wood.

The third option is to bolt the track directly to the studs. You have to do two things if you choose this method. First, make sure to order an undrilled track—you'll need to drill holes yourself at the stud locations. And second, ask the

3 MAKE WORMHOLES

Create what looks like wormholes using an awl. To make an oblong hole, tip the awl after punching it in.

supplier to recommend hardware that will avoid crushing the drywall. Most suppliers have crush plates or something similar to solve the problem.

GET THE RIGHT SPACERS AND FLOOR GUIDES

Included in the track mounting hardware package will be some sort of spacers or standoffs that will hold the track away from the wall to allow the door to slide freely. Some companies supply spacers in different lengths, while others supply adjustable-length spacers. The length of the spacers is determined by your track mounting method, whether there is trim around the door or at the floor that you must clear, and the thickness of your door. Be sure to double-check with the supplier before placing your order to make sure you're getting the correct length spacers with your hardware for your situation.

4 APPLY A BASE COAT OF STAIN
Roll or brush an even coat of light-colored stain over each board. Wipe off the excess stain with a rag.

5 ADD DARK STAIN
Dab dark stain over the board with a rag in a random pattern. Then spread out the dabs of stain to create dark areas and streaks. Finally, wipe off the excess dark stain with a different rag.

You'll also need a guide at the floor to prevent the bottom of the door from swinging. The simplest guide is an L-shaped metal bracket that mounts to the floor and fits into a groove cut in the bottom of the door. If your door doesn't have a groove in it, there are roller guides and adjustable roller guides that will work. Choose the guide that works best for your door.

MAKE SHIPLAP BOARDS

We used inexpensive 1x6 No. 2 pine boards, cut rabbets on the edges to make shiplap boards, and distressed and stained them to resemble old barn wood. When you choose boards, don't worry about knots, scratches or gouges. But try to pick boards that are straight and not cupped or warped.

We divided the width of the door by the board width to see how

6 FINISH WITH GRAY STAIN
Wipe on the topcoat of gray stain with a rag. Apply an uneven coat of stain, letting some of the previous layers show through. Wipe off the excess gray stain with a rag. Let the boards dry overnight.

many boards we would need. And then we adjusted the board width until they were all equal. When you're doing the math, remember to account for the shiplap edges.

For our 4-ft.-wide door, we cut each board 5 in. wide. Yours may be different. Cut the boards to the right width and cut rabbets on two edges of all but two boards. Cut one rabbet on two boards that will be used on the outside edges. **Photo 1** shows how we used a 3/8-in. rabbeting bit to cut the rabbets. A table saw with a dado blade will also work.

We also cut the boards to the right length before distressing

them so we could make the ends look aged. At the same time, cut the two horizontal rails and the two 3-in.-wide blocks that go under the hangers. Make the horizontal rails 2 in. shorter than your door width.

GRIND, SCRATCH AND BEAT THE BOARDS

When all the parts are cut, you're ready for the fun part—distressing the boards. **Photo 2** shows how to use a knot cup brush mounted in an angle grinder to abrade the soft wood and expose the grain. This gives the wood a weathered look. Pieces of wire from the cup can break off and cause serious injury

MATERIALS LIST
(FOR A 4-FT.-WIDE DOOR)

ITEM	QTY.
Barn door hardware kit	1
1x6 x 8' No. 2 pine boards	12
1-1/2" wrought-head nails	40
Knot cup brush for grinder ($20)	1
Tube of construction adhesive	1
Light gold stain	2 qts.
Dark stain	1 qt.
Gray stain	1 qt.
Polyurethane (optional)	1 ql.
Mini roller and cover	1
Rags	As needed
Brush or roller for poly	As needed

Labels in image: WOOD SCRAP, PENNY SPACERS

7 SQUARE THE VERTICAL SLATS

Arrange the slats on 2x4s and space them with pennies. Align the ends, and screw wood scraps to the 2x4s to hold the boards in place. Then line up the ends and check the door for square by making sure the diagonal measurements are equal.

if you're not protected, and there's a lot of dust. Make sure to wear safety goggles, hearing protection and a good-quality dust mask.

Start by nailing the board to the sawhorses with finish nails to hold it in place. The nail holes will add to the rustic appearance. Tip the grinder so the wheel is on edge and parallel to the grain to wear away the soft wood. Use the wire wheel on the edges and ends of the board to create an uneven, worn look. You can also hold the wheel flat on the surface and move it in arcs across the wood to resemble saw marks. Don't worry; you can't go wrong here. Wearing away any amount of wood will look great.

If you want to take distressing to the next level, use an awl to create "wormholes" (**Photo 3**). You don't have to put holes in every board. Some variety will add authenticity. Drag a screwdriver or other sharp object along the grain to create a fake crack. Use your hammer claw or any other tool or heavy object to create dents and gouges. When you're done distressing the boards, it's time to stain them.

ADD LAYERS OF STAIN

To achieve the look you see here, start by applying a base coat of light gold stain to the boards (**Photo 4**). We applied the stain with a mini roller to speed up the process. Wipe off excess stain with a rag. Then use a rag to apply an uneven coat of dark stain (**Photo 5**). Wipe off the excess to expose some of the base coat color. Finally, apply a thin, uneven layer of gray stain, dabbing and wiping it to create an aged look (**Photo 6**). It will look better if the stain is less consistent.

Don't worry if the finish differs from one board to another. The variation will add an authentic look when the door is assembled. Don't forget to finish the ends and edges of the boards. Let the stain dry overnight before moving on to the door assembly.

Most stain brands have colors that will work well for aging wood. Here are the colors we used for each of the coats we applied:

■ Base coat: Varathane Summer Oak
■ Second coat: Varathane Kona

Label in image: WROUGHT-HEAD NAIL

8 FASTEN THE RAILS

Measure and mark for the rails. Ours are 8 in. from the top and bottom of the door. Apply construction adhesive to the backs of the rails and place them on the door. Attach the rails with nails. We staggered the nails up and down on each board, but you can use any pattern you like.

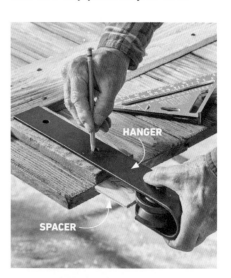

Labels in image: HANGER, SPACER

9 MARK FOR THE HANGER HOLES

Follow the manufacturer's instructions for mounting the hangers. We're using a 2-1/2-in. spacer to ensure the wheel is the correct distance from the top of the door. Mark the hole locations. Then drill holes and mount the hangers on the door.

FAMILYHANDYMAN.COM
Search for "shiplap siding" to see how to make shiplap boards on a table saw.

■ Third coat: Varathane
Weathered Gray

ASSEMBLE THE DOOR

Start by arranging the vertical boards on a pair of 2x4s placed flat on sawhorses or the floor. Arrange the 2x4s so they're lined up under the locations of the horizontal rails. Space the boards, tops and bottoms, with pennies. Screw wood scraps to the 2x4s on both sides of the door to hold the boards together while you add the horizontal rail. Check to see that the board ends are still lined up, then measure diagonally from opposite corners to make sure the door is square **(Photo 7)**. Adjust the board positions until the diagonal

measurements are equal.

Next, mark the heights of the rails on the door and attach them with construction adhesive and nails **(Photo 8)**. Since the fasteners show, we decided to use 1-1/2-in. wrought-head nails that we bought at rockler.com. Since the nails protruded slightly from the opposite side, we shortened them a bit by holding them with locking pliers and grinding off the tips on a bench grinder. You could also mount a metal grinding wheel in your angle grinder. Drill pilot holes for the nails that are near the ends of the rails to avoid splitting the wood. If you don't mind the appearance of screw heads on the opposite side of the door, you could

flip the door over and drive 1-1/4-in. screws through the boards into the rails for a little more strength.

If you prefer, you could brush on a coat of flat polyurethane. Test the finish on a scrap to see if you like it before you apply it to your door. We didn't put a finish on our door.

INSTALL THE HANGERS AND MOUNT THE TRACK

Follow the instructions included with your door hardware to install the hangers. Ours recommended using a 2-1/2-in. spacer between the door and the wheel to hold the hanger in the correct position while marking the bolt locations **(Photo 9)**. After marking the bolt locations, drill holes for the bolts; mount the hangers on the door.

The steps you take to mount the track will depend on your track support. If you've installed continuous backing between the studs or are mounting the track on a header board, then you may be using a predrilled track and can proceed to bolt the track to the wall.

If you're mounting the track over the drywall and bolting it to studs, you'll have to locate and mark the studs, and then transfer the stud locations to the track so you can drill holes for the mounting screws in the right place. The instructions should give you a formula for determining the track height. Double-check your dimensions and math before mounting the track **(Photo 10)**. You don't want to have to cut down the door or reposition the track if it's in the wrong spot.

With the track mounted, finish the job by putting the door on the track **(Photo 11)**. Mount the end stops, bottom guides and any other hardware according to your instructions.

LEVEL TRACK

10 MOUNT THE TRACK
Measure carefully to determine the track height. Hold the track level and in the correct position and mark the wall at each fastener hole. Drill pilot holes at the marks. Then attach the track to the wall with the fasteners and spacers provided in your hardware kit.

11 HANG THE DOOR
Set the door on the track. Carefully roll it to each end to determine where to place the stops. Install the stops, bottom guide and any other hardware to complete the project.

TWO-TIER SPICE DRAWER

A CLEVER WAY TO ORGANIZE YOUR COLLECTION.

You could remodel your kitchen with new cabinets, countertops and appliances, but the first thing you'll want to show off when people visit is this space-saving two-tier spice tray. When you open the drawer, you can slide the top tray all the way back into the cabinet to access the entire bottom layer; no need to lift out a separate tray. It's a clever organizer because all the spices are in one place, face up. You can use the same basic design to make a two-tier utensil drawer too.

Do a little measuring before diving into this project. You can install the 1-3/4-in.-thick tray (like the one shown) if your drawer is at least 4 in. deep on the inside. Also, these trays are most useful if your existing drawers have (or if you install) full-extension slides on the main drawer.

WHAT IT TAKES	
TIME 2 hours	**SKILL LEVEL** Intermediate
TOOLS	
Basic hand tools, drill, finish nailer, jigsaw, miter saw	

1 CUT AWAY THE TOP HALF OF THE DRAWER BACK
Use a jigsaw to cut away a little more than half of the drawer back.

DRAWER BACK

MOUNT SLIDE FLUSH TO DRAWER TOP

2 INSTALL THE TRAY SLIDES
Secure full-extension drawer slides to the top inside edges of the drawer. Install them "backward" so they extend toward the back of the drawer. It's OK if they run an inch or so beyond the back of the drawer; most cabinets have extra space in back.

Figure A
Spice Drawer

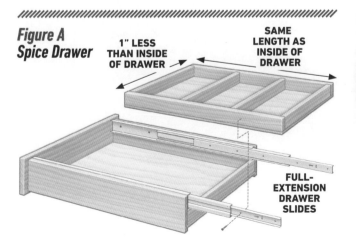

1" LESS THAN INSIDE OF DRAWER

SAME LENGTH AS INSIDE OF DRAWER

FULL-EXTENSION DRAWER SLIDES

3 BUILD THE UPPER TRAY
Since most standard drawer glides are 1/2-in. wide, build your tray 1-in. narrower (or a hair less) than the inside width of the drawer. Build your tray the same length as the inside drawer length. Install partitions according to your needs.

1/4" PLYWOOD BOTTOM

4 INSTALL THE TRAY
Attach the plywood bottom to the tray with nails or brads. Screw the tray to the drawer slides so the top of the tray is flush with the top of the drawer. Then reinstall the drawer.

ULTIMATE CONTAINER STORAGE

///

NO MORE DIGGING FOR THE RIGHT LID!

It's always a challenge to find a container with a matching lid. This rollout solves the problem by keeping all pieces neatly organized and easily accessible. Full-extension drawer slides are the key.

To simplify what can be tricky drawer slide installation, we've designed an ingenious carrier system that allows you to mount the slides and make sure everything is working smoothly before you mount the unit in your cabinet.

TOOLS AND MATERIALS

Our 24-in. base cabinet required a 4 x 4-ft. sheet of 1/2-in.-thick plywood for the rollout, plus a 2 x 3-ft. scrap of 3/4-in. plywood for the carrier. Yours may require more or less. We found high-quality birch plywood at a home center. If you have trouble finding nice plywood, consider ordering Baltic birch or Apple-Ply plywood from a home center or local lumberyard. The carrier fits under the rollout and isn't very conspicuous, so almost any flat piece of 3/4-in. plywood will work for that.

In addition to the lumber, you'll need a pair of 22-in. full-extension ball-bearing slides (sold at home centers or woodworking supply stores) and a 1/4-in. aluminum rod.

We used a table saw to cut the plywood parts, but if you're careful to make accurate cuts, a circular saw will work. You'll need a jigsaw with a plywood-cutting blade to cut the curves on the sides and dividers. We used a finish nail gun and 1-1/4-in.-long brad nails to connect the parts, but you could substitute trim-head screws if you don't mind the larger holes they leave.

WHAT IT TAKES	
TIME 1 day	**SKILL LEVEL** Intermediate
TOOLS Basic hand tools, brad nail gun (optional), drill, jigsaw, table or circular saw	

1 MEASURE THE OPENING
Measure from any protruding hinges or door parts to the opposite side to find the opening width. Also check to make sure the cabinet is at least 22 in. deep.

2 CUT THE SIDE PANELS
Cut each panel to size. Then cut the notch to form the L-shape. Start with a table saw or circular saw for the straight cuts. Finish the inside corner with a jigsaw.

MEASURE THE BASE CABINET

Most base cabinets are about 23 in. deep and will accommodate this rollout, but measure to be sure. If the measurement from the back of the face frame to the back of the cabinet is less than 22 in., you'll have to build a shallower rollout and use shorter drawer slides.

The other critical measurement is the width. Measure the clear opening width, that is, the width from any protruding hinge or door parts to the opposite side of the cabinet opening (**Photo 1**). Subtract 3 in. from this measurement to determine the width of parts **B**, **C**, **D** and **E**.

CUT OUT THE PARTS

After adjusting the size of parts **B**, **C**, **D** and **E** for the cabinet width, cut out all the parts except the carrier bottom. If using a table saw, make partial cuts to form the L-shaped sides. Remember, you can't see how far the blade is cutting on the underside, so stop short of your inside corner marks by at least an inch. **Photo 2** shows how to complete the cut with a jigsaw.

Trace along the edge of a 1-gallon paint can to draw the radius for the curve on the side panels. Trace along a quart-size can to draw the radius on the dividers. Cut the curves on the sides and dividers with a jigsaw (**Photo 3**). Smooth the curved cuts with 100-grit sandpaper.

3 *CUT THE CURVES*
Mark the curves on the side panels by tracing along a gallon paint can. Mark the dividers using a quart-size paint can. Then cut with a jigsaw.

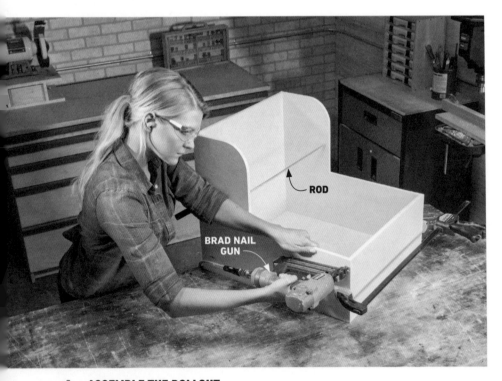

ROD

BRAD NAIL GUN

BUILD THE ROLLOUT

Mark the location of the 1/4-in. rod on the side panels using **Figure A** as a guide. Wrap tape around a 1/4-in. drill bit 1/4 in. from the end to use as a depth guide while drilling. Drill 1/4-in.-deep holes at the marks. Use a hacksaw to cut an aluminum rod 1/2 in. longer than the width of the bottom.

4 *ASSEMBLE THE ROLLOUT*
Glue and clamp the parts together. Don't forget to install the rod. Align the edges by tapping on the panels with your hand or a hammer. Then nail the parts together.

CUTTING LIST

KEY	QTY.	PART
A	2	1/2" plywood 1/2" x 22" x 18" (Sides)
B	1	1/2" plywood 1/2" x 7-1/2" x 18" (Front)
C	1	1/2" plywood 1/2" x 22" x 18" (Bottom)
D	1	1/2" plywood 1/2" x 17-1/2" x 18" (Back)
E	1	1/2" plywood 1/2" x 7-1/2" x 18" (Shelf)
F	5*	1/2" plywood 1/2" x 6" x 6" (Dividers)
G	1	3/4" plywood 3/4" x 20" x 22" (Carrier bottom)
H	2	3/4" plywood 3/4" x 2-3/4" x 22" (Carrier sides)

NOTE: These part sizes are for a 24-in.-wide base cabinet. To fit your cabinet, adjust the sizes according to the instructions in the article.

MATERIALS LIST

ITEM	QTY.
1/2" x 4' x 4' plywood	1
3/4" x 2' x 3' plywood	1
Pair of 22" full-extension slides	1
36" x 1/4" aluminum rod	1
Small package of 1-1/4" brad nails	1

Apply wood glue to all edges that meet. Then arrange the sides, bottom, front and back on a workbench and clamp them together. Work the aluminum rod into the holes. Tap the parts with a hammer to align the edges perfectly before connecting them with brad nails **(Photo 4)**. Take your time aiming the nail gun to avoid nail blowouts.

Finish the rollout by adding the dividers. First decide how many dividers you want and calculate the width of the space between the dividers. Cut a spacer block to that dimension and use it as a guide to install the dividers. Attach the dividers to the shelf **(Photo 5)**. Then measure down 7-1/2 in. from the top and make marks to indicate the top edge of the divider shelf. Line up the divider assembly with these marks and nail it in. Draw divider center lines on the back of the rollout as a nailing guide. Then attach the dividers **(Photo 6)**.

Drawer slides require 1/2-in. clearance on each side, so making

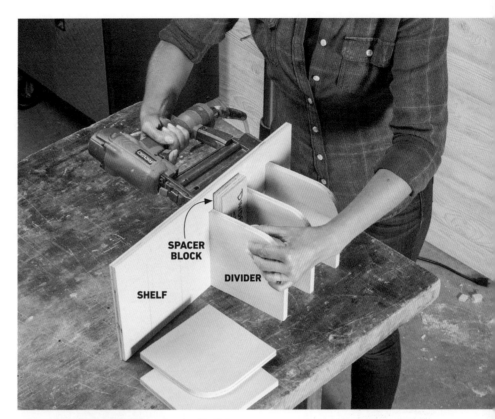

5 NAIL THE DIVIDERS TO THE SHELF
Cut a spacer the width of the desired space between dividers and use it to position the dividers as you nail them to the shelf.

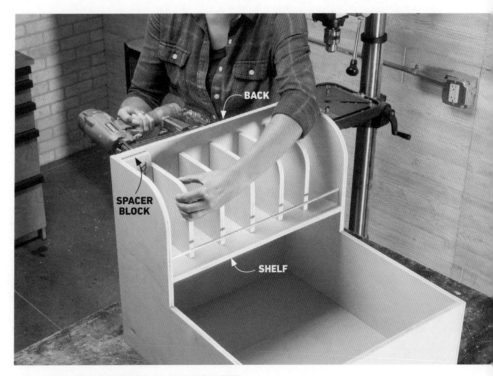

6 NAIL THE DIVIDERS TO THE ROLLOUT
Position the shelf, then nail through the sides into the shelf. Use the spacer block to align the dividers and nail through the back.

Figure A Ultimate Container Storage

OVERALL DIMENSIONS: 19" W x 17-1/2" H x 22" D

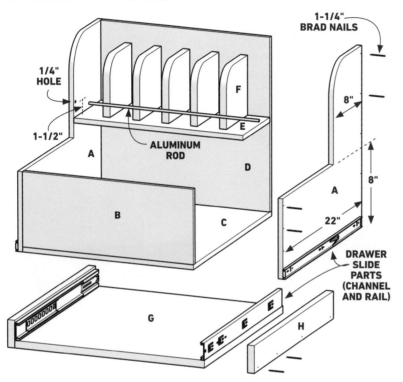

7 SCREW THE DRAWER SLIDE TO THE ROLLOUT
Separate the drawer slides and attach the rail to the rollout.
Align the rail flush to the bottom and flush to the front before
driving the screws.

the carrier exactly 1 in. wider than
the rollout will result in a perfect fit.
Measure the width of the completed
rollout and add exactly 1 in. to
determine the width of the carrier
bottom. Cut the carrier bottom from
3/4-in. plywood. Then screw the
carrier sides to the carrier bottom
to prepare the carrier for mounting
the drawer slides.

MOUNT THE SLIDES

Follow the instructions included
with your drawer slides to
separate the slides into two parts:
a channel and a rail. Usually,
pressing down on a plastic lever
releases the parts and allows
you to separate them. Screw the
rails to the drawer (**Photo 7**) and
the channels to the carrier sides
(**Photo 8**).

When you're done installing
the slides, check the fit by
carefully aligning the rails with
the channels and sliding them
together. The rollout should glide
easily on the ball-bearing slides.
If the slides seem too tight, you
can adjust the fit by removing one
of the carrier sides and slipping
a thin cardboard shim between
the carrier side and carrier bottom
before reassembling them.

MOUNT THE ROLLOUT
IN THE CABINET

Photo 9 shows fitting the carrier
assembly into the cabinet. There
will be a little side-to-side play so
you can adjust the position to clear
the hinge and door. This will probably require you to offset the carrier
slightly away from the hinge side.
Screw the carrier to the bottom of
the cabinet and you're ready to
install the rollout (**Photo 10**). Since
you've already checked the fit, it
should operate perfectly. Now load
it up with containers and lids, and
enjoy your neatly organized container rollout.

CARRIER

DRAWER
SLIDE
CHANNEL

8 SCREW THE DRAWER SLIDE CHANNEL TO THE CARRIER
Rest the drawer slide channel on the carrier and align the front flush to the front of the carrier side.

9 INSTALL THE CARRIER
Position the carrier so that the rollout will clear any hinge or door parts. Drive screws through the carrier bottom into the cabinet.

10 INSTALL THE ROLLOUT
Line up the rails and channels; slide the rollout into the cabinet. Slide it back and forth a few times to make sure it rolls smoothly.

WHAT IT TAKES

TIME
1 or 2 weekends

SKILL LEVEL
Intermediate

TOOLS
Basic hand tools, diamond hole saws (optional), drill, grout float, level, notched trowel, rubbing stone, tile nipper, tile cutter, tile saw

THE ART OF SUBWAY TILE

//
TRANSFORM YOUR BATHROOM IN A COUPLE OF WEEKENDS.

Adding tile wainscoting is a perfect DIY project. It doesn't require a huge investment in tools, the results are stunning, and tiling a wall is much easier than most other tile jobs. Unlike floors or showers, tile wainscoting doesn't have to withstand foot traffic or daily soaking, so you can set the tile directly over your existing walls using premixed mastic adhesive—no backer board, waterproofing or hard-to-mix adhesive needed! For our bathroom, we chose glazed 4 x 8-in. subway tile with matching trim pieces. The walls were already painted, providing an adequate base.

SHOP FOR TILE

First, measure your walls and draw a sketch of the room you plan to tile. Take the sketch to a home center or tile shop where the salesperson can help you order the right amount of tile. We chose to add the matching base (skirt), a cap (cornice) and a long, thin piece called a "pencil." We also ordered bullnose tile for the outside corner and special outside corner pieces for the base and cap. As you shop, you'll discover that not all tile has matching trim pieces. If the tile you select doesn't have trim pieces, you may be able to find trim in a complementary color.

Remember to choose a grout (including the color) while you're shopping. We used sanded grout to fill the 1/8-in. grout spaces on this tile, but if your grout spaces are narrower, use unsanded grout. Look for polymer-fortified grout that you mix with water.

GETTING STARTED

Before doing any tile project, it's important to check that the floor is level and the walls are flat. Use a level and straightedge to check the floor. If the it slopes, find the lowest point and mark it. Then hold the straightedge against the walls in the areas you plan to tile. If you find low areas, fill them with setting-type compound to flatten the walls before you start tiling.

Another thing to check at this stage is how your cap tile will look when it butts into your window and door moldings. If the cap protrudes past the moldings, one

SHIFT LAYOUT
TO AVOID SKINNY
TILE HERE

BASE TILE

PENCIL TILE

CAP TILE

1 PLAN THE LAYOUT

Arrange rows of tile, including the spacers, on the floor. Shift the rows left or right to determine the width of the end spaces and the locations of the plumb lines (see **Photo 2**). Then stack a column of tile, starting with the base and ending with the cap. Use this mock-up to determine the finished height of your wainscot.

OFFSET THE
TILE BY HALF
TILE WIDTH

MASTIC LINE

VERTICAL
STARTING LINE

LEVEL
LEDGER
BOARD

2 DRAW LAYOUT LINES

Install ledgers to provide a level support for the first row of tile. Then draw a stop line 1/2 in. below the top of the tile to show where to stop spreading mastic. Mark two plumb lines, offset by half the tile width, to create a running bond pattern.

MATERIALS LIST

ITEM

Tile

Tile spacers

Tile trim pieces

Mastic

Grout

Grout sponge

Caulk

Microfiber cloth

fix is to add a strip of matching wood—deep enough to hide the end of the cap tile—around the moldings (see "Pro Tip").

Planning the tile layout is critical to a great-looking job. **Photo 1** shows how to get started. Arrange rows of tile and stack all the parts on the floor to determine the exact measurements you'll need to plan the layout. Check the height measurement against light switches and outlets on the walls. Add or subtract from the wainscot height to make sure switches and outlets land above or below it.

Next, draw vertical layout lines for starting the tile. For a running bond (brick joint) pattern like ours, you'll need two vertical lines half a tile width apart. Start by assuming the first line will be centered on the wall. Then draw a layout for two rows of tile, offsetting the joints by the half tile width. Check to see what size the cut pieces on the ends of the two rows of tile will be. If any of the cuts are skinny, it will look better if you shift the layout a quarter tile width. For our 8-in.-wide tiles, we moved the starting line 2 in. off center and then drew a second vertical line 4 in. from the first (**Photo 2**). Shifting the layout like this increased the width of the skinny cut by 2 in., creating a better-looking final result.

Go through this same routine on every wall, carefully planning how the end cuts will look. Plan outside corners, taking into account how the trim pieces and bullnose tiles line up. If you're unsure, an easy

3 SPREAD THE MASTIC

Using a 1/4 x 1/4-in. notched trowel, spread only as much mastic as you can cover with tile in about 15 minutes—usually about 10 sq. ft. If you leave the adhesive uncovered too long, it will dry on the surface and become less effective. Hold the trowel at a steep angle to make the mastic ridges as high as possible.

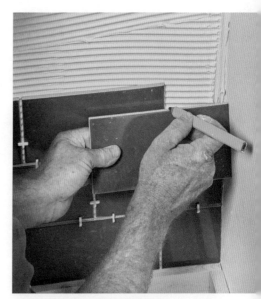

4 SET THE FULL TILES

Line up the end of the first tile with one of the plumb lines and embed the tile in the mastic. Set the rest of the full tiles in the row, resting them on the ledger and separating them with spacers. Start the next row by aligning the end of a full tile with the second vertical line. Build a stair step, alternating the tile joints as shown.

5 MARK THE END TILES

Hold each end tile in place and mark it for cutting. Subtract the width of the grout joint when you make the mark. Install the tile with the cut end against the wall.

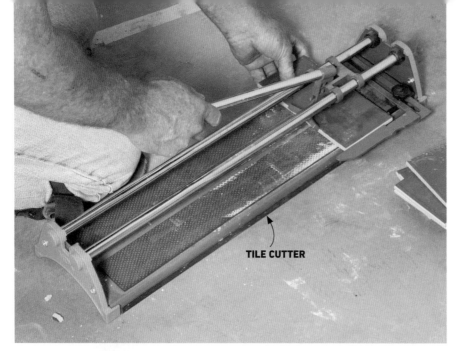

TILE CUTTER

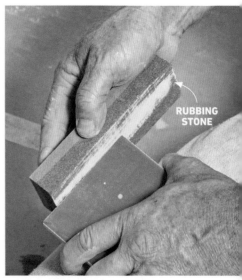

RUBBING STONE

6 CUT THE END TILES

Place the tile in the cutter with the edge against the fence. Line up the mark with the cutter. Push down gently on the cutter handle, and slide the handle forward to score the tile. Then pull the handle back until the breaker is over the center of the tile, and push down to break the tile along the scored line.

7 SMOOTH THE CUT ENDS

The cutter may leave the end of the tile a little rough. Use a rubbing stone to grind off the rough edge. Several back-and-forth strokes is all it takes.

8 MITER THE TOP CAP

The inside corners of the cap pieces must be cut at a 45-degree angle where they join in the corner. Make these cuts with a wet saw tilted to cut a 45-degree bevel.

way to do this is to draw each piece full scale on the wall to expose any potential problems.

The easiest and most accurate way to make sure your tile installation is straight and level is to screw a level ledger board to the wall and stack your tile on top. Add the height of the base tile to the width of one grout joint. Then add 1/16 in. to this measurement for a little space under the base tile. Make a mark on the wall at this height, above the lowest point on the floor, and draw a level line around the room from this mark. Align the tops of your straight ledger boards with this line and screw them to the wall. If the floor isn't level, you'll have to trim some of the base tiles to fit **(Photo 12)**.

INSTALL THE TILE

Start by spreading about 10 sq. ft. of mastic on the wall **(Photo 3)**. We used premixed water-based tile mastic and spread it with a 1/4 x 1/4-in. notched trowel. When you purchase your tile, ask the sales-

WOOD STRIP

9 INSTALL THE MITERED CAP
Embed the mitered inside corner in mastic. Use spacers under the cap to create a grout joint.

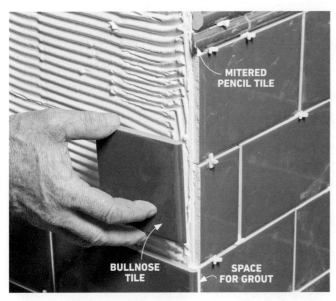

MITERED PENCIL TILE

BULLNOSE TILE

SPACE FOR GROUT

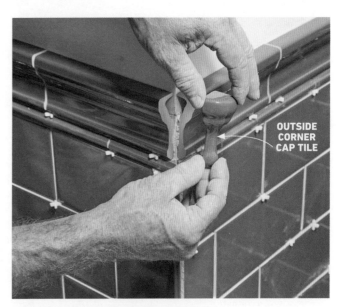

OUTSIDE CORNER CAP TILE

10 INSTALL THE BULLNOSE
Finish the outside corner with bullnose tile. When you set the tiles on the side opposite the bullnose, make sure to cut them so they're back from the corner the width of a spacer to allow room for a grout joint.

11 ADD THE CORNER CAP TILE
Spread a small amount of tile mastic on the back edges of the corner piece and press it into place. If the piece feels loose, use masking tape to hold it in position until the mastic has a chance to set up.

LEAVE GROUT SPACE

UPSIDE-DOWN BASE TILE

1/16" SHIM

12 MARK THE BASE TILE

After removing the ledger boards, cut the base tile to fit. Hold the base tile upside down and rest it on 1/16-in. spacers. Then mark for the cut, making sure to subtract for the grout joint. Cut the tile at the mark and install it.

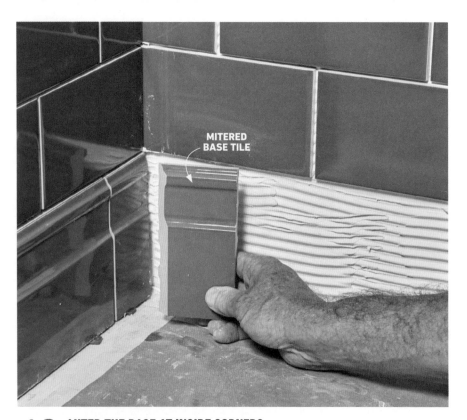

MITERED BASE TILE

13 MITER THE BASE AT INSIDE CORNERS

Cut 45-degree bevels on the baseboard pieces that meet at the inside corners. Leave a grout space between the two mitered base pieces.

person what size trowel to use. Larger tiles require larger notches. Also, if you're installing tile in a wet area, use thin-set adhesive instead.

Photo 4 shows how to get started installing the tile. Setting tile in a stair-step pattern helps keep everything lined up.

When you reach the ends, you'll have to cut tile to fit (**Photos 5** and **6**). For glazed tile like ours, with a soft bisque core, a tile cutter like the one shown in **Photo 6** is fast and convenient for making straight cuts. But if you're using porcelain, stone or glass tile, you'll have to cut it with a diamond wet saw instead. You'll also need a wet saw if you have trim pieces to miter (**Photo 8**) or if you have notches to cut.

If the cut ends of your tile will be visible, clean up the jagged edges with a rubbing stone (**Photo 7**). You'll find rubbing stones where tiling tools are sold.

If the holes for plumbing pipes fall near the edge of the tile, you can simply mark the hole location and nip away the tile with a tile nipper. Or use a wet saw to cut a series of fingers and break them off. Cutting a hole in the center of a tile is trickier. One method is to use a diamond hole saw, which comes in different sizes.

The base and cap style we chose was available in outside corner pieces (**Photo 11**), so we didn't have to miter the outside corners. But we still had to miter the inside corners. We used a wet saw for this (**Photo 8**). Remember to cut your miters short by one half of the grout joint width to allow for grout.

After you've finished installing the wall tile, let the adhesive set up for a few hours before removing the ledger boards. Then install the base tile.

Photo 12 shows how to mark a tile for cutting. Remember to

GROUT FLOAT

14 GROUT THE TILE
Mix the grout and spread it with a grout float. Remove excess grout with the edge of the float. After the grout starts to firm up, begin cleaning it with a damp grout sponge. When the grout is firm, complete the cleanup with a microfiber cloth.

subtract the width of the grout joint when you make the mark. Cut the base tiles to fit, and set them in place on top of 1/16-in. shims. Miter the inside corners of the base **(Photo 13)**. Finish up by gluing in the outside corner piece of the base.

THE LAST STEPS: GROUT AND CAULK

When you're done setting the tile, let the mastic dry overnight. The next day, mix your grout according to the manufacturer's instructions on the package. However, you should mix only enough to cover

about one wall.

Spread the grout with a grout float **(Photo 14)**, making sure to pack the joints completely. Wipe off excess grout with the edge of the float, working diagonally to the tile. Avoid getting grout in the inside corner joint or the 1/16-in. gap at the floor.

Depending on the temperature and humidity in the room, wait about 15 minutes for the grout to begin firming up (pressing your fingertip into the grout should barely leave a mark). Then begin working the grout with a damp, not wet, sponge. Wring out the

sponge frequently in clean water in a bucket (not a sink).

When all of the grout is removed from the face of the tile, and the joints are consistent and smooth, let the grout set up for an hour before polishing the tile with a damp microfiber cloth. In the meantime, you can mix more grout and begin grouting the next wall, following the same process.

Finish the project by filling the inside corners with caulk that matches the color of the grout. If you have a wood floor, don't caulk the gap at the floor.

WHAT IT TAKES

TIME
3 days

SKILL LEVEL
Intermediate

TOOLS
Basic hand tools, brad nailer (optional), drill, jigsaw, miter saw, pocket hole jig, random orbital sander, table saw

COAT RACK AND STORAGE BENCH

CLEAR ENTRYWAY CLUTTER WITH THIS STYLISH CHERRY COMBO.

If your entryway is littered with shoes, jackets, purses and backpacks, this simple bench and matching shelf may be just what you need. With coat hooks and shelves, these pieces provide an orderly area for all that clutter. Even if you already keep your entryway tidy, these stylish pieces will dress it up and give you a convenient seat while you pull on your shoes.

We'll show you how to build both pieces. They were designed for fast, easy building—they're basically plywood boxes with decorative parts added. There's no tedious precision work, no intricate joinery. Even the curved parts are simple to make. If you're an intermediate woodworker, you can handle this project, and if you have only a little woodworking experience, this is a good step-up project.

TIME, MONEY AND TOOLS

Building this set will take you two or three days, plus a few hours of finishing work. We built ours from cherry boards and cherry plywood. Cherry is expensive. Made from oak, maple or birch, our ensemble would cost less. For a more rustic look, use construction-grade pine and plywood.

This project requires two special tools: a table saw to rip solid wood to width and a pocket hole jig to make strong butt joints. If you don't own a pocket hole jig, buy one. It's a good investment and is easy to use. In addition, you'll need a drill, miter saw, random orbital sander and jigsaw. An air-powered 2-in. brad nailer isn't absolutely necessary, but it'll save lots of time and give you better results.

THE BENCH BEGINS AS A BOX

The box that forms the core of the bench is made mostly from 3/4-in. plywood. For the floor of the box, we made a grille from solid wood slats. You could save a couple of hours by using a 12 x 44-in. piece of plywood instead, but a slatted grille looks better.

Rip the grille parts to the widths shown in the Cutting List and then cut them to length. All the slats (A) must be precisely the same length, so make a

1 **RIP PARTS FOR BENCH GRILLE**
Cut all the slats to identical lengths using a bump jig. Make fine length adjustments by turning the lag screw in or out.

2 **DRILL POCKET HOLES IN THE GRILLE PARTS**
To avoid confusion, lay out the grille with the best-looking side of each piece face down. Put each part back in place after drilling.

Figure A Storage Bench
exploded view
OVERALL DIMENSIONS: 47-3/4" W x
15-1/4" D x 17-3/4" H

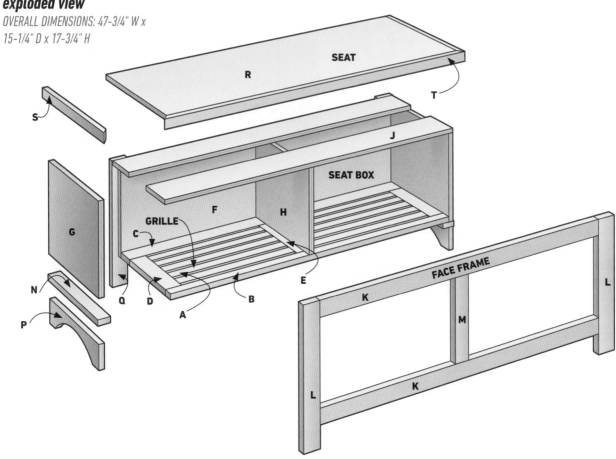

Figure B Coat Rack and Shelf
exploded view
OVERALL DIMENSIONS: 47-1/2" W x
10-3/8" D x 19-3/4" H

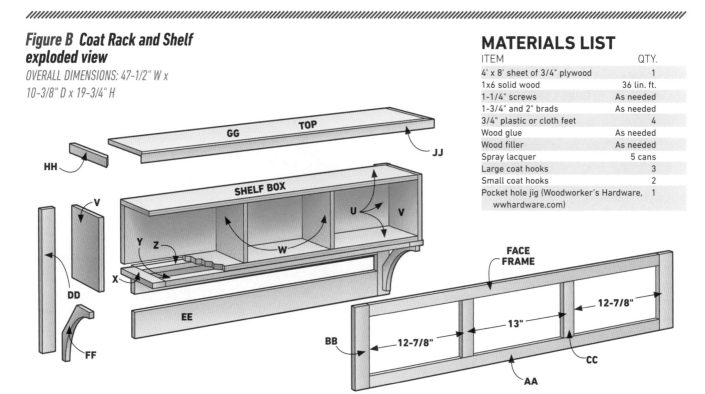

MATERIALS LIST

ITEM	QTY.
4' x 8' sheet of 3/4" plywood	1
1x6 solid wood	36 lin. ft.
1-1/4" screws	As needed
1-3/4" and 2" brads	As needed
3/4" plastic or cloth feet	4
Wood glue	As needed
Wood filler	As needed
Spray lacquer	5 cans
Large coat hooks	3
Small coat hooks	2
Pocket hole jig (Woodworker's Hardware, wwhardware.com)	1

simple bump jig from plywood scraps and a lag screw (**Photo 1**). Clamp your miter saw and the bump jig to your workbench and make the repetitive cuts.

Pocket screws make assembling the grille fast and easy (**Photos 2 and 3**). Use wood glue on your pocket screw joints later in this project, but skip the glue when assembling the grille—removing excess glue from between the slats is nearly impossible. When the grille is complete, sand all the joints flush with a random orbital

//

Plywood cutting diagram

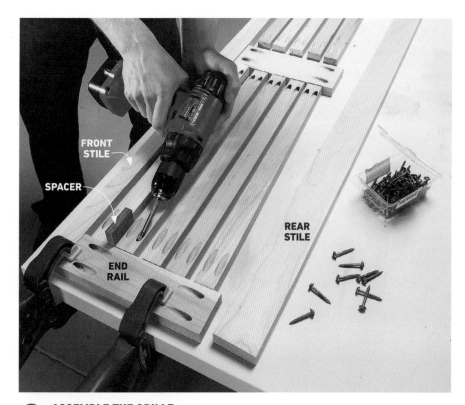

CUTTING LIST

KEY	QTY.	PART
A	10	1-1/8" x 18-1/4" (slats)
B	1	1-1/8" x 44" (front stile)
C	1	2-1/4" x 44" (rear stile)
D	2	2-1/4" x 8-5/8" (end rails)
E	1	3" x 8-5/8" (middle rail)
F	1	12-1/4" x 44" (back panel)
G	2	12-1/4" x 12-3/4" (end panels)
H	1	11-1/2" x 12" (divider)
J	2	3-3/4" x 45-1/2" (cleats)
K	2	2" x 41-1/4" (upper and lower rails)
L	2	2-1/4" x 17" (front legs)
M	1	1-3/4" x 10-1/4" (middle stile)
N	2	1-1/2" x 12-3/4" (rungs)
P	2	3-1/4" x 12-3/4" (arches)
Q	2	2-1/4" x 17" (rear legs))
R	1	14-1/2" x 46-1/4" (seat panel)
S	2	1-1/2" x 15-1/4" (side bands)
T	1	1-1/2" x 47-3/4" (front band)
U	3	8" x 44" (top, bottom, back)
V	2	8" x 9-1/2" (end panels)
W	2	7-1/4" x 8" (dividers)
X	2	2" x 8" (stiles)
Y	1	1-1/4" x 41-3/4" (front rail)
Z	1	2" x 41-3/4" (rear rail)
AA	2	1-1/2" x 41-3/4" (upper and lower rails)
BB	2	2" x 10-1/4" (end stiles)
CC	2	1-1/2" x 7-1/4" (divider stiles)
DD	2	2" x 19" (rear stiles)
EE	2	3-1/2" x 41-3/4" (coat hook rails)
FF	2	3-1/2" x 11-1/2" (brackets)
GG	1	9-5/8" x 46" (top panel)
HH	2	1-1/4" x 10-3/8" (side band)
JJ	1	1-1/4" x 47-1/2" (front band)

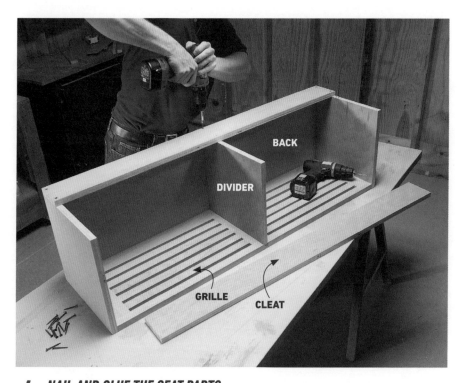

3 ASSEMBLE THE GRILLE
Using pocket screws, screw the front stile to one end rail first and then position the slats using a 7/16-in. spacer. Attach the rear stile last.

4 NAIL AND GLUE THE SEAT PARTS
Cut the plywood parts and assemble the seat box, sides, back, partition and grille with 1-3/4-in. brads and glue. Predrill and screw the cleats to the top of the box.

POCKET SCREW JOINTS

FACE FRAME

1/8" OVERHANG

sander and a 100- or 120-grit disc. Then switch to a 150- or 180-grit disc and sand the entire surface. Use this same sanding sequence on all the solid-wood bench and shelf parts.

Cut the plywood box parts following the Cutting List. If you don't have a table saw, use a circular saw and straightedge. Lightly sand the plywood parts with 150-grit sandpaper before you assemble the box with glue and brads **(Photo 4)**.

ADD PARTS TO THE BOX

To complete the bench, you just make up the remaining parts and attach them to the box. Assemble the face frame with glue and pocket screws, and sand the joints

5 ATTACH THE FACE FRAME

Assemble the face frame with glue and pocket screws, and nail it to the seat box. Remember that the face frame overhangs the sides of the box by 1/8 in.

ARCH (P)

8-1/2"

6-1/8"

BASE

TRAMMEL ARM

6 MAKE THE BENCH ARCHES

Draw an 8-1/2-in.-radius arc using an arc jig. Cut the arch with a jigsaw and sand it smooth. When you cut the arch to length, trim from both ends to center it.

3-1/4"

12-3/4"

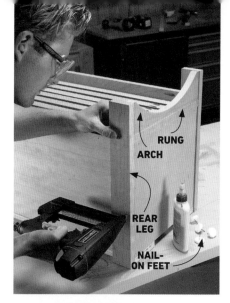

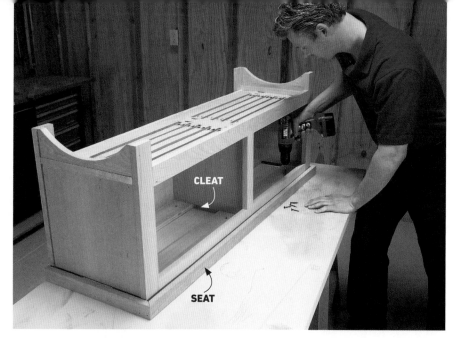

7 ADD THE RUNGS

Nail the rungs to the underside of the box. Then add the arches and rear legs. Add plastic feet or felt pads after the glue sets.

8 FINISH BUILDING THE BENCH

Cut the seat from plywood and cover three edges of it with solid wood. Fasten the seat to the bench with 1-1/4-in. screws driven through the cleats.

flush. Always make sure your parts fit the box correctly before you apply any glue. When you attach the face frame to the box **(Photo 5)**, make sure the lower rail is flush with the top of the grille. It's OK if the upper rail isn't perfectly flush with the cleat since that joint will be covered by the seat later.

Next, make a trammel to mark the arches **(P)** that fit under the bench sides **(Photo 6)**. For the trammel arm, use a 1-1/2 x 12-in. scrap. Drill a 5/16-in. pencil hole near one end of the arm, then drill a 1/8-in. screw hole 8-1/2 in. from the center of the pencil hole. For the trammel base, use an 8 x 12-in. scrap of 3/4-in. plywood. Drill a screw hole 6-1/8 in. from the long edge of the base and screw the arm to the plywood. Mark and cut the arches from pieces of wood 3-1/4 x 14 in. long. Then cut rungs **(N)**. Don't rely on our Cutting List when you cut the rungs and arches to length—instead, set them into place and mark them flush with the back of the bench.

Glue and nail them into place and add the rear legs **(Q; Photo 7)**. We nailed 3/4-in. plastic feet to

9 BUILD THE SHELF BOX

Cut out the shelf box parts. Glue and nail the bottom to the back first. Then add the dividers, the top and finally the end caps.

our bench. Plastic can stain wood finishes, so if you plan to put your bench on a wood floor, use cloth or felt pads instead.

The seat is simply a slab of plywood **(R)** banded on three sides

with solid wood **(S, T)**. Mitering the banding accurately can be difficult and frustrating. Make the joints tight by trial and error.

Start by mitering parts about 1/8 in. too long. Hold them in place

FACE FRAME

RAIL

STILE

10 ADD RAILS AND STILES

Nail rails and stiles directly to the underside of the shelf box. Assemble the face frame with pocket screws, and nail it to the front. After the glue sets, sand all the joints smooth.

BACK FRAME

11 ADD THE BACK FRAME

Assemble the back frame with pocket screws, sand the joints flush and fasten it to the shelf box. Then assemble the shelf top and attach it with glue and brads.

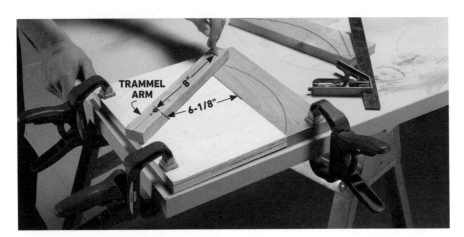

TRAMMEL ARM

8"

6-1/8"

12 BUILD THE SHELF BRACKETS

Draw an 8-in.-radius arc for the shelf brackets using the arc jig. Cut the arches using a jigsaw and the straight cuts with a miter saw set at 45 degrees.

to check the fit, and then readjust the angle on your miter saw and shave a hair off the parts again and again until they fit perfectly. Although mitered joints look best, you may prefer to band the seat with square-cut wood if you don't have experience with miters.

Screw the seat to the bench without glue **(Photo 8)** so you can remove the seat when it's time to finish the bench.

BUILD THE SHELF JUST LIKE THE BENCH

In terms of construction and techniques, the shelf is just a smaller variation of the bench. It starts with a plywood box **(Photo 9)**. The top, bottom and back of the box are identical parts **(U)**. Be sure to place the back between the top and the bottom pieces. Add rails and stiles to the underside of the box, then assemble and attach the face frame **(Photo 10)**. The back frame **(Photo 11)** provides a mounting surface for coat hooks later.

Make the shelf top just as you made the bench seat: Wrap a piece of plywood **(GG)** with solid wood banding **(HH, JJ)**. When you nail the top to the shelf box, use plenty of glue—the top will support the entire weight of the shelf when you hang it on the wall **(Photo 14)**.

Draw the arc for the shelf brackets using the same arc jig you used to make the bench arches— just be sure to reposition the screw 8 in. from the pencil hole **(Photo 12)**. If you don't have a clamp that's long enough to hold the bracket against the shelf box **(Photo 13)**, tack it into place with 2-in. brads.

A FAST FINISH

If you sanded all the parts before assembly, you won't have much prep work before finishing. Just fill the nail holes (see "A No-Curse Strategy for Invisible Nail Holes")

13 ATTACH THE BRACKETS
Glue, position and clamp the upper end of each bracket, and fasten the other end with screws driven from behind. Predrill so you don't split the bracket.

14 SECURE THE SHELF
Level and screw 2 x 8-in. cleats to wall studs. Set the shelf on the cleats and screw through the back of the shelf into the cleats using 1-1/2-in. brass screws and finish washers.

and inspect all the glued joints for glue smudges.

Cherry doesn't take stain evenly, so apply a clear finish only. With the corners and cramped spaces in the bench and shelf, brushing on a finish would be a nightmare, so we chose a lacquer finish in a spray can. Here's how to use it:

■ Wear an organic vapor respirator. Spray the lacquer outdoors or in the garage with the door open. Lacquer contains nasty solvents.

■ Spray on two very light coats, wait 30 minutes and lightly sand with 220-grit paper.

■ Vacuum off the sanding residue; apply two or more light coats until you get the look you want. There's no need to sand between coats unless specks of dust settle on the finish.

Let the finish harden overnight before you add the coat hooks and hang the shelf **(Photo 14)**.

A NO-CURSE STRATEGY FOR INVISIBLE NAIL HOLES

The wood fillers that fussy carpenters use to hide nail holes in trim aren't a good choice for furniture projects. Those fillers stay soft for years, so they're not sandable and they can rub off on clothing. Fussy furniture makers prefer fillers that dry hard. These sandable fillers are often labeled "stainable," but they usually absorb more or less than the surrounding wood, leaving light or dark dots at each nail hole.

After years of cursing at nail dots, I gave up trying to make wood fillers match wood. I gave up the cursing, too, because I discovered a technique that works every time. The key is to make the patches lighter than the surrounding finish and darken them later. These extra steps may sound like a lot of trouble, but they add only a few minutes to the process:

■ Buy the lightest color of filler available.

■ Before you fill the holes on your project, shoot a few nails into a wood scrap and fill those holes. When dry and sanded, the filler must be no darker than the wood.

■ Apply stain or clear finish to the test scrap first. In most cases, the nail patches remain lighter than the wood. If they turn darker, pretreat them so they absorb less finish by mixing two drops of wood glue with a drop of water and applying the thinned glue to the patches with a fine-tip artist's brush. Keep glue off the surrounding wood. After about 30 minutes, lightly sand each nail patch.

■ Stain and finish the wood as usual. But before you apply the final coat of clear finish, use a fine-tip marker to darken each nail patch. An art supply store is the best source for a wide variety of colors. With two or three different markers, you can match the differing wood tones in your project and the nail holes will be invisible to everyone but you.

THREE WAYS TO COVER A POPCORN CEILING

THE BEST METHOD DEPENDS ON YOUR SITUATION AND YOUR SKILLS.

Millions of homes have popcorn texture applied to ceilings. And while the texture does a pretty decent job of masking small imperfections in old plaster and drywall, it is a little out of fashion and notorious for trapping dust and cobwebs. It's also tough to make a good-looking repair with it. The good news is, however, that you've got some options for dealing with an old popcorn ceiling.

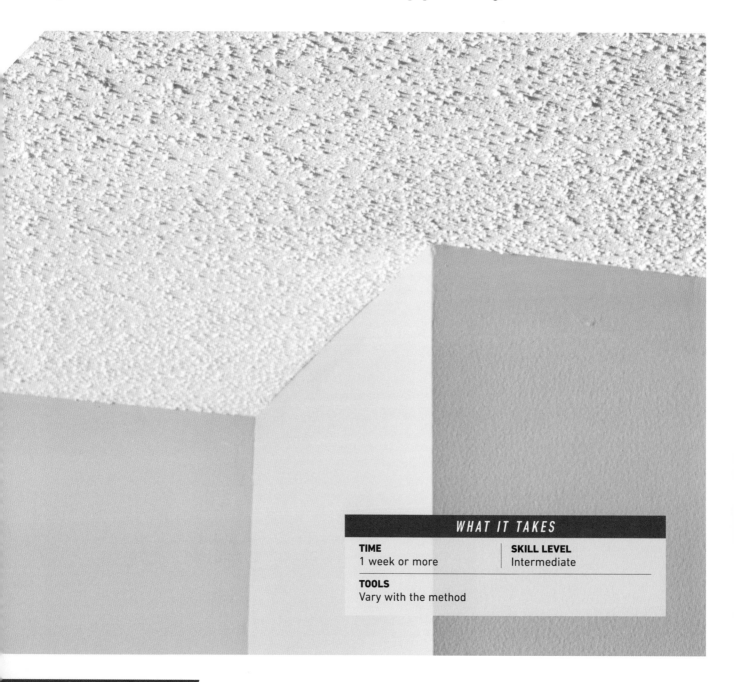

WHAT IT TAKES

TIME	SKILL LEVEL
1 week or more	Intermediate

TOOLS	
Vary with the method	

1

COVER IT WITH DRYWALL

It's not an easy project, but there are some good reasons to consider installing drywall directly over popcorn ceiling (and some good reasons not to do it).

PROS:

■ No texture to scrape off. Scraping, even wet-scraping, is hard, messy work. And if the popcorn texture is painted, it'll be even harder to scrape off.

■ Lower asbestos risk. Popcorn texture applied before 1980 might contain asbestos, which poses a lung cancer danger if it's disturbed and inhaled. Covering the ceiling with drywall minimizes your health risk because there's no scraping involved that would loosen particles.

■ No repairs to make. If you have problems like flaking texture, stains, cracks or holes, you can skip trying to fix all those things by covering them up. Hanging new drywall over the old ceiling gives you a fresh start!

CONS:

- A big job. Drywall is heavy, and lugging full sheets around—especially up and down stairs—is hard work. Plus, most of the work you'll be doing is overhead, so be ready for a sore neck and shoulders. Applying tape and joint compound to seams also takes skill and practice to master.
- Time-consuming. There's the time needed to hang the drywall, plus the time it takes to apply the tape and joint compound. It can easily take a week to finish one room.
- Finishing requires skill. Screwing the drywall to the ceiling might seem easy enough, but making your seams look good is another story. Applying tape and joint compound is a bit of an art. Remember, this is your ceiling! And ceiling flaws are much more visible than wall flaws.
- Costs money. For a 12 x 12-ft. room, your cost will be hundreds of dollars for all the materials, including drywall, joint compound, paint and the rental fee for a drywall lift.

OTHER KEY CONSIDERATIONS:

- Do you have the time? You'll need a week or more to get the drywall hung, the seams taped, and several coats of joint compound applied and then sanded. And it might take you even more time if you're a drywall newbie. Plus, don't forget you'll still have to paint the ceiling when you're done.
- Tight on space? Have you ever tried to maneuver a full sheet of drywall up a narrow staircase, around a corner and into a small room? Cutting it into smaller pieces is an option, but that means you'll have more seams to tape and finish.
- Existing crown molding? If you have crown molding on the ceiling, you'll have to remove it before installing new drywall and then reinstall it afterward. That's not a big deal, but it's one more thing you'll have to do. The good news about crown molding is that you won't have to mud and tape along the perimeter of the room because the crown molding will cover the seams between the ceiling and the walls.

KNOCKDOWN TEXTURE

A slick solution for an imperfect finish

Whether you cover your ceiling with new drywall or scrape off the texture, you're going to be left with some mudding and taping to do. And unless you're really good at it, getting a smooth ceiling will be slow or difficult, or both. Instead, consider applying knockdown texture. You basically spray texture from a hopper onto the bare drywall and knock down the high spots with a big squeegee. Your ceiling won't be perfectly smooth, but the texture hides small imperfections and looks more up to date than popcorn.

FAMILYHANDYMAN.COM
For step-by-step instructions on how to install drywall over a popcorn ceiling, how to apply knockdown texture or how to install tongue-and-groove planks, search for "popcorn," "knockdown texture" and "tongue and groove."

2 COVER IT WITH WOOD

Installing tongue-and-groove (T&G) planks on a ceiling is another good way to hide popcorn texture. Most of what you'll find in home centers and lumberyards is 1x6 or 1x8 pine or spruce, although you can special-order other kinds of wood. And if you're working solo, it's a lot easier to handle T&G boards than 4 x 8-ft. or 4 x 12-ft. sheets of drywall.

PRO:

■ Easier to install than drywall. Because T&G planks are much smaller than 8-ft. or 12-ft. sheets of drywall, you'll have an easier time installing them, especially if you're working by yourself. And because you'll be covering the old ceiling, you won't have to worry about asbestos or patching and painting the new drywall or plaster.

CONS:

■ Cost. Wood isn't cheap. Covering a 12 x 12-ft. ceiling will cost you hundreds of dollars at a minimum and can easily exceed a thousand dollars.

■ Tools. Cutting and installing T&G boards will require several power tools (a miter saw, router, pneumatic finish nailer and compressor), which can be expensive to purchase.

3

3 SCRAPE IT OFF

Scraping off popcorn texture is a lot of work, but it is totally doable and worth the effort if your ceiling is in decent shape and you're not afraid to get dirty.

PROS:

- Less work than covering the ceiling with wood or drywall. However, if the popcorn ceiling has been painted, water won't penetrate easily and you might have to dry-scrape it first—a tough and dusty job.
- Comes off easily when wet. Mist the popcorn texture with water and scrape it off while it's still wet. A bonus: If done when wet, you'll practically eliminate airborne dust.

CONS:

- Risk of asbestos exposure. Any popcorn texture applied to a ceiling before 1980 might have asbestos in it. Scraping releases asbestos fibers into the air, which can be inhaled and cause lung cancer.
- Repairs. After scraping, you might be left with lots of gouges, dings, loose drywall tape and other imperfections that you'll have to fix when you are done. And as with taping and mudding drywall, it takes time and skill to make these repairs.

WEEKEND BATH REMODEL

//
TRANSFORM YOUR BATHROOM WITH A LARGER MIRROR AND BETTER LIGHTING.

WHAT IT TAKES

TIME
1 weekend

SKILL LEVEL
Intermediate and some familiarity
with electrical projects

TOOLS
Basic electrical and hand tools, drill, noncontact voltage
tester, stud finder

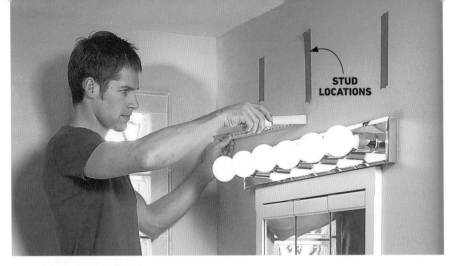

1 MARK OUT THE WALL

Determine stud locations, then make a sketch of the wall, marking the sink center and studs. Use the stud locations to plan the size of your mirror; the lights should fall between, not on, the studs.

2 REMOVE THE MEDICINE CABINET

Back out the screws inside the cabinet, tape the doors closed and lift the cabinet out of the wall.

3 REMOVE THE LIGHT BAR

Remove the cover, disconnect the wires and then unscrew the mounting plate from the wall. Make sure the power is off.

MATERIALS LIST

ITEM	QTY.
Light fixtures	2
Mirror	1
Drywall	Varies
Drywall tape	Varies
Drying compound	Varies
Junction box	1
Remodeling boxes	2
Electrical cable	Varies
Glass shelf	1

You don't have to gut a bathroom to make the room feel fresh, bright and inviting. If your sink, tile and shower are still in good shape, then handsome light fixtures and a stylish mirror may be all you need to revitalize the space.

We'll show you how to remove a medicine cabinet and strip light and then install a mirror and sconces. You'll get two big benefits: The bigger mirror will make your bathroom seem larger, and the two sconces will give you even light without deep shadows.

We needed a place for items that had been stored in the medicine cabinet, so we also installed a glass shelf and a shallow cabinet on the other side of the room.

This project doesn't require special carpentry skills or tools, but you should have basic wiring experience. Any time you open a wall, you may find unexpected pipes, electrical cables or framing. If you can't work around them, hire a pro to propose a solution.

Before getting started, apply for an electrical permit so that an inspector will check your work. Talk to your inspector about the timing of the inspection. Typically it will occur after the wiring is done but before the wall is repaired— and possibly again after the fixtures are installed.

SELECT YOUR MIRROR

Mirrors come in many sizes, so before you run off to the store, map your wall (Photo 1). The goal is to select a mirror size that looks good and leaves ample room for the sconces. Use a stud finder to locate the framing within the wall, then measure the distances from the center of the sink to neighboring walls or other cabinets.

Measure from a centerline over the sink, and then mark all the framing and clearances on a drawing. Next, mark the distances from the neighboring studs to the centerline. That'll help you position the new electrical boxes in the open stud spaces.

When you shop for a mirror, pick the widest one that will fit in the space above the sink, also making sure the light fixtures will fit into the open stud spaces on the sides of the mirror and not on top of studs. We show one of many mirror-mounting systems. Most mirrors come with the hardware and instructions for simple installation.

SELECT YOUR LIGHT FIXTURES

Choosing your sconces calls for some thought. Avoid colored globes because they'll cast less light and affect skin tones. We recommend white frosted glass to lessen the glare of the bulbs. If good makeup lighting is important, select fixtures that are rated for 100-watt bulbs. Then replace the existing light switch with a dimmer switch so you can set the lighting intensity to fit your needs and mood.

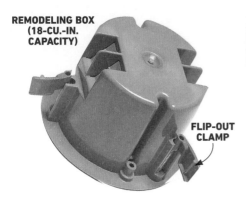

REMODELING BOX (18-CU.-IN. CAPACITY)

FLIP-OUT CLAMP

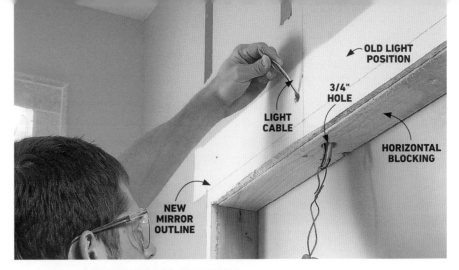

OLD LIGHT POSITION

3/4" HOLE

LIGHT CABLE

HORIZONTAL BLOCKING

NEW MIRROR OUTLINE

4 PULL THE CABLE INTO THE OPENING

Drill a 3/4-in. hole in the horizontal blocking, then fish the cable into the wall opening using a coat hanger or stiff wire. Install 2x4 backing for new drywall **(Photo 6)**.

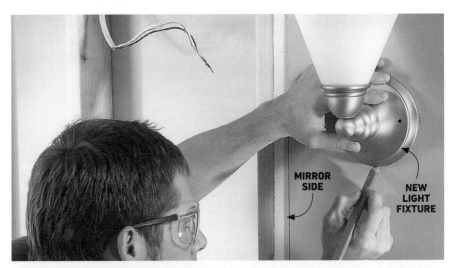

MIRROR SIDE

NEW LIGHT FIXTURE

5 MARK THE MIRROR AND FIRST FIXTURE

First, draw the edges of the mirror, making them level and at a pleasing height. Trace around the base of the first sconce.

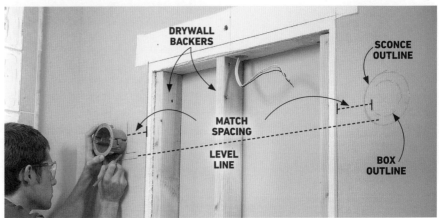

DRYWALL BACKERS

SCONCE OUTLINE

MATCH SPACING

LEVEL LINE

BOX OUTLINE

6 MARK THE SECOND SCONCE

The second sconce should be level with the first and the same distance from the mirror edge. Trace the outline of a remodeling box inside the sconce outline and cut out the box hole.

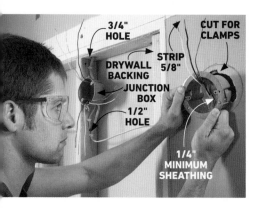

3/4" HOLE
CUT FOR CLAMPS
DRYWALL BACKING
STRIP 5/8"
JUNCTION BOX
1/2" HOLE
1/4" MINIMUM SHEATHING

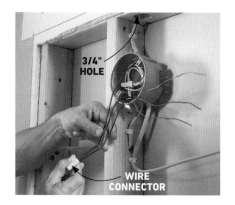

3/4" HOLE
WIRE CONNECTOR

7 INSTALL AND WIRE THE BOXES

Nail the junction box and run the existing cable to it. Then run cable to the remodeling boxes used for the sconces and tighten them in place.

8 CONNECT THE WIRES

Connect the new cable to the existing cable, black to black, white to white, and ground to ground. Screw a connector onto the exposed wires and tuck the wires into the boxes.

9 PATCH THE DRYWALL

After an inspector has approved the wiring, patch the drywall, tape the seams and sand the joints. Repaint the entire wall.

GETTING POWER TO THE SCONCE LIGHTS

DECORATIVE COVER PLATE

In most cases, you can use the same cable that fed the strip light to supply power to the new sconces. But the cable is rarely long enough to reach either sconce directly. That's why we suggest running the existing cable to a new junction box positioned close to the old light but hidden behind the mirror. From there you can feed two new cables to both new sconce boxes.

The existing cable to the light fixture usually leads from the wall switch up into and across the ceiling and then down through the framing above the old light. To find out if that's your situation, drill a 3/4-in. hole through the 2x4 at the top of the medicine cabinet recess and try to pull the cable into the opening (Photo 4). If there's enough cable to reach a new junction box, you can proceed as shown in the photos. However, according to the electrical code, the box must remain "accessible." If the box is behind the mirror, you

have to fasten the mirror in such a way that you can easily remove it.

There are three alternatives for handling the junction box:

- If the cable comes from an accessible attic above, pull the wire up into that space and mount a covered junction box in the attic.

- If the cable comes from above and is too short or the space above is inaccessible, install a new junction box at the old fixture location and cover it with a decorative cover plate painted to match the wall.

- If the cable comes through the wall studs to the old fixture, pull it back and run it to the nearest sconce box. Then run a second cable from that box to the sconce box on the opposite side.

REMOVE THE OLD CABINET AND LIGHT

Plug the sink drain to keep fasteners and debris from going down. Pull out the old medicine cabinet by removing the screws that hold the sides to the framing (Photo 2). Those screws should be obvious when you open the door. Sometimes you'll need to cut through caulk between the drywall and the cabinet frame with a utility knife.

Turn off the circuit breaker that powers the existing light. Remove the thumbnuts to access the mounting bracket screws that hold it to the wall (Photo 3). Once you have access to the wiring, check it with a noncontact voltage tester to make sure the power is off. Then disconnect the wire connectors and work the wires through the bracket as you pull the fixture mount free of the wall. If there's a cable clamp at the back of the fixture, loosen that first.

MARK THE NEW LOCATIONS

With the old cabinet removed, mark the new mirror location (Photo 5). Use a level to mark the center of the sink above the opening. Center the mirror in place and ask family members to vote on the best height. (Some mirrors come with recommended heights or even templates to help with placement.) After the position is decided, outline the mirror on the wall. Use those marks to help position one of the sconces. Trace around the sconce base 65 to 75 in. from the floor **(Photo 5)**. Or simply hold the sconce up and adjust it up and down until you find a pleasing position.

Center a remodeling box in the circle and trace around it. Then position the box on the other side to match the first **(Photo 6)**, leveling across to mark the bottom and measuring from the mirror edges to mark the side. If this position falls over a stud, readjust both boxes. Draw the second remodeling box hole, and cut out both openings with a drywall saw. Push the boxes into the holes as far as you can and mark the shoulders that surround the flip-out clamps **(Photo 7)**. Pull out the boxes and cut out those areas

as well, testing and recutting as necessary until they'll slip into the holes. You want them to fit tightly for maximum sconce support. Then set the boxes aside for now.

WIRE THE BOXES

Let the cable hang while you nail in the drywall backing, and then nail a round junction box to the center framing and feed the existing power cable into the box **(Photo 7)**. If you have to deal with more wires than we show, you'll need to calculate the box size required. Go to familyhandyman.com and search for "how to install dimmer switches" for details on box size.

Drill 1/2-in. holes through the middle of the framing and run the new cables through the sconce holes. Wherever cables run into a box, strip off 8 in. of sheathing and strip 5/8 in. of the insulation from the ends of the wires. Then slip the cables through the clamps at the back of the boxes until at least 1/4 in. of sheathing penetrates the boxes **(Photo 7)**.

Join the black (hots), white (neutrals), and bare or green ground wires as shown in **Photo 8**. In the sconce boxes, protect the wire ends with wire connectors and fold the wires into the boxes. Now you can hang drywall in the hole, tape the joints, and sand and repaint the wall **(Photo 9)**. Mount the lights following the manufacturer's instructions **(Photo 10)**.

HANG THE MIRROR

Mirrors have a variety of mounting systems. Manufacturers supply directions and often even templates to help position the wall fasteners accurately. Work off your centerline and make sure the mirror is level (or plumb). We highly recommend you discard the plastic drywall anchors that come with some units and replace them with screw-in anchors (E-Z Ancor is a brand we like) for a safer, stronger mounting system. You'll find these anchors at any home center or hardware store.

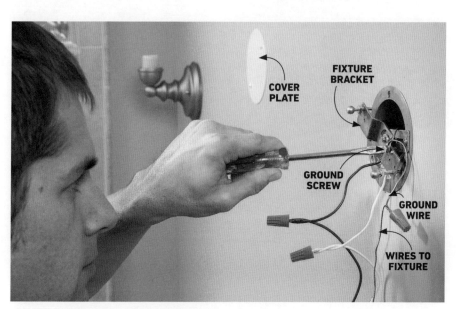

10 **MOUNT THE LIGHT FIXTURES**
Attach the fixture bracket to the box, and attach the ground wire to the grounding screw. Then connect the wires as shown and mount the fixture.

11 **HANG THE MIRROR**
Hang the mirror using wall anchors. You must be able to easily remove the mirror to access the cover plate.

ADVANCED PROJECTS

WHAT IT TAKES

TIME
10-12 days

SKILL LEVEL
Advanced

TOOLS
Basic hand tools, circular saw, compressor, drill driver, miter saw (optional), nail guns, table saw (optional)

DOUBLE-DUTY PUB SHED

THIS IS THE PERFECT SPOT FOR ENTERTAINING, WITH TONS OF ROOM FOR STORAGE.

This shed is one of the most versatile we've ever built. There's a designated area for entertaining—the bar and covered patio area make a perfect place to hang out with family and friends. There's tons of storage space thanks to the steep roof and sturdy lofts. And the high-tech materials used in the building, including reflective roof sheathing and prefinished floor panels, add to the shed's comfort and convenience. Of course, if you don't want a bar, you can instead install a bank of windows in its place. In fact, without too much additional work, you could simply eliminate the front porch and build a bigger shed that would provide even more storage space.

TOOLS, TIME AND MATERIALS

In addition to common building materials that you'll find at most home centers and lumberyards, we used some special products from LP Building Solutions (see "Materials for a Better Shed") that you may have to order if you want to duplicate this shed exactly as shown here.

The windows are shop-built using plastic utility window sash that we found at a local home center. Search for "barn sash" online if you can't find it locally. The swing-up bar door is site-built. The entry door on the side is a standard prehung exterior door that's readily available at most home centers.

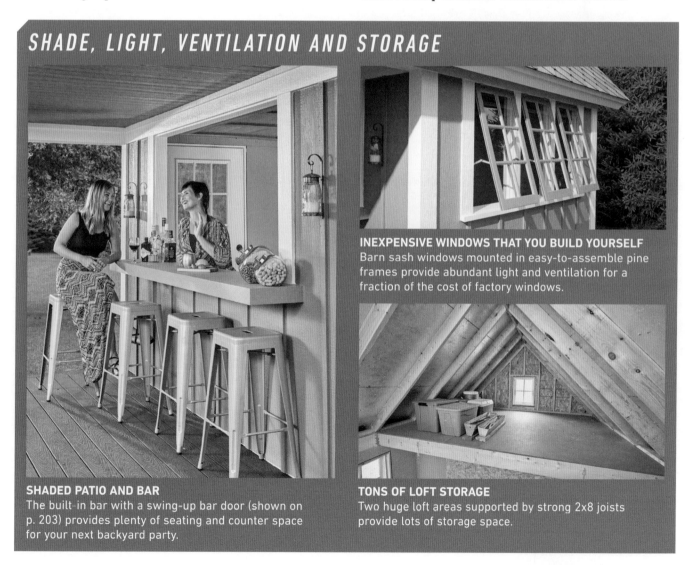

SHADE, LIGHT, VENTILATION AND STORAGE

INEXPENSIVE WINDOWS THAT YOU BUILD YOURSELF
Barn sash windows mounted in easy-to-assemble pine frames provide abundant light and ventilation for a fraction of the cost of factory windows.

SHADED PATIO AND BAR
The built-in bar with a swing-up bar door (shown on p. 203) provides plenty of seating and counter space for your next backyard party.

TONS OF LOFT STORAGE
Two huge loft areas supported by strong 2x8 joists provide lots of storage space.

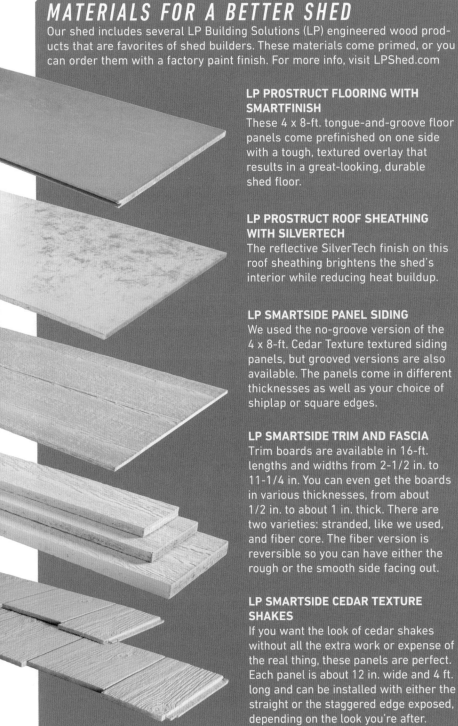

MATERIALS FOR A BETTER SHED

Our shed includes several LP Building Solutions (LP) engineered wood products that are favorites of shed builders. These materials come primed, or you can order them with a factory paint finish. For more info, visit LPShed.com

LP PROSTRUCT FLOORING WITH SMARTFINISH
These 4 x 8-ft. tongue-and-groove floor panels come prefinished on one side with a tough, textured overlay that results in a great-looking, durable shed floor.

LP PROSTRUCT ROOF SHEATHING WITH SILVERTECH
The reflective SilverTech finish on this roof sheathing brightens the shed's interior while reducing heat buildup.

LP SMARTSIDE PANEL SIDING
We used the no-groove version of the 4 x 8-ft. Cedar Texture textured siding panels, but grooved versions are also available. The panels come in different thicknesses as well as your choice of shiplap or square edges.

LP SMARTSIDE TRIM AND FASCIA
Trim boards are available in 16-ft. lengths and widths from 2-1/2 in. to 11-1/4 in. You can even get the boards in various thicknesses, from about 1/2 in. to about 1 in. thick. There are two varieties: stranded, like we used, and fiber core. The fiber version is reversible so you can have either the rough or the smooth side facing out.

LP SMARTSIDE CEDAR TEXTURE SHAKES
If you want the look of cedar shakes without all the extra work or expense of the real thing, these panels are perfect. Each panel is about 12 in. wide and 4 ft. long and can be installed with either the straight or the staggered edge exposed, depending on the look you're after.

You'll need standard DIY tools including a circular saw and a drill to build this shed. A framing nail gun and compressor will speed up the framing. Since a lot of trim and siding need to be nailed up, we used a coil siding nailer loaded with galvanized ring-shank siding nails. A miter saw and table saw aren't required but will make your cuts more accurate.

This is a big shed, but it's no more complicated than a small one. If you have experience with deck building or other small carpentry projects, you shouldn't have any trouble finishing it. There are a lot of materials to cut and hoist, though, so you'll want to round up a few helpers. Expect to spend five or six weekends completing the project.

GETTING STARTED
Check with your local building department to see whether a permit is required. Also find out if there are rules about where your shed can be located on the lot.

Take the Materials List (online, see "Familyhandyman.com" on p. 197) to a lumberyard or home center, and go over it with a salesperson to see what items you may have to order. Then set up a delivery so you'll be ready to build when your help arrives. A few days before you plan to dig, call 811 for instructions on how to locate buried utility lines.

BUILD THE FLOOR
We built this shed on a wood floor supported by treated 6x6s. But you could substitute a concrete slab or provide footings or another type of support for the floor joists.

Start by laying out the perimeter of the shed, either with stakes and a string line or with a rectangle built with 2x4s to represent the outside edges of the 12 x 16-ft. floor. Now measure in 8-3/4 in. from the short sides and drive stakes to mark the center of the trenches. Drive a third pair of stakes to mark the center beam.

Dig trenches about 12 in. wide and about 10 in. below where you want the bottom edge of the joists to end up. Pour 4 in. of gravel into the trenches and level it off. Make sure the gravel in all three trenches is at the same height. Then cut the 6x6s to 12 ft. long and set them in the trenches. Measure to make sure the 6x6s are parallel. Then measure diagonally from

Figure A Double-Duty Pub Shed

OVERALL DIMENSIONS (INCLUDING OVERHANGS):
14' 6" W x 15' T x 18' 1" D

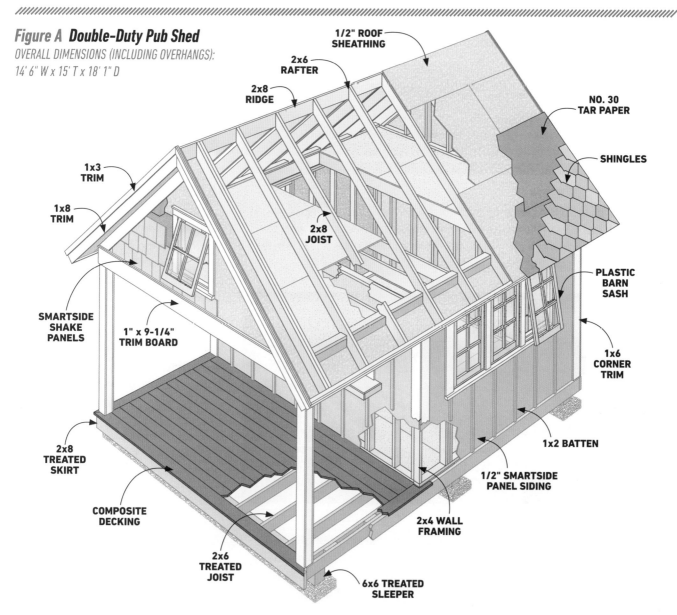

1/2" ROOF SHEATHING

2x6 RAFTER

2x8 RIDGE

NO. 30 TAR PAPER

SHINGLES

1x3 TRIM

1x8 TRIM

2x8 JOIST

SMARTSIDE SHAKE PANELS

1" x 9-1/4" TRIM BOARD

PLASTIC BARN SASH

1x6 CORNER TRIM

2x8 TREATED SKIRT

1x2 BATTEN

COMPOSITE DECKING

1/2" SMARTSIDE PANEL SIDING

2x4 WALL FRAMING

2x6 TREATED JOIST

6x6 TREATED SLEEPER

the ends of the outside 6x6s to make certain they're square. The diagonal measurements should be equal. Finally, level the 6x6s (**Photo 1** and **Figure B** online).

Next, frame the floor with 2x6s. Start by cutting the 12-ft.-long rim joists for the front and back and marking the joist locations. Cut the joists and nail them to the rim joists. When you're done, square the joists (**Photo 2**). Use a taut string line or sight down the 12-ft. rim joist to make sure it's straight. Then drive toenails through the joists into the 6x6s to hold the joists in place.

We used tongue-and-groove LP ProStruct Flooring with SmartFinish for the shed floor (**Photo 3**).

BUILD THE WALLS

Using **Figure C** (online) as a guide, chalk lines on the floor to indicate the inside edges of the walls. These lines will provide a reference for straightening the bottom plate of the walls after the walls are standing. Cut the top and bottom wall plates, and mark the stud locations on them (**Figures D–G** online). Build the side walls (**Photo 4**). Stand them up and brace them

temporarily. Then build and stand the front and back walls. After nailing the walls together at the corners, install temporary diagonal braces on the inside to hold the walls plumb (**Photo 5**).

There are two 4x4 posts at the front of the shed that support the

FAMILYHANDYMAN.COM

Get detailed plans and a Materials List online: familyhandyman. com/DoubleDuty PubShed.pdf.

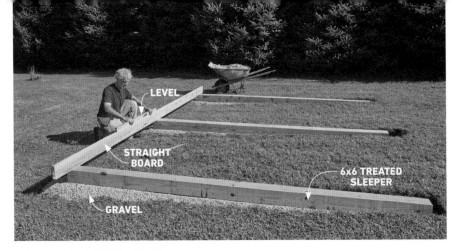

LEVEL

STRAIGHT
BOARD

6x6 TREATED
SLEEPER

GRAVEL

1 LAY THE FOUNDATION

Rest treated 6x6 sleepers on beds of gravel. Use a long, straight board and a level to make sure the 6x6s are level from end to end, and level with each other. Pound the tops with a sledgehammer or heavy board to adjust the heights of the 6x6s.

2x6
JOISTS

2 SQUARE THE FLOOR FRAME

Build the 2x6 frame on top of the 6x6s. Measure diagonally to be sure the frame is square. Diagonal measurements from opposite corners should be equal. If not, rack the frame until they are. Then nail or screw the four corners to the 6x6s to hold the frame square.

4x8
FLOORING

3 INSTALL THE FLOORING

Fasten the first sheet in the back corner with construction adhesive and deck screws. Finish the row with a half sheet. Start with a full sheet from the opposite end so the seams are staggered.

front half of the roof. Secure the bottoms of the posts to the deck frame with metal post anchors. Tie the tops of the posts together with the second (top) 2x4 plates that run over the tops of the walls. Miter the ends of the 2x4 plates over the posts and attach them with screws **(Photo 6)**.

ADD CEILING JOISTS AND ATTIC FLOORING

The next step after installing deck boards on the front porch **(Figure M** online and **Photo 7)** is to build the attic floor. The 2x8 joists covered with sheets of flooring material provide storage space in the attic. We left a 4-ft.-wide opening for easy access to the front and back loft areas, but you could also cover the entire area with a floor and provide an access door or pull-down ladder instead.

Start by marking the joist locations on the two side rim joists using **Figure H** (online) as a guide. Then cut and install the joists **(Photo 8)**. Before you cover the joists with the 4 x 8-ft. sheets of flooring, plumb and brace the 4x4 posts with diagonal 2x4s. Also, stretch a string or mason's line from front to back along the top edge of the outside joist to make sure the walls and joists are straight. The attic floor needs to be square and have straight sides. If not, the rafters won't fit correctly.

INSTALL THE SIDING

Double-check the corners and the front posts to make sure they're plumb. Then cut and install the 4 x 8-ft. sheets of siding **(Photo 9)**. Follow your siding manufacturer's instructions for spacing and nailing the siding. Make sure you remember to install metal drip cap flashing (visible in **Photo 9**) over the 2x8 skirt board before installing the siding.

FRAME THE ROOF

Start by cutting the 2x8 ridge board to length and marking the rafter locations on both sides using **Figure K** (online) as a guide. Also mark the rafter locations on the floor along both sides of the shed. Next, set the ridge on temporary 2x4 posts and brace it with diagonal 2x4s **(Photo 10)**. The top of the ridge should be 76 in. from the floor. Cut a pair of rafters **(Figure J** online) and set them in place to test the fit. Make any needed adjustments, and when you have a pair of rafters that fit perfectly, mark one of them as a pattern. Use the pattern to trace the rafter cuts on the remaining 2x6s and cut out the rafters.

Stretch a string along the top of the ridge as a guide to keep the ridge straight as you install the pairs of rafters **(Photo 10)**. The 2x4 blocks nailed to the floor between the rafters help position the rafters and make them easier to secure. Add the 2x6 subfascias before you install the four overhang rafters at the front and back of the shed.

When the roof frame is done, you can build the front and back gable walls **(Figure L** online). The front wall requires an opening for the gable-end window **(Photo 11)**. Finish the roof construction by covering the rafters with sheathing **(Figure N** online and **Photo 12)**.

TRIM OUT THE EXTERIOR

Start by nailing the soffit boards to the underside of the rafters. Then add the 1x8 fascia boards that cover the 2x6 subfascias and overhanging rafters. Finish the overhang trim by installing the 1x3 roof molding over the 1x8 fascias **(Photo 13)**.

Next, install the 1 x 9-1/4-in. trim board that fits against the soffit and runs around the perimeter of the shed and porch. This wide trim

SIDE WALL

4 BUILD THE WALLS
Cut the plates and mark the stud locations on them. Build and stand up the side walls. Then build and stand up the front and back walls.

DIAGONAL BRACE

4' LEVEL

5 PLUMB AND BRACE THE WALLS
Make sure the walls are firmly nailed together at the corners. Then use a level to plumb the corners while you attach temporary diagonal bracing to the inside of the walls. Brace all four walls. You can remove the bracing after you install the siding panels.

MITERED PLATES

6 FASTEN THE PLATES OVER THE POSTS
Run the second top plate on each side of the shed out over the posts. Cut miters on the plates where they join over the posts. Connect the plates to the posts with screws.

COMPOSITE DECKING

2x8 CEILING JOISTS

7 INSTALL THE DECKING

Start by cutting and installing the perimeter boards. Leave a 1-in. overhang. Notch and miter the perimeter boards to fit around the post. Then space the remaining deck boards with a 16d nail and screw them to the joists. We used the Cortex hidden fastening system.

8 SET THE CEILING JOISTS

Mark the joist locations on two rim joists and nail the rims to the top plate. Make sure they are set in 1-1/2 in. from the outside edge of the wall to allow space for the second rim joist. Attach the joists with screws or nails driven through the rim joists. Then add the second rim joist and install joist hangers on every joist.

forms one side of the false beam that runs around the porch ceiling. Add a 2x4 frame to the underside of the porch ceiling to create the false beam. Then nail the grooved panels to the porch ceiling and cover the 2x4 false beam with trim (**Photo 14**). You can install the corner boards at this stage, but the battens will have to wait until after you've built and installed the windows. **Figures S–V** (online) show details for the siding and trim installation.

ASSEMBLE THE WINDOWS

We built inexpensive windows for the shed using plastic barn sash mounted in 1x4 pine frames (**Photo 15** and **Figures Q** and **R** online). Start by measuring the sash and building a 1x4 frame that's 1/4 in. wider and taller than the sash. Cut 10-degree angles on the bottom of the sides to provide a sloping sill. Cut 1x2 stops to fit in the frame; position them to hold the sash flush with the outside edge of the 1x4 frame. Then attach galvanized screen door hinges to the frame, set the sash in place and drill holes for the fasteners. Since

the plastic isn't strong enough to hold wood screws, we drilled holes through the sash and attached the hinges with machine screws, washers and nuts.

Connect three windows to form the window assembly for the side wall (**Figures R** and **U** online). Use a pair of 2x4s as spacers between each window. Screw through the window frames into the spacers to hold the windows together. Tip the triple window assembly into the window opening. Shim under the windows until about 3/8 in. of the top frame is exposed on the outside. Shim between the studs and the window frame to level and plumb the window unit and to adjust the frame until there's a consistent space between the window frame and the sash. Make sure the window frames are flush to the siding. Then screw through the frames into the studs to hold the windows in place. We added Stanley Storm Window Adjuster hardware to the windows to hold them open and to lock them.

Rip a 2x4 to 2 in. wide with a 10-degree bevel on each side to form the sill piece. Cut the sill to extend 3-1/4 in. past the window

SIDING

1/2" SPACER

DRIP CAP FLASHING

9 SIDE THE WALLS

Measure and cut the siding panels so that the seams align over wall studs. Rest the bottoms of the panels on a temporary 1/2-in. spacer to provide space between the siding and the drip cap. Nail the siding to the studs.

frame on each end and attach it to the wall under the windows with long screws. Then cut and install the 1x4 trim pieces that fit between the top trim and the sill **(Photo 16)**.

The front window is similar, except it's smaller and contains only one sash. Use the same process to build and install it.

INSTALL THE DOOR AND FINISH THE TRIM

If your prehung door has exterior trim, pry it off. The wide trim board running around the shed, under the soffit, will take the place of the top door trim. Place the door in the opening to check the fit. The top doorjamb should rest against the wide trim board. Use wooden or composite shims between the side jambs and the 2x4 framing to square the door frame. Place shims behind each hinge and at the top, middle and bottom of the latch side. Adjust the shims until there's an even space between the door and the doorjambs on the top and sides. Then drive screws through the doorjambs into the framing at the shim locations to secure the door. Finish the door installation by adding 1x4 trim boards to each side.

Finish the exterior trim by nailing 1x2 battens over the stud locations and installing the corner boards if you haven't done so already.

ADD THE SHAKE PANELS

The front and back gable ends are covered with panels resembling cedar shakes. After installing a metal drip cap over the 1x2 that caps the wide trim board, install the shakes according to the manufacturer's instructions **(Photo 17)**. Follow the manufacturer's instructions for details about panel placement and how much caulk space to leave between the panels and trim.

2x8 RIDGE
2x6 RAFTERS
TEMPORARY SUPPORT
TEMPORARY BRACE

10 FRAME THE ROOF
Mark the rafter locations on the ridge and set the ridge in place on temporary posts. Cut the rafters and install them in pairs, making sure the ridge stays straight as you screw or nail the rafters to the ridge.

STUD LOCATION

11 FILL IN THE GABLE FRAMING
Mark the stud locations on the bottom plate. Then use a level to transfer the stud locations to the top plate. Measure to find the stud lengths.

TEMPORARY BLOCK

12 INSTALL THE SHEATHING
Screw blocks to the subfascia to support the first row of roof sheathing while you nail it to the rafters. Space the sheathing about 1/8 in. between sheets to allow for expansion. Stagger the seams between rows.

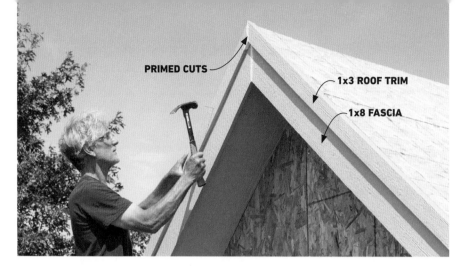

PRIMED CUTS

1x3 ROOF TRIM

1x8 FASCIA

13 INSTALL THE SOFFIT AND FASCIA

Nail the soffits to the underside of the rafters. Then nail the 1x8 fascia boards to the subfascia and gable-end rafters. Add 1x3 roof molding flush to the top of the sheathing.

FALSE BEAM

BEAM TRIM

14 BUILD THE FALSE BEAMS

Frame down with 2x4s to create a false beam. After covering the ceiling with siding sheets, wrap the side and bottom of the false beam and add 1x2 trim around the ceiling.

PLASTIC BARN SASH

1x2 STOP

SCREEN DOOR HINGE

10° ANGLE

1x4 FRAME

15 ASSEMBLE THE WINDOWS

Cut the 1x4s, including a 10-degree angle on the bottoms of the side pieces; screw them together. Add 1x2 stops. Screw a pair of hinges to the frame. Set the sash into place and use the hinges as a guide to drill holes for the machine screws to attach the sash.

16 TRIM THE WINDOWS

Rip 10-degree angles on the sill piece and screw it to the wall under the windows. Then cut 1x4s to fit between the top trim and the sill, and nail them on.

BUILD THE BAR AND THE BAR DOOR

The bar consists of a frame of 2x2s and 2x4s covered on the top and bottom with plywood and finished with a wood edge (**Photo 18** and **Figure P** online). For extra strength, use screws to attach the frame. Shim under the 2x4s if needed to level the bar top before installing the plywood.

When you're done building the bar, add jambs to the sides and top and then install exterior trim. Cut the jamb material to fit, and nail the pieces to the sides and top of the bar opening. Then add 1x6 trim to both sides of the bar opening to finish it off.

The bar door attaches to the inside of the shed with hinges and swings up to open. To build the door, simply cut a piece of siding material to the right size. Then attach the frame and batten boards with glue and screws (**Photo 19** and **Figure P** online).

To install the bar door, rest it on blocks so that the bottom is

CEDAR SHAKE PANEL

METAL DRIP CAP

3/4" PLYWOOD

18 BUILD THE BAR
Screw the 2x2 and 2x4 frame to the framing. Then cover the top and bottom with plywood. Finish the bar by covering the face with trim, mitered at the corners.

17 COVER THE GABLES WITH SHAKES
Follow manufacturer's instructions for installing the shake panels. Provide space for caulk at the ends; stagger joints according to the instructions.

2-1/4 in. below the bar top. Add a 1-1/4-in.-thick strip of wood along the top of the door to provide a hinge attachment point. Then screw strap hinges to the wood strip and to the door (Photo 20). Remove the temporary support blocks when you're done attaching the hinges.

We mounted a pair of locking hasps on the interior side of the bar door to secure it when it's closed. Then we added eye bolts to the door edges and to the ceiling above the door to provide a way to hang the door when it's open.

FINISHING UP
Before you shingle the roof, install a metal drip edge. Then nail a row of starter shingles along the bottom of the roof. Install the rest of the shingles according to the package instructions.

Before painting, we filled spaces on the exterior with acrylic caulk. Then we rolled and brushed two coats of top-quality acrylic exterior paint onto the trim and siding.

CONSTRUCTION ADHESIVE

19 ASSEMBLE THE BAR DOOR
Cut a sheet of siding according to the dimensions given in Figure P online. Glue and screw 1x6s and 1x4s to the siding to create the bar door.

HINGE ATTACHMENT STRIP

SWING-UP BAR DOOR

TEMPORARY BLOCKS

20 MOUNT THE BAR DOOR
Rip a strip of 2x4 to 1-1/4 in. thick and nail it along the top of the opening to provide a fastening location for the hinges. Support the door on temporary blocks while you attach the strap hinges to the door.

STONE WATERFALL

//

THIS ARTESIAN WATERFALL REQUIRES ALMOST NO MAINTENANCE, AND YOU CAN BUILD IT IN A WEEKEND.

If you're looking for an eye-catching feature for your patio, deck or even front entry, this natural-looking artesian waterfall will do the trick. This project was designed around a special stone, one with a 1-in. hole drilled through it. Water from the pump gurgles up through the hole and overflows the stone. To reduce maintenance, there's no collection pond. A gravel-filled reservoir below collects the overflow for recirculation. Since no sunlight can reach the water in the reservoir and support algae growth, the water stays pristine. You'll have algae growing near wet areas, but it only contributes to the natural look.

Here you'll learn how to select and drill a boulder that'll mimic a natural artesian well. Also, you'll learn how to construct a simple under-gravel reservoir using 5-gal. pails. The decorative choices—the top-dressing stones, fountain (drilled) stone and plants—are left to your own creative eye and inspiration.

The whole building process is simpler than you might think, and you don't need any special skills or tools, but it's not a completely no-sweat job. You'll have to dig an 8 x 10-ft. hole about 2 ft. deep and dump in gravel. That's the only genuinely heavy work. Once you've gathered the materials, you can easily have this project up, running and finished in a day. Your waterfall doesn't have to be as large and elaborate as this one. You can design a smaller version that will cost much less. All you need is one water-spouting boulder resting in a small area of decorative stone for a beautiful conversation piece for your garden.

THE PLANNING STEPS

The water basin is a two-tiered hole: a shallow end where the boulders rest and a deeper end that serves as the reservoir **(Figure A)**. The 5-gallon pails **(Photos 5–8)** create a large reservoir volume, so you don't have to add water often. They also reduce the amount of coarse gravel needed to fill the hole. All of the pails but the one containing the pump are positioned about 5 in. below the surface to leave room for potted, water-loving plants. Elevate the pump pail so the lid lies just

WHAT IT TAKES

TIME	**SKILL LEVEL**
1 day	Advanced

TOOLS
Basic hand tools, drill with spade or twist bit, rotary hammer drill with 1-in. masonry bit (rental), shovel

below the surface for easy pump access. Drill all the pails with holes sized to keep the gravel out **(Photo 5)** but let the water seep in.

If you build a smaller waterfall with fewer 5-gallon pails, monitor the water level more frequently. If the reservoir goes dry, the pump may be ruined.

Begin your search for waterfall stone by contacting local stone suppliers who can either custom-drill stones or have a selection of predrilled stones (search "natural stone") to purchase. Prices for 1-ton stones with natural basins, plus delivery and placement charges, will vary greatly.

Deciding on the fountain stone (the stone with the hole in it) is the hard part. Bring several gallons of water with you and pour water over your stone selections to see how it flows. Adjust the stone to alter the flow. Look for a stone that has natural chutes or channels if you're seeking a "stream-like" flow, or one that has a natural basin if you're after a gurgling-up-from-the-ground look. Pick a stone

that's less than 15 in. thick at the waterfall hole location; that's the limit for available drill shafts.

You'll also need boulders that support and surround the fountain stone. If you don't have a source for drilled stones, buy a stone and drill it yourself. It's easier than you think. (See "Drilling a Stone.")

SELECT A SITE AND DIG THE HOLE

Pick an area that has no more than a few inches of slope over the length and width of the water feature you plan to build.

Roughly assemble your fountain and other decorative large stones, and cluster the 5-gallon pails to locate the deep end of the basin **(Photo 1)**. Use a rope to shape a natural-appearing perimeter for the basin and gravel bed. Keep in mind that a larger basin means more digging! The excavation shown here is about 4 ft. wide and 8 ft. long. Dig the deeper part of the hole with steep sides and a flat bottom to leave plenty of room for the pails. Use the depth of the

pails as a guide to the proper depth **(Photo 2)**.

LAY IN THE PADDING AND POND LINER

The whole purpose of the pond liner padding is to protect the waterproof liner from punctures, but it won't offer complete protection. Cut off roots flush with the bottom and sides of the hole, and dig out sharp stones. Lay indoor/outdoor or any other old carpeting beneath the padding to further protect the liner **(Photo 3)**, especially where the pails and heavy stones will sit. Then line the entire hole with the

//

Figure A Stone Waterfall details
OVERALL DIMENSIONS:
8' W x 10' L x
2' D

POND LINER

LINER PAD

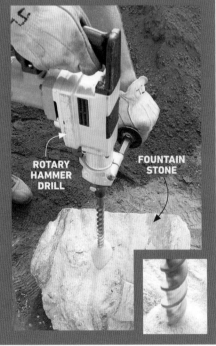

ROTARY HAMMER DRILL

FOUNTAIN STONE

liner pad **(Photo 3)**. If you need to cut it to fit the contours better, go ahead. Just do your best to keep folds to a minimum and avoid large voids between the soil and the pad.

Work in your socks when you're installing the pond liner to reduce the chance of damage. Start by unfolding the liner and centering it over the hole. Work the liner well into the transition between the bottom and the sides, folding neat, flat pleats wherever necessary to help it fit **(Photo 4)**. The weight of the fill and water will push the liner into any remaining small voids. Add another layer of carpeting or pond liner scraps under the boulder and pail positions to further guard against punctures **(Photo 5)**.

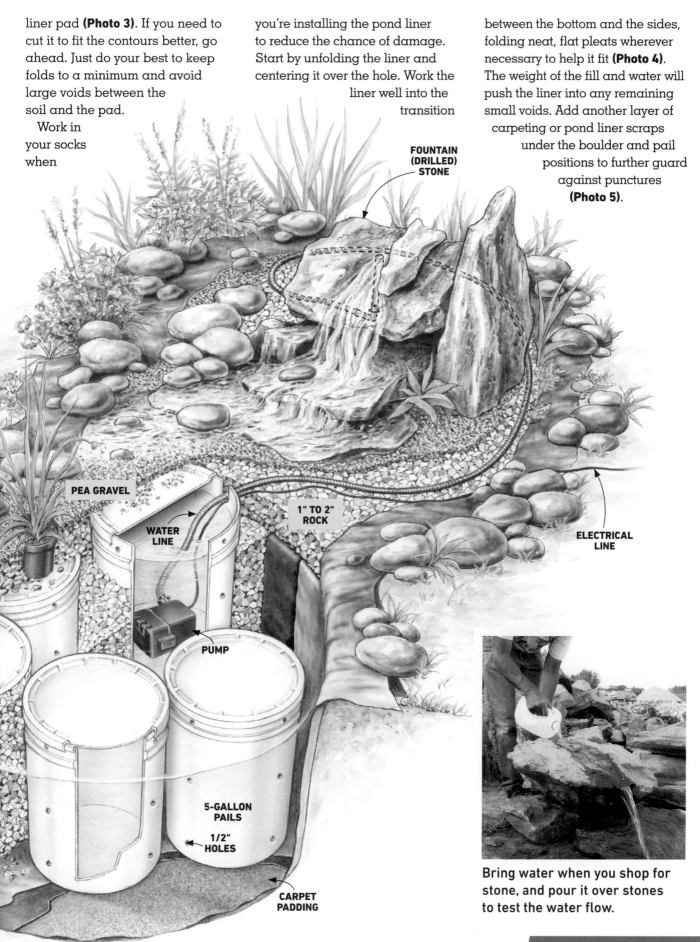

FOUNTAIN
(DRILLED)
STONE

PEA GRAVEL

WATER
LINE

1" TO 2"
ROCK

ELECTRICAL
LINE

PUMP

5-GALLON
PAILS

1/2"
HOLES

CARPET
PADDING

Bring water when you shop for stone, and pour it over stones to test the water flow.

1 DETERMINE THE LOCATION AND LAYOUT

Group the pails and roughly assemble the stone waterfall. When you're satisfied, mark the edges with spray paint.

CAUTION:
Call 811 or visit call811.com to locate underground lines before you dig.

2 EXCAVATE THE SITE

Dig the reservoir end of the hole 6 in. deeper than the pail height, and the waterfall end 6 in. deep overall.

ADD THE PAILS AND FILL IN THE HOLE

Use either a spade bit or a twist bit to drill 1/2-in. drain holes in all the pails as shown in **Photo 5**. To make accessing the pump easier, cut off the lid-locking rim of the pump-containing pail **(Photo 6)**. When you start backfilling around the pails, they'll want to shift a bit, so keep a foot on the lids while you shovel a few inches of rock around each base. Be sure to keep the height of the pump pail about 2 in. below grade level **(Photo 7)**. Stop filling at this point. The pea gravel will fill the final 2 in.

LAY IN THE TOP-DRESSING ROCK AND ARRANGE THE FOUNTAIN AND FILLER STONES

Hook up the pump to the water line and rest the pump on the bottom of the pump pail **(Photo 8)**. Position the larger base rocks at this point, and then pour the pea gravel around them and top off the rest of the feature **(Photo 9)**. Arrange the fountain stone and other stone supports or features in the shallow end of the hole. Use a flowing garden hose near the hole in the fountain

MATERIALS LIST

ITEM	QTY.
1"-2" smooth round stones for the main filler stone	1,000 lbs.
Indoor/outdoor carpeting or any other old carpeting you may have on hand	Small roll
Pond liner padding and waterproof liner	As needed
5-gallon pails with lids	5
Pea gravel	25 bags
Corrugated pond tubing	
Tubing clamps	2
1" male adapter	1
Silicone caulk	1 tube
1" elbow	1
Spray paint	1 can
Pond foam	1 can
Aluminum foil	As needed
300-gph water pump	1
Fountain stone	As needed

CORRUGATED POND TUBING

stone, and tinker with the stones until the flow pattern approximates the look you're after **(Photo 10)**. When you're satisfied, tip over the fountain stone to expose the hole, cut the water line to length and clamp on the plastic fittings **(Photo 11)**. Test-fit the fitting end in the fountain hole; you may have to grind or chisel off the plastic barbs on the fitting to make it tight. Coat the fitting with silicone caulk and slip it into the hole. Let it set for an hour and then reset the stone.

Now fill the reservoir by laying a garden hose on the gravel and running water until the pump pail is full. Rest the pump at the bottom of the pail and then plug it in for a test run. Readjust the stones as needed to get the ideal flow.

If you stack boulders and smaller stones to form a more elaborate waterfall, use expanding pond foam between the stones to stabilize the pieces. Protect the stones from overflowing foam by tucking aluminum foil in the areas you want to keep free of foam **(Photo 12)**. Start with small amounts of foam, and try to keep it out of sight by shoving the dispensing tube deep into the

CARPETING

LINER PAD

3 ADD CARPETING AND THE LINER PAD
Lay carpeting in the bottom of the hole. Then lay in the liner pad, folding it to follow the contours of the hole.

TUCK INTO CREVICES

POND LINER

4 TOP WITH THE LINER
Unfold the liner and center it over the hole. Push it into recesses and pleat it wherever necessary to fit it against the sides of the hole.

ADDITIONAL PADDING

1/2" HOLES

5 POSITION THE PAILS
Drill four columns of 1/2-in. holes around the middle and near the bottom and top of each pail. Snap on the lids and rest the pails in the hole.

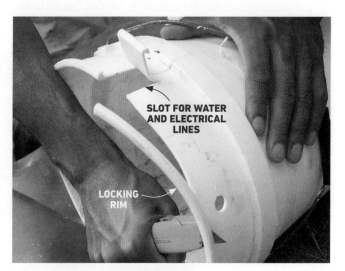

SLOT FOR WATER AND ELECTRICAL LINES

LOCKING RIM

6 REMOVE THE PUMP PAIL RIM
Cut off the rim from the pump pail, and cut and fold down a 1-1/2-in.-wide x 2-in. flap at the top for the water line and electrical cable.

7 ADD GRAVEL TO THE HOLE

Backfill around the reservoir pails with 1-in. to 2-in. gravel, resting the pump pail on the gravel so its top is 2 in. below grade level. Keep the gravel 2 in. below grade.

8 CONNECT THE WATER LINE TO THE PUMP

Route the water line to the waterfall location, avoiding areas where heavy stones will rest.

9 POUR IN PEA GRAVEL

Level the pea gravel until it's even with the edges. Then use a steel rake to even out the surface.

Figure B Fountain fittings

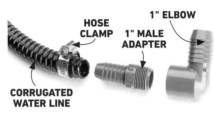

crevices. After the foam sets (about two hours), tear away the foil and cut off any exposed foam with a knife or saw.

If water "sticks" to the side of the stone as it runs off, let the stone dry and then apply a bead of silicone to the water side of the stone. The silicone will repel the water and help it "fall."

Finish the water feature by trimming off the overhanging liner and pad even with the rim of the hole. The liner is best cut with a utility knife and the pad with scissors. Add whatever other top-dressing or perimeter stones and plants you wish.

If you live in a cold climate, take your pump in for the winter and store it in a pail of water to keep the seals wet. Don't worry about draining the reservoir; freezing won't hurt it.

SELECTING A PUMP

A 300-gph (gallons per hour) water pump will give you the type of flow you see on page 204. If you'd like a smaller, gurgling flow, buy a 200-gph pump or install a restrictor valve at the pump that will allow you to adjust the flow.

A low-voltage pump was used here because it's safer and the wiring is easier to install. In fact, you need to bury the cable only an inch or two below grade. For a standard 120-volt pump, however, you'll have to apply for an electrical permit, bury the wire much deeper and install a GFCI-protected outlet.

10 POSITION THE BOULDERS

Place and roughly adjust the boulders using a garden hose placed near the fountain hole to simulate the water's path. Then flip over the boulder to access the underside of the hole.

11 ATTACH THE FOUNTAIN FITTINGS

Cut the water line to length and attach the fountain fittings. Coat the plastic elbow with silicone caulk and work the fittings into the hole on the underside of the fountain stone.

12 CHECK THE WATER FLOW

Test the flow by filling the basin and running the pump. Shim the stones as necessary, then fill around the stones with pond foam to lock them into place.

13 FINISH IT UP

Scoop out the pea gravel and set in potted pond plants. Finish the water feature with decorative top-dressing and perimeter edging stones.

BACKYARD OASIS

PLACE THIS SHADED RETREAT THAT'S SURPRISINGLY EASY TO BUILD NEXT TO YOUR DECK OR ANYWHERE IN YOUR YARD.

If you treasure your time outdoors, this simple shelter is the perfect retreat for you. It's open and airy, yet it'll shade you from that hot afternoon sun as well as keep you dry on a rainy day.

We designed it so you can easily connect it to your existing deck. Or you could build it freestanding in your yard. In either case, it'll quickly become your favorite destination!

We'll show you how to assemble this structure step by step. Don't be intimidated by the post-and-beam design. It's not difficult to build, and we'll walk you through the key details. We've simplified the steps with goof-proof techniques—like positioning the posts with a 2x4 frame and shaping the ends of beams with a circular saw. If you've tackled jobs like basic deck building or wall framing, you can build this shelter.

You'll need a miter saw and a table saw to make the angle cuts on the walls. A brad nailer will save you time but isn't absolutely necessary. You'll need at least three full weekends to complete the job.

PLAN YOUR RETREAT

The floor can stand as little as 14 in. above ground to about 8 ft. above ground, but if you build it more than 4 ft. above ground, you'll have to add diagonal knee braces between the posts and the floor (consult a structural engineer on this detail). The floor can be level with your deck, or it can stand higher or lower and include stairs.

When you apply for a building permit, ask your inspector about local requirements, including how deep to dig footings. Be sure to include bridge plans. For a bridge more than 4 ft. long or 4 ft. wide, your inspector may require you to strengthen the deck itself. A few days before you dig the footing holes, call 811 or visit call811.com to have underground utility lines marked.

Most home centers carry only treated lumber 6x6s. If you want a different wood, you may have to order it.

POSITION POSTS PERFECTLY

A layout frame makes positioning footings and posts foolproof **(Photo 1)**. Later, it helps you determine post heights and position the floor framing **(Photo 4)**.

Screw two 2x4s (94-1/2 in. long) between 14-ft. 2x4s to form a square with inside dimensions of 94-1/2 x 94-1/2 in. Square the frame by taking diagonal measurements and add a diagonal brace **(Photo 1)**. Rest the frame's legs on the deck, position the frame and make sure it's parallel to the deck. Then clamp or screw the legs to the deck. Support the other end with upright 2x4s. Roughly level the frame.

Hang a plumb bob from each corner of the frame to locate footings **(Photo 2)**. The plumb bob locates the outer corner of each post, not the center. Mark the footings using spray paint.

Slide the frame out of your way so you can dig the holes. But first trace around the frame's legs on the deck with a pencil to mark their exact positions. When the holes are complete, move the frame back into

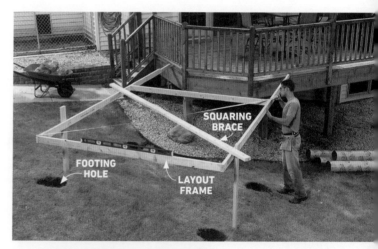

SQUARING BRACE

FOOTING HOLE

LAYOUT FRAME

1 MARK THE FOOTING LOCATIONS
Position the post footings using a layout frame as your template. Square, brace and level the frame, and then mark the post locations and dig the post holes.

WHAT IT TAKES	
TIME 6 days	**SKILL LEVEL** Advanced
TOOLS Basic hand tools, brad nailer (optional), drill, handsaw, miter saw, plumb bob, table saw	

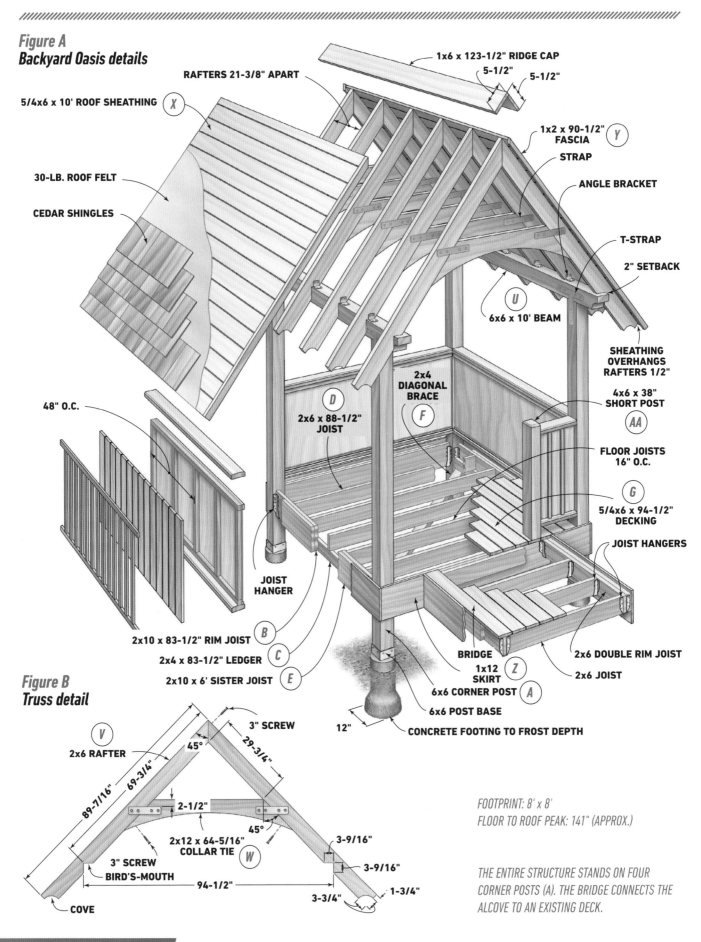

Figure A
Backyard Oasis details

1x6 x 123-1/2" RIDGE CAP

5-1/2"

5-1/2"

RAFTERS 21-3/8" APART

5/4x6 x 10' ROOF SHEATHING X

1x2 x 90-1/2" Y
FASCIA

STRAP

ANGLE BRACKET

30-LB. ROOF FELT

T-STRAP

2" SETBACK

CEDAR SHINGLES

U

6x6 x 10' BEAM

SHEATHING
OVERHANGS
RAFTERS 1/2"

2x4
DIAGONAL
BRACE

4x6 x 38"
SHORT POST

AA

48" O.C.

D

2x6 x 88-1/2"
JOIST

F

FLOOR JOISTS
16" O.C.

G

5/4x6 x 94-1/2"
DECKING

JOIST HANGERS

JOIST
HANGER

2x10 x 83-1/2" RIM JOIST B

2x4 x 83-1/2" LEDGER C

2x10 x 6' SISTER JOIST E

BRIDGE

1x12
SKIRT Z

6x6 CORNER POST A

6x6 POST BASE

CONCRETE FOOTING TO FROST DEPTH

12"

2x6 DOUBLE RIM JOIST

2x6 JOIST

Figure B
Truss detail

V

2x6 RAFTER

45°

3" SCREW

29-3/4"

89-7/16"

69-3/4"

2-1/2"

45°

2x12 x 64-5/16"
COLLAR TIE W

3-9/16"

3-9/16"

3" SCREW
BIRD'S-MOUTH

94-1/2"

3-3/4"

1-3/4"

COVE

FOOTPRINT: 8' x 8'
FLOOR TO ROOF PEAK: 141" (APPROX.)

*THE ENTIRE STRUCTURE STANDS ON FOUR
CORNER POSTS (A). THE BRIDGE CONNECTS THE
ALCOVE TO AN EXISTING DECK.*

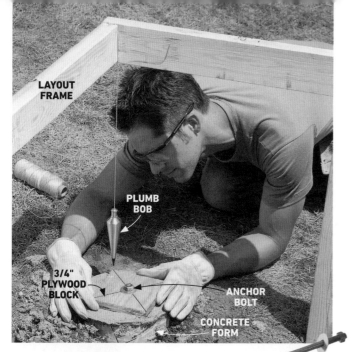

LAYOUT FRAME

PLUMB BOB

3/4" PLYWOOD BLOCK

ANCHOR BOLT

CONCRETE FORM

ANCHOR BOLT

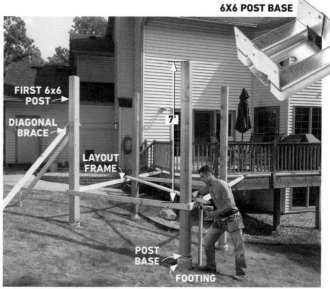

6X6 POST BASE

FIRST 6x6 POST

DIAGONAL BRACE

LAYOUT FRAME

7'

POST BASE

FOOTING

2 ADD CONCRETE

Fill the footings with concrete and position the anchor bolts using 5-1/2-in. square bolt blocks. When the concrete hardens, remove the blocks and bolt on the post bases.

3 SET THE POSTS

Cut the posts **(A)** to length, and screw the first post to its base and to the frame. Add stakes and braces to hold it plumb. Set the other posts and plumb each of them.

MATERIALS LIST

ITEM	QTY.
6x6 cedar (corner posts; lengths vary)	4
6x6 x 10' cedar (beams)	2
4x6 x 8' cedar (short wall posts)	1
2x6 x 8' cedar (wall bases and caps, rafters)	19
2x12 x 12' cedar (collar ties)	3
5/4x6 x 10' cedar (decking, roof sheathing)	49
1x12 x 8' cedar (skirt)	4
1x6 x 10' cedar (wall boards)	12
1x2 x 8' cedar (rails, battens, fascia)	30
2x10 x 8' pressure-treated (rim joists)	4
2x10 x 12' (sister joists)	2
2x4 x 8' (joist ledgers)	2
2x6 x 8' (floor joists)	5
2x4 x 12' (diagonal brace)	1
2x2 x 8' (wall plates and studs)	13
4' x 8' T1-11 plywood (wall sheathing)	3
2x4 x 14' (frame; see Photo 1)	3
2x4 x 8' (frame, bracing, stakes; see Photo 3)	6

NOTE: This list doesn't include materials for roofing, bridge or railings.

HARDWARE, ETC.	
Anchor bolts, washers and nuts	4
Joist hangers (for 2x10s)	8
Post bases (Simpson ABA66Z or similar)	4
Angle brackets (Simpson A23 or similar)	12
Straps (Simpson OHS or similar)	24
T-straps (Simpson OHT or similar)	8
5/8" x 2" lag screws	48
5/8" x 2-1/2" bolts and nuts	48
8" tube forms	4
3" galvanized nails, 2" deck screws, joist hanger nails, 10d galv. nails, 6d galv. finish nails	As needed
Cement mix	As needed
Construction adhesive	As needed

NOTE: Everything you need is available at home centers, except the straps and T-straps.

position. Double-check to make sure the frame is square, perfectly positioned and level. Add extra vertical supports so the long 2x4s won't sag.

POUR THE FOOTINGS AND SET THE POSTS

Pour 12 in. of concrete into each hole, set the tube forms into place, backfill around them and then fill them with concrete. To position the anchor bolts perfectly, cut four 5-1/2 x 5-1/2-in. bolt blocks from plywood **(Photo 2)**. Drill a 5/8-in. hole at the center of each block, insert the anchor bolt and add the nut. Set each bolt into the wet concrete. Then stand up and eyeball the block to make sure it's parallel to the layout frame. The blocks leave impressions in the concrete. When the concrete hardens, use those impressions to position the post bases.

Next, cut the posts to length. To determine the length of each post, measure from the post base to the layout frame and then add 7 ft. to that measurement. A 7-1/4-in.

circular saw won't cut through a 6x6, so cut from all four sides and finish with a handsaw.

Recheck the position of the layout frame. Set one of the back posts first. Add braces to hold it plumb. Set the other posts **(Photo 3)**, then check each one with a level. If a post is out of plumb, don't simply shove it into position—the layout frame will push the others out of plumb. Instead, slip a wrench inside the post base and loosen the nut on the anchor bolt. The oversized bolt hole in the base lets you move the base slightly and plumb the post. Don't forget to retighten the nut.

FRAME A STURDY FLOOR—FAST

Measure down from the layout frame to mark the position of the floor framing on each post **(Photo 4)**. Toe-screw each rim joist **(B)** into place; add the joist hangers. Be sure to inset the rim joists 1-1/2 in. from the outer edges of the posts. Remove the layout frame, but leave the post braces in place

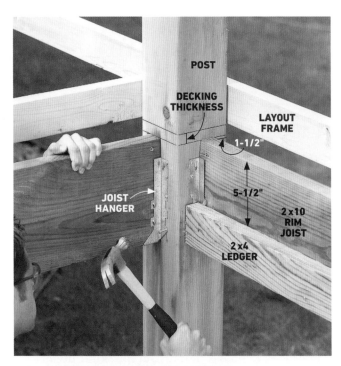

4 INSTALL RIM JOISTS AND LEDGERS

Mark the thickness of the decking below the layout frame. Install 2x10 rim joists at that height using joist hangers. Nail 2x4 ledgers to two rim joists. Remove the layout frame.

5 INSTALL FLOOR AND SISTER JOISTS

Nail 2x6 floor joists into place. Drive in shims to straighten a bowed rim joist. Nail additional 2x10 "sister" joists (see **Figure A**) alongside each rim joist, then install the decking.

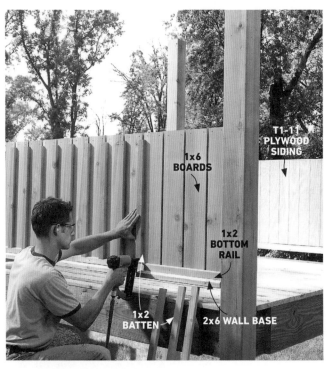

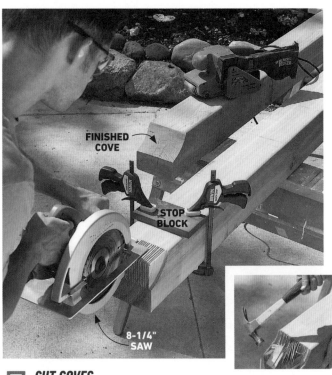

6 BUILD THE SIDEWALLS

Frame the sidewalls as detailed in **Figure C**. Cover the insides of the walls with plywood siding and the outsides with boards and battens.

7 CUT COVES

Cove the beams with an 8-1/4-in. circular saw, using a stop block to ensure uniform cuts. Break out the chips and smooth the cove with a 100-grit sanding belt.

until you install the sidewalls.

To support the floor joists, add ledgers **(C)** to two of the rim joists **(Figure A)**, driving 10d nails every 4 in. Using ledgers is easier and faster than using joist hangers.

Set the floor joists **(D)** on the ledgers and nail them into place **(Photo 5)**. Then add the sister joists **(E)**. Nail the diagonal brace **(F)** to the undersides of joists. Lay the deck boards flush, as you would on any deck.

STIFFEN THE STRUCTURE WITH SOLID SIDEWALLS

The walls that surround the alcove aren't just for looks; they also stiffen the structure and make it safer.

Build the sidewalls **(Photo 6)**, but leave the rear wall off until the roof trusses are in place. **Figure C** shows all the details. To start, install the 2x2 wall framing **(H, J, K)**. Chamfer the wall cap **(L)** and base **(M)** by tilting your table saw blade to 45 degrees. Check the posts for plumb before you nail on the plywood siding **(P)**. Next, nail on the 1x6 boards **(Q)**. Then tilt

your table saw blade to 15 degrees and bevel the 1x2 bottom rails **(R)** so they'll shed rainwater. Add the top rails **(T)** after all the battens **(S)** are in place. To install the wall caps **(L)**, apply construction adhesive to the inner and outer top rails. Then predrill and drive screws up through the rails and into the cap. To avoid dents from dropped tools, we left the caps off until later.

CUT PERFECT COVES AND SET THE BEAMS

Coved ends give the beams **(U)** a more graceful look than square-cut ends. And there's a fast way to do it using a circular saw **(Photo 7)**. We first tried a 7-1/4-in. saw but found that a slightly larger cove cut with an 8-1/4-in. saw looked better and was well worth the rental fee.

Before you cut coves, determine the position of the stop block. We clamped our block 5-5/8 in. from the ends of each beam, but that measurement will differ with a different saw. Clamp your stop block to a 6x6 scrap left over from the posts. Cut until the saw

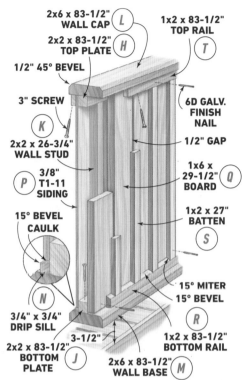

**2x6 x 83-1/2"
WALL CAP** L

**1x2 x 83-1/2"
TOP RAIL** T

**2x2 x 83-1/2"
TOP PLATE** H

1/2" 45° BEVEL

3" SCREW K

**6D GALV.
FINISH
NAIL**

1/2" GAP

**2x2 x 26-3/4"
WALL STUD**

**1x6 x
29-1/2"
BOARD** Q

**3/8"
T1-11
SIDING** P

**1x2 x 27"
BATTEN** S

**15° BEVEL
CAULK**

**15° MITER
15° BEVEL** R

**3/4" x 3/4"
DRIP SILL** N

**2x2 x 83-1/2"
BOTTOM
PLATE** J

3-1/2"

**1x2 x 83-1/2"
BOTTOM RAIL**

**2x6 x 83-1/2"
WALL BASE** M

bumps against the block, then measure the length and depth of the cut. Adjust the stop block until the length and depth are equal. Measure the position of the block and use that measurement to position the block on the beams.

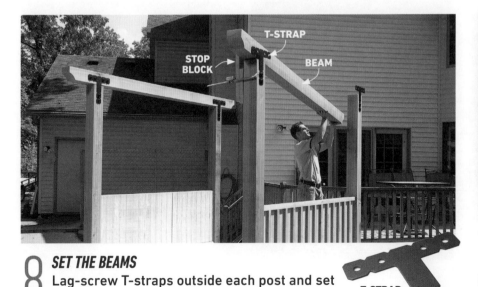

**STOP
BLOCK**

T-STRAP

BEAM

T-STRAP

8 SET THE BEAMS
Lag-screw T-straps outside each post and set the beams. Then add the inside straps. Clamp stop blocks to the posts so the beam can't fall off while you position it.

**65-7/8"
LONG**

**COLLAR
TIE**

**64-5/16"
PLASTIC
1x2**

45°

2x12

9 CUT THE ARCS
Trace arcs on collar ties using a flexible arc jig. Cut the arcs with a jigsaw and smooth them with a belt sander. Cut the 45-degree ends with a circular saw.

DRILL GUIDE 5/8" BIT

BOLT HOLE

RAFTER

COLLAR TIE

CRIB

STRAP

10 ASSEMBLE THE TRUSSES
Cut the rafters as shown in **Figure B** and assemble the trusses on a 2x4 crib. Drill perpendicular bolt holes using a simple 1x4 drill guide.

RIDGE BRACE

FIRST TRUSS

TRUSS BRACE

11 SET THE TRUSSES
Set the first truss, level it and brace it to the deck. Set the second truss, then screw on a temporary ridge brace to hold the trusses upright.

When you cut the coves, hold the saw flat against the beam; if you tip down the back of the saw, you'll cut too deep.

Set the beams on the posts **(Photo 8)** and fasten them to the posts with T-straps. We spray-painted the heads of our lag screws black before installing them and touched them up with an artist's brush after.

BUILD FANCY ROOF TRUSSES WITH BASIC SKILLS
Building the six trusses is simple but time-consuming. Consider building them in your garage before you break ground for this project. **Figure B** shows you all the details you'll need.

First, mark an arc on the 2x12 collar ties **(W; Photo 9)**. Screw blocks to a 2x4 and bend a spring stick between them. Plastic molding makes a perfect spring stick. Slide the jig to the left or right to avoid knots in the 2x12 and select the most attractive part of the board.

Next, cut the rafters **(V)**. To assemble the trusses quickly and consistently, build a simple 2x4 crib that will hold the truss parts in position **(Photo 10)**. Join the parts with 3-in. screws. Line up the straps using a 4-ft. level. Mark the bolt-hole locations by drilling shallow holes. Then set the strap aside and finish the holes using a guide to hold the drill bit perfectly vertical so the holes match up on both sides **(Photo 10, inset)**. The guide is simply two square blocks screwed together. Bolt on the straps.

PRO TIP
Sand and stain the truss parts and roof sheathing before you assemble them.

SET THE TRUSSES AND SHEATHE THE ROOF

Mark the truss locations on top of both beams. Set the front truss first, fastening it with angle brackets **(Figure A)**. Then set and brace the remaining trusses **(Photo 11)**.

The bird's-mouths may fit so tightly over the beams that it's difficult to set the trusses. Here's how to solve that problem: After the first truss, fasten only one side of each remaining truss. That way you can tug the beams inward as you set each truss. (To allow this, you must build the back wall only after the trusses are installed.) Fasten the loose side of each truss and build the back wall before you sheathe the roof with deck boards **(X)**. Start at the bottom of the rafters, overhanging the first board by 1/2 in. and spacing the boards 1/4 in. apart. These boards will be visible from below, so lay the best side face down. Cover the ends of the sheathing with fascia trim **(Y; Photo 12)**. Use short roofing nails that won't pop through the underside of the sheathing.

FASCIA

12 **SHEATHE AND SHINGLE THE ROOF**
Sheathe the roof with 5/4-in. deck boards. Nail 1x2 fascia trim to the sheathing at the front and back, then shingle the roof. Take safety precautions on the steep roof.

CAUTION: The roof is too steep to stand or kneel on. At the very least, you'll need roof jacks and a 2x10 plank (see **Photo 12**). Scaffolding makes the job easier and safer.

THE BRIDGE AND RAILINGS

The bridge is basically a small deck (see **Figure A**). After you frame and deck the bridge, add the 1x12 skirt boards **(Z)**.

The front walls are just shorter versions of the walls shown in **Figure C**. If you can't find 4x6s for the front wall posts **(AA)**, you can cut them from 6x6s using a 10-in. table saw. To extend the deck railing, you'll have to cut out a section of the existing railing and add two new railing posts, copying the existing ones. Then install the new railing, again copying the existing design. We finished all the exposed wood with transparent deck stain.

FAMILYHANDYMAN.COM
To find more information online, search for "deck footings," "deck boards," "deck stairs," "roof safety" and "shingle installation."

CLASSIC GARDEN ARBOR

CUT PERFECT, OLD-STYLE JOINTS WITH STANDARD TOOLS, AND KEEP ALL THE FASTENERS OUT OF SIGHT.

This timber garden arbor can be a special place to get away for a quiet retreat, or it can serve as a delightful lawn sculpture that you can view from your kitchen window.

Building it is enjoyable too. The main structure goes together like an old-fashioned timber frame, with tenons and notches cut into wooden 6x6s with a circular saw and handsaw. The main posts are anchored in the ground with concrete, and the roof and sides are made of dimensional treated lumber screwed to the treated 6x6s. The project shown took about three days to build with plenty of break time. Three weeks later, after the wood had ample time to dry out, an exterior oil stain was applied.

SHOPPING FOR TREATED LUMBER

When you're looking for lumber at your local home center, make sure to pick out 6x6s that are fairly dry and free of twists and large cracks. The same goes for the other treated dimensional lumber you'll need for this project.

However, don't be disturbed by the green color of the wood at this stage. A quality semi-transparent oil stain will give you a nice, warm wood tone.

STAND THE TWO END ASSEMBLIES AND FILL IN THE CONCRETE

To get this structure to behave and end up square, measure the holes carefully and dig each one about 16 in. deep and 12 in. wide with a posthole digger.

TIP: If you're wondering what to do with the extra dirt, lay a tarp right next to where you're digging and dump the soil right onto it. Then drag it around to any location on the lot that needs a bit of fill.

Join the front posts as a pair **(Photo 2)**, then do the same with the rear. Stand the rear assembly (get a friend to help) and stick the bottoms of the posts into the rear holes. Now drive some stakes into the ground while one person holds the assembly. Plumb the posts with temporary braces fastened to the stakes and posts, then level the horizontal ties at the bottom with shims. Once this assembly is secured, insert the front post assembly into the front post holes and fasten it to the rear assembly with the 2x2 horizontal side supports as shown in **Photo 3**. With the front secured to the rear assembly, make sure the front posts are at right angles to the rear posts and the diagonal

> **CAUTION:**
> Call 811 or visit call811.com to locate underground lines before you dig.

WHAT IT TAKES

TIME
4 days

SKILL LEVEL
Advanced

TOOLS
Basic hand tools, belt sander, block plane, chisel,
7-1/4-in. circular saw, 10-in. circular saw (optional),
drill driver, coarse file, handsaw, jigsaw, level

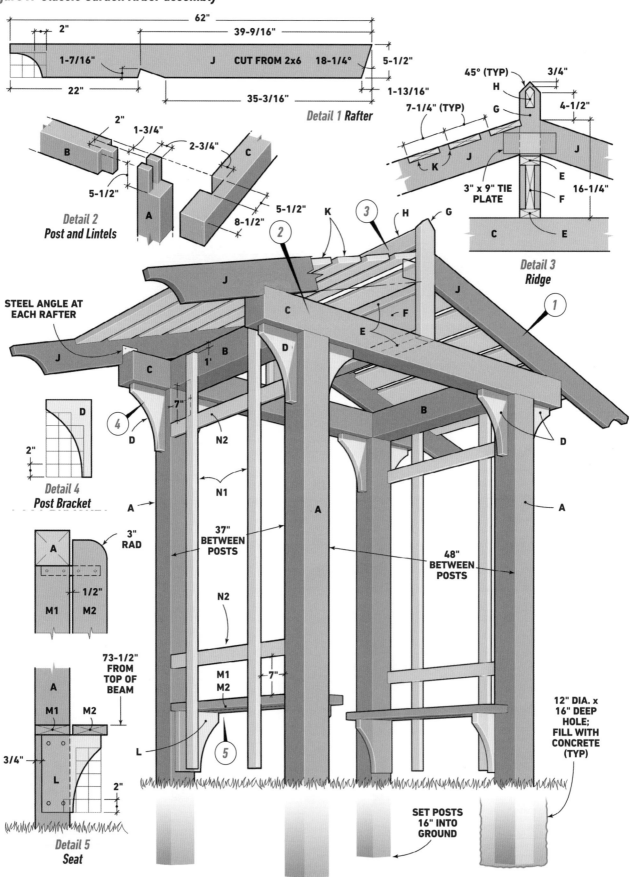

Detail 1 Rafter

62"
39-9/16"
2"
1-7/16"   J   CUT FROM 2x6   18-1/4°
5-1/2"
22"
35-3/16"
1-13/16"

**Detail 2
Post and Lintels**

2"
1-3/4"
B
2-3/4"
C
5-1/2"
A
5-1/2"
8-1/2"

**Detail 3
Ridge**

45° (TYP)   3/4"
H
4-1/2"
7-1/4" (TYP)
G
J   J
K
3" x 9" TIE PLATE
E
F
16-1/4"
C   E

STEEL ANGLE AT EACH RAFTER

**Detail 4
Post Bracket**

D
2"

**Detail 5
Seat**

A
M1   M2
3" RAD
1/2"

73-1/2" FROM TOP OF BEAM

A
M1   M2
3/4"
L
2"

1'
B
C
7"
D
D
N2
4
N1
A
37" BETWEEN POSTS
N2
M1 M2
7"
L
5

48" BETWEEN POSTS
A
F
E
J
B
A
A
D

12" DIA. x 16" DEEP HOLE; FILL WITH CONCRETE (TYP)

SET POSTS 16" INTO GROUND

CUTTING LIST

KEY	QTY.	PART
A	4	5-1/2" x 5-1/2" x 105-1/2" Treated posts
B	2	5-1/2" x 5-1/2" x 42-1/2" Treated side lintels
C	2	5-1/2" x 5-1/2" x 76" Treated front and back lintels
D	8	1-1/2" x 7-1/4" x 12" Post brackets
E	2	1-1/2" x 3-1/2" x 45" Center beam flanges
F	1	1-1/2" x 7-1/4" x 45" Center beam
G	2	1-1/2" x 3-1/2" x 22-1/2" Ridge beam supports
H	1	1-1/2" x 3-1/2" x 45" Ridge
J	4	1-1/2" x 5-1/2" x 62" Rafter
K	14	1" x 5-1/2" x 45" Roof lattice
L	4	1-1/2" x 9-1/4" x 12" Seat braces
M1	2	1-1/2" x 5-1/2" x 37" Outer seat slats
M2	2	1-1/2" x 5-1/2" x 45" Inner seat slats
N1	4	1" x 2-11/16" x 80" Vertical side lattice
N2	4	1" x 2-11/16" x 37" Horizontal side lattice

MATERIALS LIST

ITEM	QTY.
6x6 x 10' treated posts and lintels	6
2x2 x 8' supports	2
2x4 x 8' treated beam flanges, ridge beam and ridge supports	2
2x4 x 10' braces, supports	6
2x6 x 8' treated seat slats	2
2x6 x 12' treated rafters	2
2x8 x 12' treated beam and brackets	1
2x10 x 8' treated seat braces	1
5/4x6 x 8' roof and side lattice	11
Simpson A-23 steel angles	4
Simpson TP39 tie plates	2
80-lb. bags of concrete mix	3
1/4" x 3-1/2" lag screws, washers	16
10d nails	2 lbs.
1-5/8" screws	2 lbs.
3" deck screws	2 lbs.

measurements between the posts are equal. Add additional braces if necessary.

Mix the cement for your posts in a tub or wheelbarrow. Mix no more than two bags at once and then mix more as needed. About three 80-lb. bags were used here, but the amount depends on the hole diameter and depth. Dump the concrete into each hole and then pack it around the posts with a scrap 2x2. Bring the concrete up to grade level **(Photo 4)** and then berm it slightly to keep water from collecting at the bottoms of the posts every time it rains.

1 CUT THE POST NOTCHES
Cut the 6x6s to length and then cut the notches in the tops with a circular saw. First cut lengthwise, then make the crosscut and finish the cut with your handsaw. Clean the bottom of each notch with a sharp chisel.

2 ATTACH CROSSTIES
Screw temporary 59-in.-long 2x4 crossties to the posts near the top and 16 in. up from the bottom.

LOCK THE LINTELS TOGETHER WITH 3-IN. SCREWS

Tenons and mortises are usually held together with dowel pins, but because this structure is exposed to the weather, it's best to lock them into place with 3-in. galvanized screws driven at angles from above. As you place each lintel, you may find that you'll need to either squeeze or separate the top ends of the posts a bit to get them to fall into place. This is because one or more of the posts may be slightly out of plumb. Screw in the brackets **(D)** as shown in **Photo 10**.

PRO TIP
You can cut the notches into the 6x6s **(Photo 1)** with a standard 7-1/4-in. circular saw and a sharp handsaw, but a rented 10-in. circular saw will make quick work of it. Be aware, however, that these saws are heavy and a bit awkward to handle. If you decide to use the smaller circular saw and handsaw, use the handsaw to get the extra depth you can't get with the circular saw and to clean up the notches.

TEMPORARY 2x2 HORIZONTAL SUPPORT

BRACE

DIAGONAL BRACE

REAR ASSEMBLY

FRONT ASSEMBLY

LEVELING SHIM

3 DROP POSTS IN HOLES

Tip and drop the rear assembly into the 16-in.-deep x 12-in.-dia. holes. Screw temporary supports to stakes and then to the assembly to plumb it. Once the rear assembly is level and plumb, drop the front assembly into the holes and screw it to the back assembly with temporary 2x2 horizontal supports top and bottom. Square the legs by measuring and making the diagonals equal between opposite legs.

MAKE THE CENTER BEAM FROM 2x4S AND A 2x8

Screw the 2x4 parts (E) to the center 2x8 (F) to create an I-beam that'll run from front to back and support the roof members. Get the beam positioned 1-1/2 in. from the outer edge of both front and rear lintels (Photo 11). Screw it into place with 3-in. screws.

Next cut the ridge supports and the ridge, and fasten them as shown in Photo 12. The top ridge has a 45-degree bevel on each top edge. Make a mark 7/8 in. down

4 POUR CONCRETE AROUND THE POSTS

Mix cement and pour it into each hole around the post. Let the concrete set for two days before continuing.

TENON

SIDE LINTEL (B)

(A)

(A)

5 ADD THE SIDE LINTELS

Remove the braces, cut the side lintel tenons with your circular saw and handsaw, and lower each lintel into the front and back post notches. Screw the joints together with 3-in. deck screws.

6 USE A 10-IN. SAW

It's easier to cut the notches in the front and back lintels with a 10-in. circular saw, which you can rent.

7 CLEAN UP THE NOTCHES

Break out the chips and clean the bottoms of the notches with a sharp chisel. Finish smoothing them with a coarse file.

8 INSTALL THE FRONT AND BACK LINTELS

Set the front and back lintels onto the post tops so they're flush with the posts. If needed, use a hammer and wood block to persuade them. Attach with 3-in. screws angled in from the top.

9 MAKE THE POST BRACKETS

Cut the post brackets with a jigsaw and then smooth the curves with your belt sander (80-grit works best).

10 ATTACH THE BRACKETS

Screw brackets to posts with 3-in. deck screws. Drill a pilot hole to avoid splitting the brackets.

11 ATTACH THE CENTER BEAM TO THE LINTELS

Cut and assemble the parts for the center beam, and then center and screw it to the front and back lintels.

from the top edge of the 2x4 ridge board on each side.

Temporarily nail the ridge to the sawhorse tops, then set your circular saw at a 45-degree bevel and cut along the line on one side. Then pull the nails and reposition the ridge so that you can cut the other side. Screw the ridge to the ridge supports, making sure it rests 3/4 in. down from the top of the ridge supports.

Cut the remaining roof parts and assemble them as shown in **Photos 13–15**.

SAND THE ARBOR TO REMOVE ROUGH EDGES

This isn't a fine piece of furniture, but you will have a few rough edges and corners that could give you splinters. Examine the corners and edges, and sand them smooth with 100-grit sandpaper. You may have to wait a week or more to sand if your treated wood is still moist; otherwise, it will just gum up your paper.

Once the project is dry to the touch, find an oil stain that suits your taste and brush it on. Have a rag or two handy so you can catch the drips and runs, and be sure to use drop cloths if you're staining over a walkway or other things you want to protect. One coat of stain should be sufficient. You'll need to plan to recoat your arbor in about three years.

12 SECURE THE RIDGE SUPPORT AND RIDGE
Screw the ridge support **(G)** to the center beam and then fasten the ridge to the support with 3-in. deck screws.

13 CUT AND NOTCH RAFTERS
Cut the rafters **(J)** as shown in **Figure A** using your jigsaw and circular saw. Complete one, then use it as a pattern for the rest.

14 ATTACH THE RAFTERS
Measure down 4 in. from the top of the ridge support, make a horizontal mark with your square and align the top edges of the rafters with your mark. Screw the rafters to the support. Then use Simpson A-23 angles on the back side of each bird's-mouth notch to connect the rafter to the beam.

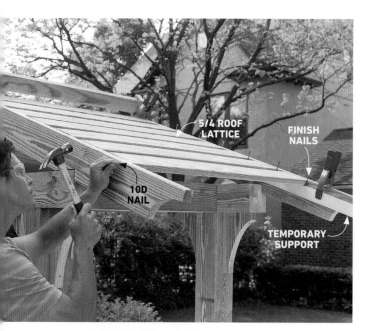

15 ADD THE ROOF LATTICE
Clamp a temporary support 1 in. down from the top of the rafter to guide the roof lattice board. Tap in nails every 7-1/4 in. Nail into the edge of the rafters with 10d casing nails.

16 ATTACH THE SEAT BRACES
Predrill and screw the seat braces to the inside faces of the four posts using 1/4 x 3-1/2-in. lag screws.

17 INSTALL THE SEAT SLATS
Fasten the 2x6 seat slats to the braces with 3-in. deck screws. Leave a 1/2-in. space between the boards and round over the outside edge of the inner slat with a 3-in. radius cut.

18 BUILD THE SIDE LATTICE
Rip 5/4x6 decking in half. Round over the edges with a block plane and sandpaper. Screw the vertical parts to the side lintels and back of the seat. Screw the horizontal parts to the inside face of the verticals with 1-5/8-in. deck screws.

WHAT IT TAKES

TIME
2 weeks

SKILL LEVEL
Advanced

TOOLS
Basic carpentry tools, circular saw, drill, power miter box, reciprocating saw, rolling scaffold system, staple gun, table saw

SCREEN PORCH

///

BEAT THE BUGS AND SPEND MORE TIME OUTDOORS THIS SUMMER.

A screen porch is a major improvement, but it's also a big project that could consume most of your spare time during the summer. To avoid that, we've kept this porch design simple. You can build it with standard dimensional lumber, and it doesn't require heavy beams or complex joints. The simple 2x4 walls are light and airy looking. Two horizontal bands of 2x4s, set 10 in. from the tops and bottoms of the walls, add a design element and stiffen the 2x4 framing enough to support the hand-built trusses. With this design, there's no need to precisely align the overhangs. And the exposed rafters and open soffit look great on many house styles.

We opted to use cedar for the decking and ceiling, but it's expensive. If you need to cut costs, you could save money without sacrificing quality by substituting treated decking for the floor or using tongue-and-groove pine on the ceiling.

Even though it's a large project, most of the construction is straightforward. If you have experience building decks or sheds, you'll be able to tackle this job with confidence. We'll show you the key steps for building the porch. Study the drawings and photos for more details.

You'll need a full set of basic carpentry tools, a circular saw and a drill to build this porch. In addition, a reciprocating saw, a table saw and a power miter box will make the job go quicker and give you better results. To reach high places safely and easily, we recommend renting a rolling scaffold system **(Photo 8)** for a month.

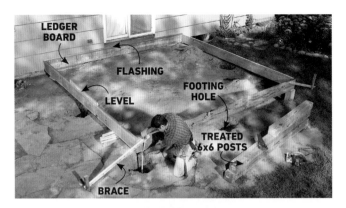

LEDGER BOARD

FLASHING

LEVEL

FOOTING HOLE

TREATED 6x6 POSTS

BRACE

1 ASSEMBLE THE PERIMETER JOISTS
Bolt the ledger to the house. Nail the perimeter joists together, and level and square the assembly. Measure, cut and set the 6x6 posts.

SECOND OUTSIDE JOIST

2 HANG THE JOISTS
Cut the joists to length and nail them into place with a pair of nails at each end. Then slide joist hangers onto the ends of each joist and nail the hangers.

PLAN IN ADVANCE TO AVOID HEADACHES

You can add this porch to almost any house, but attachment details may vary from what we show here. On most two-story houses, you won't have to worry about tying in to the roof, but you may have to situate the porch carefully to avoid covering a window. Our house roof sloped 5 in. per foot (a 5/12 slope) and extended 18 in. at the overhang. Your roof may vary from this, and the details of how the porch will tie in may vary as well.

If you're not sure how to neatly join the porch and house roofs, we recommend hiring an architect to help work out the details. Another option is to build a full-size mock-up of a roof truss out of inexpensive and lightweight 1x4s. Figure out where the top of the wall plate would be if you built the porch according to our plans **(Figures A–H)**. Then support the mocked-up truss at this height to see how the porch overhang meets the roof. If you don't like the way the overhangs intersect, adjust the level of the deck slightly, alter the wall height or change the width of the overhang.

Contact your local building inspections department to find out what's required to obtain a building permit. Start this process at least a month before you plan to build. This will allow enough time to work through any problems.

BUILD THE DECK SQUARE AND LEVEL

Start by marking the ledger board location on the house wall. We located the top of the ledger board 90 in. below the bottom of the soffit. On our house, this left a 6-in. step down from the patio door to the deck surface.

Remove the siding. Attach the ledger with 1/2 x 4-in. galvanized lag screws **(Figure D)**. Make sure the ledger is perfectly level. If it needs to attach to concrete, predrill holes and insert lead shield lag screw anchors before installing the lags. After mounting the ledger, use stakes and string lines to outline the deck frame according **Figure B** dimensions and mark the footing locations.

A few days before you plan to dig the footings, call 811 or visit call811.com to have underground utilities marked in the vicinity of the porch. Your local building department will specify how large and deep the footings should be for your climate and soil

SAW GUIDE

WALL SHEATHING

SLOT FOR WALL

3 CUT AWAY THE SIDING
Make a mark 1-5/8 in. from the deck on both sides. Then make another mark 5-1/8 in. inside the first mark. Draw plumb lines up from these marks and cut a 5-1/8-in. slot through the siding but not the sheathing.

conditions. Pour a concrete pad in the bottom of each footing hole after they've been inspected. Let the concrete set overnight.

Next, choose the six straightest 2x10s for the perimeter beams. Cut the 2x10s for the two side beams to length and nail the pairs together. Use 16d stainless steel or double-dipped galvanized nails for all of the joist framing and to attach the joist hangers to the ledger board. Rest one end of each side beam

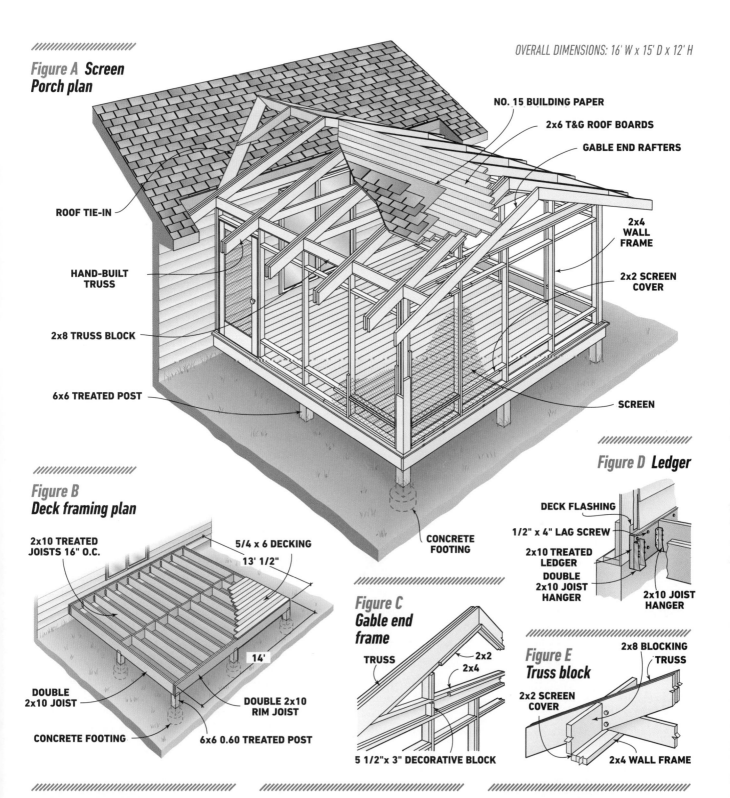

Figure A Screen Porch plan

- NO. 15 BUILDING PAPER
- 2x6 T&G ROOF BOARDS
- GABLE END RAFTERS
- ROOF TIE-IN
- 2x4 WALL FRAME
- HAND-BUILT TRUSS
- 2x2 SCREEN COVER
- 2x8 TRUSS BLOCK
- 6x6 TREATED POST
- SCREEN
- CONCRETE FOOTING

Figure B Deck framing plan

- 2x10 TREATED JOISTS 16" O.C.
- 5/4 x 6 DECKING
- 13' 1/2"
- 14'
- DOUBLE 2x10 JOIST
- DOUBLE 2x10 RIM JOIST
- CONCRETE FOOTING
- 6x6 0.60 TREATED POST

Figure C Gable end frame

- TRUSS
- 2x2
- 2x4
- 5 1/2"x 3" DECORATIVE BLOCK

Figure D Ledger

- DECK FLASHING
- 1/2" x 4" LAG SCREW
- 2x10 TREATED LEDGER
- DOUBLE 2x10 JOIST HANGER
- 2x10 JOIST HANGER

Figure E Truss block

- 2x8 BLOCKING TRUSS
- 2x2 SCREEN COVER
- 2x4 WALL FRAME

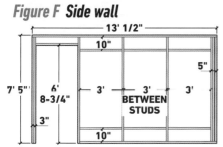

Figure F Side wall

- 13' 1/2"
- 10"
- 5"
- 7' 5"
- 6' 8-3/4"
- 3'
- 3'
- 3'
- BETWEEN STUDS
- 3"
- 10"

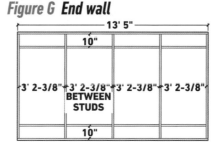

Figure G End wall

- 13' 5"
- 10"
- 3' 2-3/8" 3' 2-3/8" 3' 2-3/8" 3' 2-3/8"
- BETWEEN STUDS
- 10"

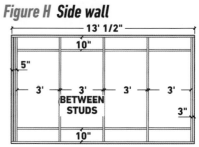

Figure H Side wall

- 13' 1/2"
- 10"
- 5"
- 3'
- 3'
- 3'
- 3'
- BETWEEN STUDS
- 3"
- 10"

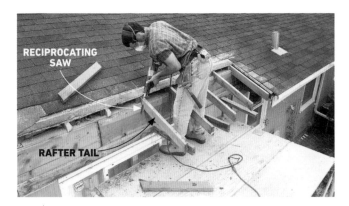

RECIPROCATING SAW

RAFTER TAIL

PLYWOOD SHEETS

4 CUT BACK THE OVERHANG
Mark the roof portion that overhangs the deck. Then cut the roof sheathing back even to the edge of the house and pry it off. Cut the rafter tails flush with the house wall.

5 ASSEMBLE THE TRUSSES
Screw two sheets of plywood to the deck and mark truss shapes on them **(Figure J)**. Screw stop blocks along each truss's rafter lines and crosstie line. Assemble the trusses.

in the double joist hangers and prop them up level with a stack of wood **(Photo 1)**. Nail through the joist hangers into the beams at the house to hold them in place. Then connect the opposite ends of the two beams at the front with a 2x10 cut to the same length as the ledger. Adjust the resulting frame until the diagonal measurements are equal. Brace the frame against stakes pounded into the ground to hold the frame square while you install the treated posts, joists and decking **(Photo 2)**. Sight along the outside rim joist occasionally, and adjust the lengths of the joists as needed to make sure the front rim joist is straight.

CUT AWAY THE OVERHANG AND SIDING TO MAKE WAY FOR THE PORCH
If your house has an overhang, you'll have to cut it back flush to allow the innermost truss to fit against the wall. Start by removing the soffit and fascia boards above the deck and several feet to each side of the deck. It's easier to remove extra soffit and fascia boards and then patch them back after the porch is done than to calculate cutoff points now.

After the soffit boards are removed, use a level to draw plumb lines from the house wall to the underside of the roof boards, in line with the outside edges of the porch. Mark the two points. Then drive a long screw or nail up through the roof boards at the two marks. Snap a chalk line between the nails, and remove the shingles below and about 6 in. above the line. Chalk a new line and remove nails along the line. Then saw along the line and pry off the roof boards **(Photo 4)**. Be sure to wear safety glasses and hearing protection when you're sawing. Finally, cut the rafter tails flush to the house wall.

You'll have to decide whether to cut a slot where each porch wall

meets the siding **(Photo 3)**. If your siding is stucco, brick or stone, you may want to butt the walls to the siding. **Photo 3** shows how to cut a slot for a wall. Set the saw blade just deep enough to cut through the siding only. Remove the siding. Waterproof the slot with No. 15 building paper.

PRIME AND PAINT THE PARTS AHEAD OF TIME
Prime and paint the truss parts, wall frame and screen stops before assembly. Prime the wood with a special stain-blocking primer such as Zinsser's oil-based Cover Stain. Then brush on a coat of acrylic exterior house paint. Make sure to prime every cut end as you work; otherwise, these

Figure J Truss details

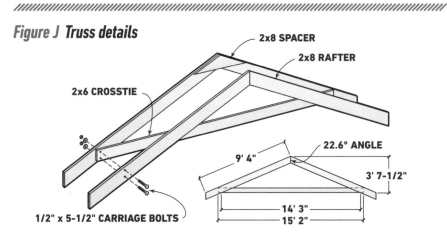

2x8 SPACER
2x8 RAFTER
2x6 CROSSTIE
22.6° ANGLE
9' 4"
3' 7-1/2"
14' 3"
15' 2"
1/2" x 5-1/2" CARRIAGE BOLTS

CROSSPIECE
CROSSPIECE SPACER
2-3/4" SCREWS

LEVEL
TEMPORARY DIAGONAL BRACE

6 ASSEMBLE THE WALL PARTS

Cut the wall parts and screw them together. Use the crosspieces as spacers to position the posts. Screw the crosspieces between the posts. Use a spacer block to get perfect alignment (inset).

7 INSTALL THE WALLS

Stand the walls, and screw the wall corners together. Align the walls flush to the deck and screw them down. Finally, plumb and brace them.

areas will absorb moisture and cause staining. We prefinished the roof boards with an oil finish.

CONSTRUCT A JIG TO ASSEMBLE THE ROOF TRUSSES

It's easiest to assemble the roof trusses first using the deck platform as a work surface. Screw two sheets of plywood to the decking and use the dimensions in **Figure J** to chalk lines indicating the tops of the rafters and the bottom of each 2x6 crosstie. Cut triangular blocks and screw them to the plywood to hold the rafters in alignment as you assemble the trusses (**Photo 5**). Cut a rafter using the dimensions in **Figure J** and use it as a pattern to mark the remaining

rafters. Place a pair of rafters in the jig and screw the tops together. Next, screw the 2x6 crosstie and 2x8 spacer to the pair of rafters. Keep the crosstie screws clear of the bolt hole locations. Complete each truss by screwing another pair of rafters on top. Check the ends and tops of the rafters as you assemble the trusses to make sure they're perfectly aligned. The trusses must be identical so that your roof boards and soffit trim will line up. Finally, elevate each truss on blocks of wood while you drill a pair of 1/2-in. holes into each end of the crosstie for the carriage bolts (**Figure J**). Run the 1/2 x 5-1/2-in. carriage bolts through the rafters and crosstie ends, and tighten the nuts.

FRAME THE WALLS ACCURATELY FOR SMOOTH ASSEMBLY

Because the wall framing for this porch is the finished surface, it's worth taking a little extra time to make the framing material look good. To do that, we chose the nicest cedar 2x6s we could find and then ripped them into 3-1/2-in. and 1-1/2-in. boards. This created sharp, clean edges. (We also ripped off all the factory rounded edges.)

Cut the studs and crosspieces to length, and screw the walls together (**Photo 6** and **Figures F–H**). We used a power miter saw for clean, square cuts, but a circular saw will work too. Use a crosspiece as a spacer when you're attaching the

MATERIALS LIST

ITEM	QTY.
80-lb. bags of cement mix	10
6x6 x 4' 0.60 treated posts	5
2x10 x 14' treated joists, blocking	17
5/4x6 x 14' cedar decking	28
2x4 x 14' cedar plates, crosspieces and gable end*	14
2x2 x 14' cedar screen covers*	14
2x4 x 8' cedar uprights*	21
2x2 x 8' cedar screen covers*	21
2x2 x 14' gable end frame	2
2x4 x 14' cedar (rip for sill)	2
2x4 x 16' cedar (rip for sill)	1
2x6 x 8' cedar corner boards	4
2x4 x 16' SPF (spruce, pine or fir) bracing	5
1x4 x 16' roof brace	1
2x8 x 12' SPF rafters	22

2x6 x 16' SPF crossties	5
2x8 x 16' SPF gussets	1
2x8 x 16' SPF truss blocking	2
2x8 x 8' SPF tie-in ridge	1
2x8 x 10' SPF tie-in plates	2
2x6 x 10' SPF tie-in rafters	1
1x2 x 8' SPF truss furring	2
2x10 x 14' SPF or cedar trim board	2
2x10 x 16' SPF or cedar trim board	1
4x8 x 3/4" CDX plywood	2
2x6 x 16' tongue-and-groove cedar	46
1x3 x 12' cedar trim	2
1x3 x 16' cedar trim	2
1x6 tongue-and-groove cedar	48 ft.
Ice and water membrane	300 s.f.
No. 15 building paper	400 s.f.
Shingles	400 s.f.
10' lengths of metal drip edge	5
10' lengths of valley flashing	3

4' aluminum screening	150 ft.
36" screen door	1
Post brackets	5
Double inverted-flange beam hangers	2
2x10 joist hangers	18
Joist hanger nails	5 lbs.
16d double-dipped galvanized nails	5 lbs.
12d galvanized box nails	5 lbs.
3/8" x 4" galvanized lag screws	22
2-5/8" deck screws	6 lbs.
3" weather-resistant deck screws	5 lbs.
1/2" x 5-1/2" galvanized carriage bolts, nuts and washers	20
1" galvanized roofing nails	10 lbs.
5/16" staples	1 box
2-1/2" screen door hinges	3
Screen door closer	1
Screen door latch	1
*Option: Rip these pieces from 2x6s.	

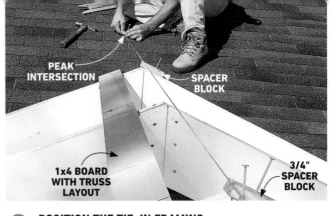

8 INSTALL THE TRUSSES

Stand a truss against the house. Plumb and brace it. Set the outside truss; screw a 1x4 brace to it. Stand and brace the remaining trusses. Toe-screw all the trusses to the top wall plate.

9 POSITION THE TIE-IN FRAMING

Stretch a mason's line across the peaks of the trusses to position the roof tie-in framing. Use 3/4-in.-thick spacer blocks to raise the line to the correct tie-in framing height.

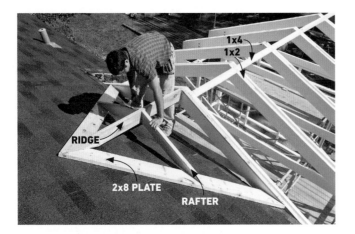

10 BUILD THE TIE-IN FRAMING

Cut 2x8 plates and nail them to the roof. Measure for the ridge. Cut the ridge and a pair of rafters, and nail them to the plates. The framing should be exactly 3/4 in. above the top of the trusses.

11 ATTACH THE ROOF BOARDS

Bevel the first roof board and nail it flush to the ends of the trusses. Nail the remaining tongue-and-groove roof boards to the trusses. Cut the last board on each side to fit at the peak.

studs to the top and bottom plates (**Photo 6**). Then cut a 10-in. spacer block to position the crosspieces for assembly (**Photo 6, inset**).

PLUMB AND BRACE THE WALLS

The key to standing the walls is to check and double-check along the way to make sure they're straight along their top and bottom plates, perfectly plumb and square, and securely braced (**Photo 7**).

Start by positioning the walls with their outside edges flush to the deck; screw them down. Next, screw the corners together, making sure the top plates of adjacent

walls are even with each other. Use a long level to plumb the walls while you attach diagonal braces to hold the walls in position (**Photo 7**). Leave the braces in place until after the roofing is complete.

Round up a couple of strong helpers to assist in setting the trusses. Start by marking the positions of the trusses on the top plate and on a 16-ft. 1x4 (you'll use the 1x4 to brace and position the tops of the trusses as you stand them up). The first truss simply butts to the house wall. The outermost truss aligns with the edge of the top plate, and the three interior trusses are centered

on the studs below. Set the first truss against the house, carefully centering it so that 1-1/2 in. of the bottom 2x6 overhangs the top wall plates on each side. Screw the truss to the top plate. Then use a straightedge and level to stand the truss perfectly plumb and brace it to the roof (**Photo 8**). Make sure this brace is securely screwed to the roof and the truss because the remaining trusses will be supported by this truss until the roof tie-in framing is complete.

Lift the remaining trusses onto the tops of the walls and rest the trusses on the first truss. Slowly and carefully slide the outermost

Figure K
Corner details

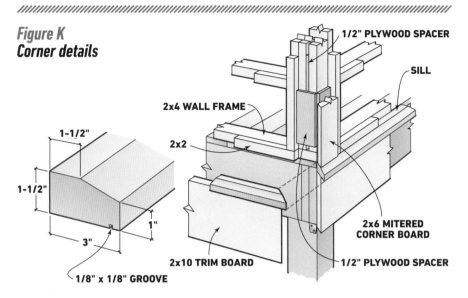

1-1/2"

1-1/2"

3"

1"

1/8" x 1/8" GROOVE

1/2" PLYWOOD SPACER

SILL

2x4 WALL FRAME

2x2

2x6 MITERED CORNER BOARD

2x10 TRIM BOARD

1/2" PLYWOOD SPACER

truss to the outside end of the porch. Align the marks on the 1x4 with the truss at the house and outermost truss, and screw the 1x4 to the trusses. Center the outermost truss on the walls and toe-screw it to the top plate of the walls. Stretch a string line between nails at the peaks of the two trusses. Align the remaining trusses with the string line and the marks on the 1x4 and top plates, and screw the trusses in.

LINE UP THE TIE-IN FRAMING WITH THE PORCH

One of the trickiest parts of the porch construction is joining the two roofs. The key is to extend lines from the new porch and mark where they intersect the existing roof. Do this by using a taut string line or a long, straight board. Remember to raise the tie-in framing on the existing house roof 3/4 in. above the porch framing to compensate for the difference in thickness of the 3/4-in. plywood and 1-1/2-in. roof boards **(Photo 12)**.

Start the tie-in framing by locating the point where the peak intersects the existing roof **(Photo 9)**. Then cut the 2x8 roof plates. If you're not good at calculating

roof angles, start by estimating the angles and cutting the plates an extra 6 in. long. Then set them in place, re-mark the angles and recut them until they fit. Screw the roof plates through the roof boards into the rafters below. Next, measure for the ridge, estimate the angle and cut it a little long. Trim the angle to fit, and screw the ridge rafter to the first truss and roof plates. Complete the tie-in by installing a pair of rafters **(Photo 10)**.

Photo 11 shows installation of the roof boards. Set your table saw or circular saw to 23 degrees, and rip a bevel on the groove edge of the first board. Align the board with the ends of the trusses and nail it with 16d galvanized nails. Install the remaining boards, making sure to snug the joints tight before nailing them. Let the boards hang out past the last truss to form the gable end overhang.

When you're done installing the roof boards, snap a chalk line at the gable (outer) end and saw the boards to leave an 18-in. overhang. Finish the gable end overhang by installing a pair of rafters and the 1x3 trim. Hold the gable end rafters tight to the underside of the cutoff roof boards and screw through the roof boards

12 COVER THE TIE-IN FRAMING
Use 3/4-in. plywood. Add blocking as needed to fill in the triangular areas between the existing roof and the new roof.

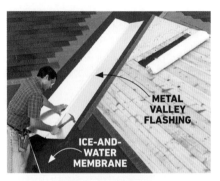

13 SHINGLE THE ROOF
Adhere an ice-and-water membrane barrier along the eaves and up the valleys. Then nail metal valley flashing over the top. Add No. 15 building paper, then shingles.

14 ADD TRIM BOARD AND SILL
Nail a 2x10 trim board over the outside joist, 1-1/2 in. below the top surface of the deck. Cut a 2x4 sill piece to width and bevel the top on a table saw. Miter the ends and nail the sill to the top of the 2x10 trim board.

15 INSTALL SCREENING

Cut lengths of screening and staple them to the framing. Start by tacking the two corners, making sure the screen is square to the opening. Then stretch the screen slightly and staple the sides, top and bottom. Place 1/4-in. staples every 3 in.

16 ADD TRIM TO SCREENING

Cut 2x2s to fit and screw them to the framing to cover the staples along all the edges. Frame and screen the outer gable end following **Figure C**.

to hold the rafters in place. Then cut 1x3 trim to cover the end grain of the roof boards. Extend the trim around the corners, and return it along the roof edge to the house.

PAY ATTENTION TO FLASHING AND ROOFING DETAILS

Building the tie-in framing on top of the existing shingles is a good way to keep the house waterproof as you construct the porch, but when it comes time to install the roofing, you'll have to cut the shingles along each of the valleys with a hook-blade utility knife. Then pry loose the cut shingles to make a wide path for the valley flashing **(Photos 12** and **13)**.

We won't go into roofing details here. In general, cover the eaves and valley with strips of waterproof membrane **(Photo 13)** and install the metal valley flashing. Place roofing nails about 12 in. apart along the edge of the metal valley. Cut a short piece of metal valley to complete the top on each side, overlapping it about 6 in. onto the long piece. Staple No. 15 building paper

to the remainder of the porch roof, starting at the bottom and working up. Overlap each row 3 in. on the one below. Follow the manufacturer's instructions for starting, overlaps and nail placement. Use 1-in.-long galvanized roofing nails to avoid nailing through the tongue-and-groove ceiling.

FINISH UP THE PORCH GABLE ENDS

Cover the triangular opening in the truss above the house wall by building a 2x2 frame and nailing 1x6 tongue-and-groove boards to the back. Then slide the frame into the opening and screw it into place. Fill the triangular space above the outside wall with a 2x4 frame **(Figure C)**. Staple screening to it and cover the screens with stops, just as with the walls below. Practice on scraps to make accurate patterns for the steep angles. Then transfer the angles to the actual framing members. You may have to cut these angles with a handsaw; they're too steep for a miter saw unless you build a special jig.

INSTALL THE SCREENS AND SCREEN DOOR

The charcoal aluminum screening we used is strong and long lasting, but you have to handle it carefully to avoid creases and dents. Carefully unroll the screen on a large work surface and cut lengths about 3 in. longer than you need. Reroll each piece and carry it to its location. **Photo 15** shows how to staple the screening to the framing. After you stretch and staple each section, cut off the excess screen with a sharp utility knife. Cover the edges with 2x2 trim pieces **(Photo 16)**. We screwed these on to allow for easy removal for future screen repairs.

If you use a wood door as we did, start by trimming it just enough to fit in the opening. Then set it in place and mark the door for final fitting. Use a sharp plane or belt sander to trim the door. You may have to repeat this process a few times to get a good fit. Nail 1/2 x 2-in. wood stops to the framing at the door opening. Then hang the door using galvanized or brass screen door hinges, and mount a latch and door closer.

WHAT IT TAKES

TIME	**SKILL LEVEL**
Varies	Advanced
TOOLS	
Varies	

BASEMENT FINISHING

REMODELING PROS GIVE SLICK SOLUTIONS.

Finishing a basement is a dream project for many DIYers. You can add beautiful living space and save thousands of dollars by doing the work yourself. But you're also guaranteed to run into unusual problems.

We met with pros from all the trades and asked how to solve some of the problems likely to be encountered when working in the basement. They gave us some great quick-fix tips as well as helpful strategies for conquering major hurdles. Our goal is to help you avoid unfortunate pitfalls and assist you in creating a comfortable, high-quality living space that will last a lifetime.

BOOST THE AIRFLOW

The coldest room in the basement is usually the room farthest from the furnace. Boost the airflow on long duct runs with an in-line duct fan. These fans are easy to install, but they do require a power supply. Some are hardwired and some plug into an outlet, but either way you'll need to leave an access to the junction box, which can be accomplished with a panel or a cover plate. In-line fans can run 24/7, they can be installed with an optional thermostat or they can be wired to turn on when the furnace fan turns on. You'll find a 6-in. fan like the one shown here at home centers, but 4-in. and 8-in. fans are also available.

BUILD WALLS ON THE FLOOR

If you have enough space, it's easier to build the walls on the floor and then tip them up into place. Build and install the perimeter walls first; then build the interior walls, stacking them in a corner as you go. Don't install interior walls until they've all been built so you won't frame yourself out of open floor space.

IN-LINE DUCT FAN

VENT PIPE

J-HOOK PIPE HANGER

DRAIN-PIPE

RUN PIPES BEHIND WALLS

It's a lot easier to run plumbing behind a new wall before the wall is nailed into place so you don't have to drill a bunch of holes through studs for the pipes.

Assemble the pipes and tape them to the foam insulation temporarily. Tip up the new wall and hang the pipes on studs before nailing the wall permanently into place. That will make it easier to attach the hangers. The downside of this method is that you will lose a little floor space.

HIDE THE SERVICE PANEL

Sometimes the electrical service panel is located on a wall that will eventually be in a finished living space. Instead of paying big bucks to move it, simply hang a photo, painting or other piece of art over it.

PLANE DOWN ANY SAGGING JOISTS

Hold a straightedge across joists to make sure they form a flat surface for the ceiling. If any joist sags 1/4 in. more than the one next to it, you'll end up with a noticeable bump in your basement ceiling. Snap a line from the bottom edge of one end of the joist to the other, and use a power plane to shave the board straight.

Before you start, make sure there are no nails or screws embedded in the wood. Make several passes, each shorter than the next, until you cut down to the line.

Power planers are loud, so be sure to wear hearing protection. You should also wear a dust mask and safety glasses. A planer can be rented if you don't own one. If you have several sagging joists or joists that bow upward, see "Form a Flat Ceiling."

STRAIGHTEN BOWED STUDS

Use a 4-ft. level or some other straightedge to check for bowed studs. Even if you personally checked every stud in every wall when you built it, new lumber can twist and bow as it dries.

If a stud is bowed in, fill the gap with drywall shims made from paperboard (think cereal boxes), as shown here. Start by using longer strips, then add layers of shorter strips until the gap is filled.

If the stud is bowed out and you can get to the back side of it, use a reciprocating saw to slice into the side that's bowed in. Cut far enough so the back side opens up when you press on the front side. Insert a shim in the kerf to hold the stud where you want it. Drive a nail through the separated area to keep the shim in place and to add a little strength to the stud.

DRYWALL SHIMS

BOWED IN

BOWED OUT

SHIM

ANEMOMETER

TEST THE AIRFLOW

It's a lot easier to troubleshoot poor airflow problems before you hang the drywall. Our pros recommend using an anemometer to check the airflow at each register first. This ABM-100 Smartphone Anemometer is made by AAB (it requires a phone with a headphone jack). After downloading the free app, all you do is answer a few simple questions about your ducts and hold your phone in front of the register box. The numbers, which tell volume and velocity, will depend on the size of the room and the size of the ducts.

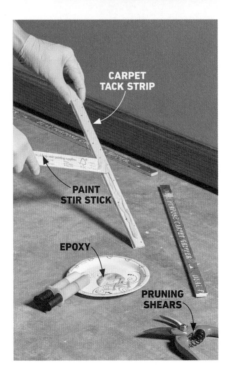

CARPET TACK STRIP

PAINT STIR STICK

EPOXY

PRUNING SHEARS

GLUE DOWN THE CARPET TACK STRIP

Ready to install carpet? You can buy a tack strip made specifically for concrete, but it's always hit-or-miss whether the nails in the strip will penetrate. For a guaranteed solid connection, pull the nails out of the strip and glue the strips down with epoxy.

It's rare for both the floor and the strips to be perfectly straight, so cut the strips into halves or thirds (pruning shears work well). It's easier to get smaller pieces to lie flat. Wipe the floor clean before you start. Construction adhesive will also work, but you'll need to wait a couple of days before installing the carpet.

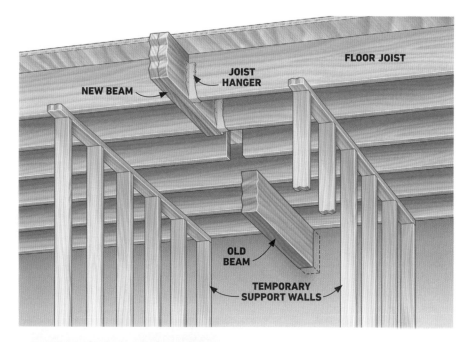

NEW BEAM · **JOIST HANGER** · **FLOOR JOIST** · **OLD BEAM** · **TEMPORARY SUPPORT WALLS**

RAISE A BEAM

Is that head-bonkingly-low beam stopping you from finishing your basement? You may be able to get the beam mostly out of the way by raising it to the same level as the floor joists. You'll need an engineer to tell you whether you can reuse the existing beam or need a bigger one. A lumberyard will be able to refer you to an engineer. Build temporary walls to support the joists before you remove the existing beam. Cut out a space in the joists for the new beam. Slide in the new beam and support each end. Finish by attaching the floor joists to the beam with joist hangers.

USE SCREWS ON HARD LUMBER

Old lumber gets hard and brittle, so nailing into it can be extremely frustrating, even for the pros. A pneumatic nail gun will penetrate old wood, but it also tends to split it. If you need to connect new walls to old existing walls or attach soffits to old floor joists, make sure you have some self-tapping construction screws on hand before you start. Screws work better on old wood and create a super strong connection. However, you may still have to predrill screw holes when you're working with really brittle wood.

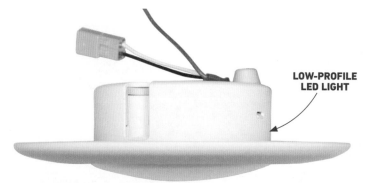

LOW-PROFILE LED LIGHT

INSTALL SKINNY LIGHTS

Many basements have low ceilings, which is why recessed lights work so well. But sometimes ducts, pipes or beams get in the way, leaving no room for the cans that house the lights. That's where LEDs come in. You can buy low-profile LED recessed lights that look like typical recessed lights but fit into standard round electrical boxes. They're sold at home centers and lighting stores.

FILL THE LOW SPOTS

No matter what type of finish flooring you choose, the floor underneath must be smooth and flat. You don't want to feel bumps under the carpet or hollow spots under plank flooring. And an uneven surface is a common cause of cracked tiles, especially large tiles. Holes deeper than 1 in. and large cracks need to be patched, but uneven sections and low spots can be filled with self-leveling underlayment.

Vacuum and then mop the floor first; let it dry, and then roll out the recommended primer. Unless you have less than 10 sq. ft. to fill, get a helper so you have one person to mix the underlayment and the other to work it around with a squeegee. Don't do the mixing right next to the area you're working on; the dust could interfere with adhesion.

SELF-LEVELING UNDERLAYMENT

FORM A FLAT CEILING

The bottom edges of floor joists are not always on the same plane, especially in older houses. You could spend two days trying to plane them all into alignment or you could sister new lumber onto the existing joists. Make sure the flooring system is structurally sound and doesn't need additional bracing before establishing the new basement ceiling height (search for "structural repairs" at familyhandyman.com).

Install a straight 2x4 on the worst joist, and use that as a reference to snap lines on walls. Nail on new, straight boards to the sides of the joists even with the lines on the wall. To work in large rooms, pull a string tight and use it as a guide. It's easier to avoid ducts, plumbing pipes and electrical wires if you nail up 2x4s. Use larger-dimension lumber if the joist spaces are relatively uncluttered and you want a stiffer floor on the first level.

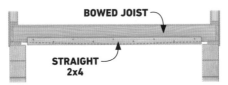

BOWED JOIST

STRAIGHT 2x4

CARPET PAD

DUCT TAPE

QUIET NOISY PIPES

If you've never spent much time in your unfinished basement (why would you?), you may have really noisy drainpipes and not even know it. Before you bury them behind drywall, have a helper run water, drain bathtubs, empty a washing machine and flush toilets while you hang out and listen for loud swooshing noises. If you do have a noisy pipe, wrap it with carpet padding. Use a quality duct tape or zip ties to hold it in place. If the home center near you doesn't sell carpet padding by the foot, stop by your local carpet store where you may be able to get some free scraps.

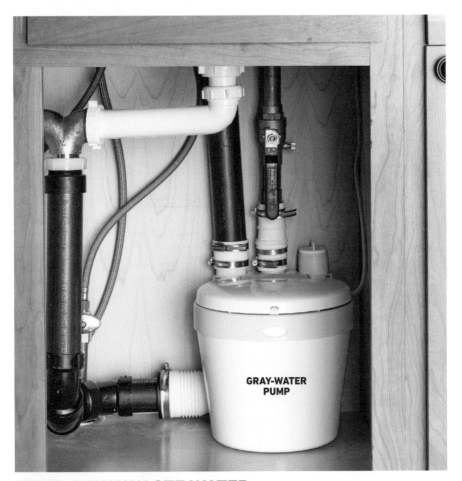

GRAY-WATER PUMP

PUMP AWAY WASTE WATER

Running supply lines to a basement wet bar is easy, but sometimes there's not an easy way to install a drainpipe. The solution: Get a gray-water pump and direct sink water wherever you want. These pumps are easy to install and small enough to fit inside a cabinet—they'll work for dishwashers and laundry sinks as well—but they're not made for solids, so always keep a strainer in the basin. The one shown here is a Saniswift made by Saniflo.

LET A PRO PLAN THE DUCTWORK

A poor heating and cooling design could seriously reduce the comfort of your new basement space, so don't guess at the number, size or placement of new ducts. Instead, hire a professional HVAC contractor to draw up a plan. A local contractor can supply you with a comprehensive custom plan and cost estimate.

WHAT IT TAKES

TIME	SKILL LEVEL
4 days	Advanced

TOOLS
Basic drywall and hand tools, drill driver, grout float, notched trowel, score-and-snap tile cutter or tile saw

SHOWER UPGRADES

BUILD A WATERPROOF TILED SHOWER AND THREE CONVENIENT BUILT-INS.

Showers used to be simple boxes since it was feared that any special architectural features could lead to a leak—and expensive repairs. But modern tiling materials, especially spreadable waterproof membranes, have put these fears to rest. Now you can add a bench or other structure with confidence and make showering more convenient and pleasant.

Here you'll learn how to build in three features: a bench, a shelf and an alcove. Included are the key planning steps and the waterproofing and special tiling techniques.

This project isn't for a tiling rookie. You should have some hands-on tiling experience before tackling a complex project like this one, but if you have

rudimentary framing skills, and have successfully tiled floors, backsplashes or simple shower surrounds, the advanced techniques shown here will enhance your skills.

Framing, sheathing and tiling a shower like this one will take you about four full days. The tiling alone will take two days. It pays to rent or buy a score-and-snap tile cutter if you're using 4 x 4-in. tiles like those shown. But if you're using natural stone or larger tiles and your tile layout requires lots of cuts, especially notching, rent a tile saw for a day. You can score and snap glass tile (small mosaic tiles only), but you'll break about every 10th tile—not a big deal if you plan the tile layout well and have to cut only a few.

PLAN THE LAYOUT

The first step in planning is to make sure you have enough space in your shower to add a bench. You'll need to leave at least 3 ft. of shower area so you can still move around. This bathroom originally had a 5-ft. tub, which was torn out and replaced with a 4-ft. shower base. This left a 1-ft. space for the bench and the overhead shelf at the end of the shower.

The key to an exceptional tile job is to plan the shower with the actual tile you intend to use. Use the tile to decide on exact dimensions and positions of benches, alcoves and even wall thicknesses so you can use whole tiles as much as possible and minimize cutting.

A foolproof method is to draw a full-scale template of each wall on rosin paper (**Figure A** and **Photo 1**). Be sure to draw the walls including the thickness of the backer board and any plywood that's needed, like on the bench seat. Then mark existing studs that outline alcove positions.

Next, lay the tile on the template to decide on the heights, widths and depths of shower features like benches, alcoves and shelves.

Try to wind up with full tiles outlining or covering those features whenever possible. Notice that this alcove is surrounded by full tiles. Those tiles determined the final position and size of the alcove. (It's easier to deal with cutting the tiles that cover the back of the alcove than the ones that border it.) Notice also that the exact height of the bench allowed for full tiles to be placed around it—no cutting needed.

Also adjust the thicknesses of walls and ledges for full tiles.

You can fur out the 2x4 wall with strips of 1/2-in. plywood so the glass tile will cap the end without any cutting. Choose framing and sheathing thicknesses to achieve the same aim with the shelf edge. If possible, plan the tile for the large wall expanses so that you'll have columns of similar-width tiles at both ends of each wall. Study **Figure A** to make all of this clear. You won't be able to avoid all tile cutting, of course. The goal is to simplify the tile work as much as possible. The more effort you put into planning the project, the easier it will be to install the tile. And you'll be rewarded with a first-class tile job.

Figure A
Shower Upgrades layout objectives

1. Shelf rests on full tile
2. Thickness matches face tile
3. Adjust alcove width for full field tiles
4. Plan height for full field tiles
5. Start alcove at top of tile row
6. Fur out as needed to avoid cutting tiles
7. Full tiles define bench height
8. Start with full tiles at base

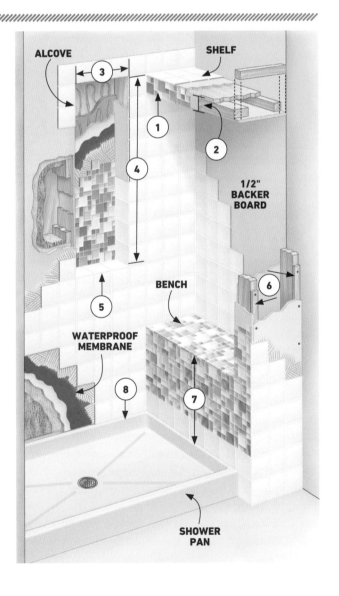

1 LAY OUT ON ROSIN PAPER
Plan the framing and tile layout for each wall on rosin paper cut to match the size of each wall.

FRAME THE SHOWER

If you have a space between the shower base and the wall, as shown in **Photo 2**, start by framing a continuous wall, floor to ceiling, between the base and the wall. If there's no framing behind the ceiling for anchoring the wall, just screw it to the drywall and then add a bead of construction adhesive around the ceiling plate. Next, frame in the alcove. Use your template to establish the height of the top and bottom, and then add blocking there. Fur out the side(s) if needed to accommodate the tile sizes within and/or surrounding the opening. If your alcove is on an outside wall, glue 1-in.-thick foam insulation against the outside sheathing using special foam adhesive.

Frame the bench with a 1/4-in. slope so water won't pool. Cap the bench with 3/4-in. plywood, screwing it with 1-5/8-in. screws. Lastly, add 2x6 blocking to anchor any shelves and any missing blocking at inside corners.

Cement board tile backer is commonly used for shower walls, but shown here is a drywall-type tile backer called DensShield. It's slightly more expensive than cement board but much easier to work with. You score it, snap it and cut it just like drywall.

Whatever material you use, anchor it with 1-1/4-in. cement board screws spaced every 4 in. at seams and every 6 in. elsewhere. If you have a premade shower base, keep the bottom row of backer board just above the lip. The tile will hang down over the lip to direct water into the base.

Next, lay a strip of alkali-resistant fiberglass mesh tape

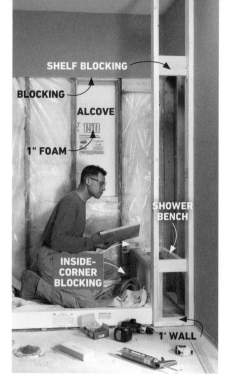

2 INSTALL BLOCKING

Add blocking to the top and bottom of the alcove, shimming the sides as needed, and fill in the back with foam board. Frame the end wall and then the bench.

over all seams and corners. It has adhesive on one side, but many brands don't stick very well. If you have trouble, use staples to hold it in place. Mix about a quart of thin-set mortar to the consistency of creamy peanut butter and trowel it over all the seams with a 6-in. putty knife. Try to avoid big buildups, which keep the tile from lying flat.

ADD WATERPROOFING MEMBRANE

Any area that will be exposed to lots of water should be coated with two coats of a brush-on waterproofing membrane (available at some home centers and all tile stores). Use disposable brushes and let the first coat dry thoroughly before recoating. The product shown goes on pink and dries to red when it's ready for a second coat (**Photos 4** and **5**). Focus on areas that will get the

3 TAPE AND MUD DRYWALL

Cover all seams and corners with fiberglass mesh tape. Embed the tape with a thin layer of thin-set.

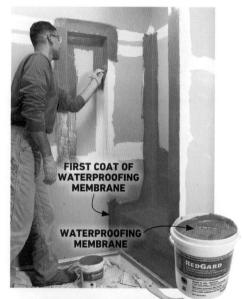

4 USE WATERPROOFING MEMBRANE

Coat water-prone areas with two coats of waterproofing membrane.

lion's share of showerhead water, especially corners, horizontal bench surfaces and recessed alcoves. For extra protection, also coat all the screw heads in areas

TILE THE ALCOVE AND WALL

Mix about a quart of thin-set at a time (follow the directions on the bag). Comb the thin-set onto the back of the alcove with a 1/4-in. notched trowel **(Photo 5)**. Then press the mosaic tile sections into the thin-set. Lightly tap the tiles with a grout float to embed each small tile evenly with its neighbors **(Photo 11)**. Look closely for thin-set that works its way out between the tiles. Wipe it off with a damp rag; it's hard to scrape off after it sets.

Use your template as a guide to snap exact tile layout lines on the wall. First establish lines for the rows of tiles surrounding the alcove. Then dry-stack and measure tiles to get an exact measurement from the bottom of the alcove to the top of the first row of tile. Draw a level line and screw a 1x2 ledger to the wall **(Photo 7)**. The ledger will ensure a perfectly straight bottom course of tiles and keep them from sliding down before the adhesive sets. (You'll remove the ledger and add the bottom row of tiles later, cutting them to height if needed.)

Begin setting the field (wall) tile following your layout lines. Dip tiles in water before sticking them to the wall so they form a better bond with the thin-set **(Photo 8)**. After you set each tile, give it a little rap with your fist to better embed it. Continually check the rows of tile for straightness. When

5 **TILE THE BACK OF THE ALCOVE**
Spread thin-set on the back of the alcove with a 1/4-in. notched trowel, and then embed the mosaic tile into the adhesive.

6 **FIX SAGGING TILES**
Support sagging tiles with shims or nails until the adhesive sets. Tamp tiles level with a grout float **(Photo 11)**.

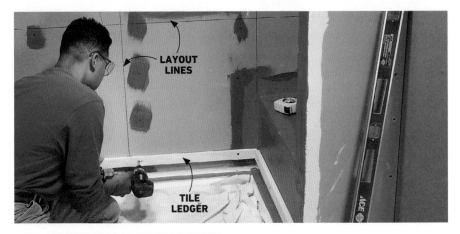

7 **MARK KEY WALL TILE LOCATIONS**
Lay out the critical tile lines with a chalk line. Screw a 1x2 ledger to the studs to support the second row of tiles.

8 **SET THE FIRST TILES**
Spread thin-set up to the horizontal layout line and around one corner of the alcove. Set those tiles and then continue tiling the wall, leaving out the row of tiles directly behind the shelf.

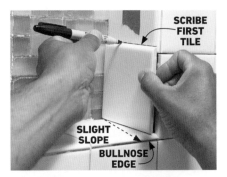

9 **TILE THE ALCOVE BOTTOM**
Tile the alcove bottom first with bullnose-edged tile, sloping it slightly toward the shower. Scribe the bottom side tiles to get the proper angle, then finish tiling the sides and top.

that'll get deluged. As with the thin-set, try to avoid creating big buildups.

the thin-set is still fresh, you can even out rows just by pushing a level against several tiles at once **(Photo 12)**. Finish tiling the wall, cutting the top row to fit as needed. Leave out the row of tiles where the shelf will rest **(Photo 8)**.

Tile the alcove sill, then the sides and top. For drainage, slightly slope the sill tiles toward the shower by piling on a little extra thin-set on the back side. Match the slope on the bottom side tiles by taping the bottom tile even with the row above it and scribing the angle with a full tile (see **Photo 9**).

TILE THE BENCH

Starting at one end, set the mosaic on the face of the bench. If there's a gap at the other end, cut the tile into strips and slightly expand the grout lines between rows **(Photo 10)**. Small variations in the width of the lines won't be noticeable. Lay tile on the seat to gauge the final grout line width between the seat and face tile. Add the seat tile, working from front to back, aligning grout lines with the face tile. Make sure the seat tile edges align with the surface of the face tile—they shouldn't be backset or overhanging. Finish tiling the rest of the field tile above the bench, stopping at the shelf **(Photo 12)**.

ADD THE SHELF

Build the shelf 1/8 in. narrower than the opening so you can tip it into place. Leave off the plywood top but add backer board to the underside. Rest the

TILE FRONT FIRST

10 DO THE BENCH FRONT FIRST
Cut the mosaic tiles into strips so you can adjust spacing to get a better fit with less cutting.

TILE LEDGER

12 CONTINUE WITH LARGE TILE
Add the rest of the field tile, stopping at the underside of the shelf. Align tile edges at outside corners with a straightedge.

shelf on the field tile; screw it to the blocking behind the backer board with two 3-in. screws at each side. Screw the 3/4-in. plywood top to the framing with 1-5/8-in. screws **(Photo 13)**. Add the backer board to the top and front edge. Tile the edge first, supporting it with a ledger screwed to the shelf's underside **(Photo 14)**. Remove the ledger after an hour or so, then finish tiling the underside, the top and the field tile above the shelf. Last, remove the 1x2 ledgers and add the bottom row of tiles.

GROUT FLOAT

11 TILE BENCH AND WALL END
Set mosaic tiles evenly into the thin-set on the bench and the end of the short wall using a grout float.

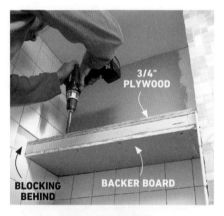

3/4" PLYWOOD

BLOCKING BEHIND **BACKER BOARD**

13 BUILD THE SHELF
Frame it, add backer board, rest it on the tile and screw it to the blocking. Add 3/4-in. plywood. Cover exposed wood with backer board.

SUPPORT LEDGER

14 TILE THE SHELF
Screw a support ledger to the shelf's underside (for the lip tile). Tile the underside, top and rest of the wall. The next day, grout the tile and caulk all inside corners.

MURPHY BED AND BOOKCASE

//

THIS IS A COZY EXTRA BED WHEN YOU NEED IT AND A HANDSOME SHOWPIECE WHEN YOU DON'T.

When William Lawrence Murphy filed patents for his space-saving bed in the early 1900s, he couldn't have known that he was solving a 21st-century problem: the need for a home office or hobby space along with extra sleeping space for guests. And although his invention has been improved over the last century, the basic idea is still brilliant.

Building a Murphy bed requires some precision— you have to install the hardware exactly according to the instructions. But the woodworking here is actually simpler than that required for many bookcases. There are no dadoes, mortises or tricky joints. And all the door frames are impostors. They look exactly like classic rail-and-stile frames, but each is just 1/4-in.-thick solid wood applied to plywood. The bookcases that flank the bed are optional.

WHAT IT TAKES

TIME	SKILL LEVEL
4 weekends	Advanced

TOOLS
Basic hand tools, brad nailer (or micro pinner), drill, jigsaw, miter saw, router with a pattern bit, table saw

DESIGNED TO PAMPER YOUR GUESTS

A Murphy bed can be super simple: Some are just upright boxes that contain a fold-down bed. But this is a deluxe version. Aside from the handsome design and storage spaces, we included some features to make guests comfortable, including pullout tables mounted on drawer slides, display lights inside the side cabinets that also act as night-lights, and a touch knob on the headboard so guests can switch on lights above the bed.

Lights built into the side cabinets aren't just decorative; they can act as night-lights.

A pullout tabletop on each side of the bed functions like a nightstand—the perfect spot to set a book or a cup of bedtime tea.

Just touch a knob on the headboard to operate the dimmable reading lights above the bed.

BEFORE YOU BUILD

Don't begin this project until you have the Murphy bed hardware on hand—you may have to alter our design slightly to suit different hardware. Also, be sure the room and its furniture will accommodate the bed. As built, ours protrudes 80 in. from the wall.

Most of the materials you'll need are available at home centers. The exceptions are the Murphy bed hardware and the 1/4-in.-thick solid oak. You can order the hardware (we bought ours at rockler.com) as well as the 1/4-in. hardwood (walllumber.com is one source). Or you can resaw thicker boards to make 1/4-in. hardwood.

BUILD THE BED FRAME

You will want a large assembly table for this project. A full sheet of 3/4-in. plywood screwed to a pair of sturdy sawhorses will do the trick. Otherwise, you'll need to work on the floor. Assemble the struts **(GGG)** from stock that's at least 1/4 in. too long and trim them to final length after assembly. Then join them to the frame sides **(HHH)** with screws **(Photo 1)**.

The rest of the bed frame is made from oak plywood **(G–J)**. The bed rails get 1-1/2-in. edging **(KK)** on the end and 3/4-in. edging on the top **(LL)**; see **Photo 2**. For the curves on the rails, create a plywood template **(Photo 3)**. Use

the template to position hardware holes **(Photo 4)** and to mark the curves. Rough-cut the curves with a jigsaw. Smooth the curves by sanding or by running a pattern router bit along the template.

Attach the head rail, foot rail and side rails to the inner bed frame. Cut two pieces of plywood for the bed face panels **(A)**. Trim one side and the top edge (where the foot of the bed will be) of each panel with 1/4-in. edging. Lay the two panels face down on your bench and butt the two pieces together so the hardwood edges are to the outside. Lay the assembled bed frame on top of the panels and attach with screws **(Photo 5)**.

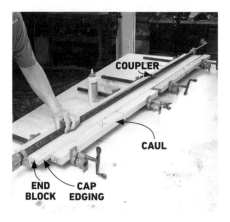

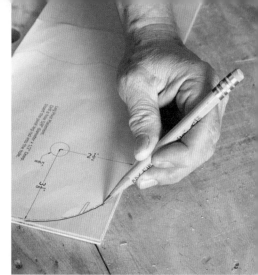

1 BUILD THE INNER FRAME

The inner frame forms the core of the fold-down bed frame. Assemble the L-shape struts with glue and brad nails. Then fasten them to the sides with screws.

2 ASSEMBLE THE SIDE RAIL

The side rails are built from plywood strips edged with solid wood. Clamp the top edging in place using cauls to distribute the pressure. You'll need a long clamp to attach the end block edging.

3 MAKE A TEMPLATE FOR THE SIDE RAILS

Trace along the paper template, then cut a template from 1/4-in. plywood. The plywood template serves double duty as a drilling guide and a routing pattern.

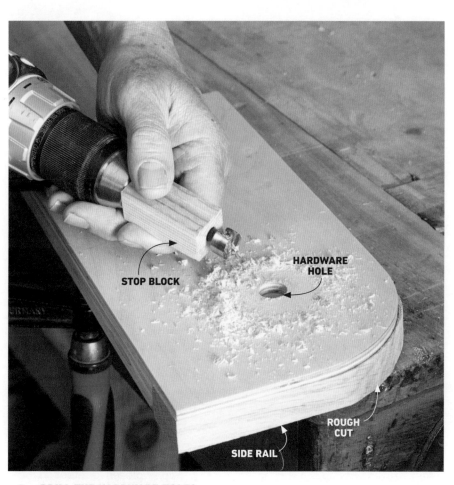

4 DRILL THE HARDWARE HOLES

The template positions the holes perfectly. A stop block ensures the correct depth. Rough-cut the curve, and then finish it with a router and a pattern bit guided by the template.

MURPHY BED HARDWARE

Hardware kits include folding legs that support the foot of the bed, pivots that allow the bed to swing down and, most important, gas pistons that operate like the pistons on a hatchback to lift most of the weight of the bed when you close it.

There are lots of online sources for Murphy bed hardware. We ordered ours from rockler.com and were impressed with both the quality of the hardware and the detailed instructions. Twin-, full- and queen-size kits are available. Aside from the hardware, we also purchased lighting kits designed especially for Murphy beds and bookcases.

With a helper, carefully turn over the bed frame assembly so it's face up on your bench. Rip the stock for the faux panels and drawers **(UU–BBB)** to width. Use 1/8-in. spacers to create gaps between the faux doors and drawers, and attach with glue and brads or pins **(Photo 6)**. Be sparing with the glue to avoid squeeze-out, which is tough to clean up. Go ahead and mount the pulls and knobs. Be careful to avoid the inner frame structure when placing your hardware. Remove all the hardware until after the cabinet is finished. Cut and fit the mattress supports **(X)**. Don't screw these into place until final assembly.

BUILD THE CABINETS

Cut the bed cabinet plywood parts **(B, C, E)**. Glue and clamp 3/4-in. hardwood edging **(MM)** on the bed cabinet verticals. Add 1/4-in. edging to the top and bottom edge of the headboard. Lay out and drill for the hardware. If you plan to add the light fixtures, now is the time to cut the 2-7/8-in.-dia. holes in the bed header panel. Follow the instructions in the kit. Screw and glue the mounting cleats **(JJJ)** to the ends of the header board. Add the header front and back **(BB)** according to the instructions. Wait to assemble the bed cabinet.

The bookcases on either side of the bed cabinet are assembled with the same screw and cleat system that is used for the bed cabinet. Cut the plywood parts **(F, N–R, U)** and cleat stock **(KKK–NNN)**. Then cut 1/4-in.-deep by 3/8-in.-wide rabbets along the back edges of the middle and bottom shelves and on the cabinet sides between the two shelves. Assemble the side cabinets with screws **(Photo 7)**.

Cut the face frame and pullout parts for the side cabinet **(DD–**

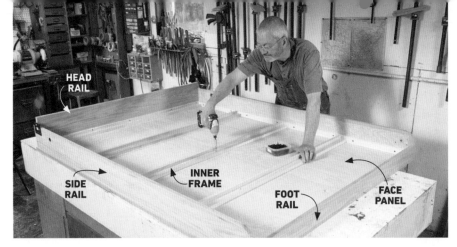

HEAD RAIL · SIDE RAIL · INNER FRAME · FOOT RAIL · FACE PANEL

5 ASSEMBLE THE BED FRAME
Connect the rails to the inner frame and mount the frame on the face panels. Cut and fit the plywood that will cover the inner frame, but don't fasten it yet. Flip the entire bed frame over so you can cover the face panels with false doors and drawers.

1/8" SPACER · DRAWER FRONT · DOOR FRAME · FACE PANEL

6 ADD FALSE DOORS AND DRAWERS
To dress up the face panels, glue on thin boards that form false door frames and drawer fronts. Position the parts with spacers and tack them in place. A brad nailer will work, but a micro pinner is best because the nail heads are tiny and barely distinguishable.

HH). Build the face frames using pocket screws or dowels. Then clamp and glue the face frames to the cabinets. Cut and glue the hardwood edge on the middle shelf. Then construct and mount the pullouts.

Add the faux panel frames **(CCC–EEE)** to the doors, and then mount the doors. If you're planning to use Euro-style cup hinges, be sure you order the hinges that are made for thick doors (see the rockler.com list on p. 255). Cut and fit the backs **(Y)**.

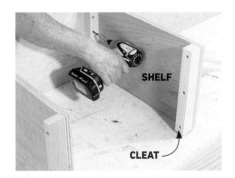

SHELF · CLEAT

7 BUILD THE SHELF UNITS
Join the fixed shelves to the side panels with screws and cleats. The other shelves rest on adjustable supports.

CONSTRUCT THE CABINET TOPS

Cut the parts for the three cabinet top and fascia assemblies (**D, K–M, S, T, V, W, PP–TT**). Assemble the fascia boxes with screws and glue. Cut and fit the 1/4-in. oak fascia with mitered corners (**Photo 8**). Trim the 1/2-in. plywood in the same manner. Attach the fascia trim board to the bottom of the fascia boxes, then screw the box down onto the top of each cabinet. If you're using lights, use a jigsaw to make a 4-in.-dia. hole in the bottom of each fascia trim board. Cut the top parts (**D, M, CC**). Cut a 15-degree bevel on the top trim on the table saw. Cut and miter the top trim to fit. Wait to attach the tops until installation. Drill ventilation holes for the lights in the cabinet tops.

INSTALLATION

You'll need at least one helper for this. The Murphy bed can be disassembled as much as you need to get the bed into the room. The only thing remaining that's large and cumbersome is the bed frame. If the bed has to wind its way through a narrow staircase or other obstacle, consider leaving off the middle drawer and the two horizontal dividers on the faux front. These are the elements that bridge the two face panels and once installed cannot be easily dismantled for moving. You can reassemble the bed frame in the room and add the drawer and horizontal dividers at that point.

Before installation, reattach all the bed hardware but leave off the bed stops, pulls and handles. Place a pad on the floor about 2 ft. in front of the wall where the bed will be mounted. Lay the bed frame face down on the pad, with the head of the frame toward the wall. Mount the bed cabinet sides

8 BUILD THE FASCIA BOXES
Build simple plywood boxes and cover them with 1/4-in.-thick solid wood. Tack the fascia into place, and use clamps and cauls to hold them flat.

9 ASSEMBLE THE BED CABINET
Place cardboard or padding on the floor, then assemble the cabinet and bed frame face down on it. Stand up the cabinet and add the header.

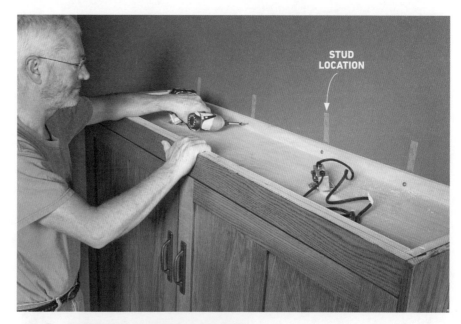

10 SCREW THE CABINET TO THE WALL
Make sure the cabinet is square—you may need to nudge the top slightly left or right to square it. Then drive at least three 3-in. screws into studs.

to the bed frame on the metal pivots. At this point, the cabinet verticals should also be face down alongside the bed frame. Attach the headboard using screws.

With a helper on the other side, lift the cabinet up to the vertical position. Be sure the leg support

is folded up before you lift the cabinet (**Photo 9**). Then attach the bed header assembly to the top. Next, lift the bed frame into the vertical position while your helper holds the cabinet. Be careful: Until the cabinet is attached to the wall, you need someone holding

Figure A **Murphy Bed**
OVERALL DIMENSIONS: 104" W x 82-3/4" H x 18-1/4" D

MATERIALS LIST

ITEM	QTY.
4' x 8' x 3/4" oak plywood	5
4' x 8' x 1/2" MDF	1
4' x 8' x 1/4" oak plywood	2
3/4" solid oak*	60 bd. ft.
Murphy Bed hardware kit	1
Light kits	2
Pulls	4
Backplates	4
Square knobs	5
100-lb. slides	2 pairs
Thick door frameless inset hinges	2 pairs
3/4" poplar	12 bd. ft.

*Includes material for resawing into 1/4"-thick stock.

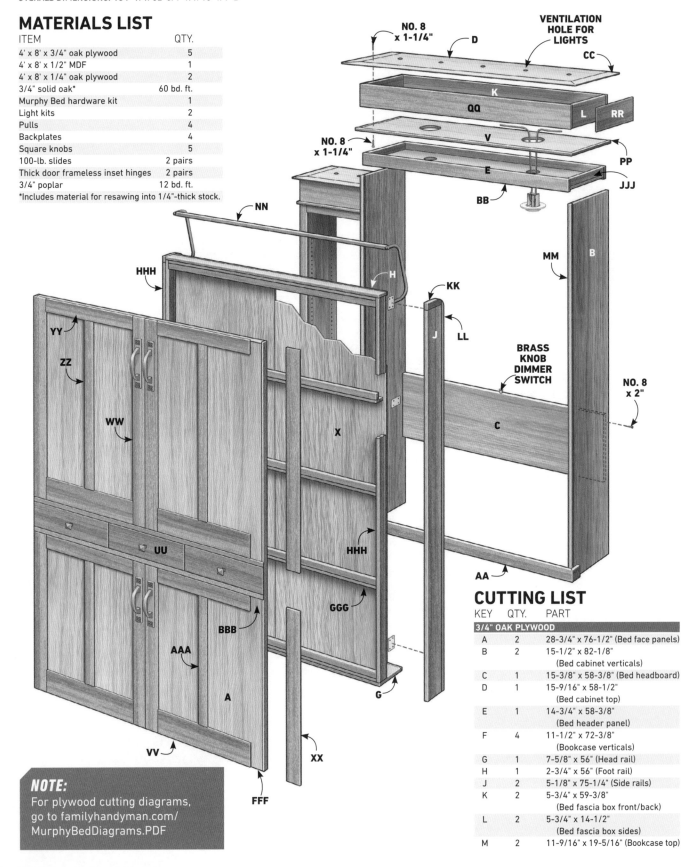

NO. 8 x 1-1/4"

VENTILATION HOLE FOR LIGHTS

BRASS KNOB DIMMER SWITCH

NO. 8 x 2"

NO. 8 x 1-1/4"

NOTE:
For plywood cutting diagrams, go to familyhandyman.com/MurphyBedDiagrams.PDF

CUTTING LIST

KEY	QTY.	PART
3/4" OAK PLYWOOD		
A	2	28-3/4" x 76-1/2" (Bed face panels)
B	2	15-1/2" x 82-1/8" (Bed cabinet verticals)
C	1	15-3/8" x 58-3/8" (Bed headboard)
D	1	15-9/16" x 58-1/2" (Bed cabinet top)
E	1	14-3/4" x 58-3/8" (Bed header panel)
F	4	11-1/2" x 72-3/8" (Bookcase verticals)
G	1	7-5/8" x 56" (Head rail)
H	1	2-3/4" x 56" (Foot rail)
J	2	5-1/8" x 75-1/4" (Side rails)
K	2	5-3/4" x 59-3/8" (Bed fascia box front/back)
L	2	5-3/4" x 14-1/2" (Bed fascia box sides)
M	2	11-9/16" x 19-5/16" (Bookcase top)

N	4	11-1/2" x 18-1/2" (Bookcase top/bottom shelves)
P	2	11-1/4" x 18-1/2" (Bookcase middle shelves)
Q	2	11-1/4" x 13-1/2" (Pullouts)
R	4	10-1/2" x 18-1/4" (Adjustable shelves)
S	4	4-3/4" x 19-3/4" (Bookcase fascia box front/back)
T	4	4-3/4" x 10-1/2" (Bookcase fascia box sides)
U	2	15-3/8" x 16-1/4" (Doors)
1/2" BIRCH PLYWOOD OR MDF		
V	1	16" x 59-3/8" (Bed fascia trim boards)
W	2	12" x 19-3/4" (Bookcase fascia trim boards)
1/4" OAK PLYWOOD		
X	2	28" x 75" (Mattress supports)
Y	2	19-1/4" x 19-3/8" (Bookcase back)
3/4" OAK		
Z	1	5-3/4" x 60" (Bookcase base)
AA	1	2-3/8" x 80" (Bed base)
BB	2	2-3/4" x 58-3/8" (Bed header front/back)
CC	1	2-3/4" x 182" (Top trim)
DD	4	2" x 72-3/8" (Face frame stiles)
EE	4	2" x 16" (Face frame rails)
FF	2	3/4" x 16" (Middle shelf edges)
GG	2	1-3/4" x 15-7/8" (Pullout fronts)
HH	4	1-1/2" x 11" (Pullout sides)
JJ	4	1-1/4" x 18-3/8" (Adjustable shelf trim)
KK	2	1-1/2" x 5-1/8" (Side rail end trim)
LL	2	3/4" x 76-1/2" (Side rail edges)
MM	2	3/4" x 82-1/8" (Bed cabinet edges)
NN	1	3/4" x 54-1/4" (Leg support rail)
PP	1	1/2" x 168" (Fascia trim)
1/4" OAK		
QQ	1	5-3/4" x 59-7/8" (Bed fascia front)
RR	2	5-3/4" x 16-1/4" (Bed fascia sides)
SS	2	4-3/4" x 20" (Bookcase fascia fronts)
TT	2	4-3/4" x 12-1/4" (Bookcase fascia sides)
UU	3	4-3/4" x 19-1/4" (Bed panel drawer fronts)
VV	4	4" x 22-15/16" (Bed panel bottom rails)
WW	4	3" x 40" (Bed panel upper stiles)
XX	4	3" x 30" (Bed panel lower stiles)
YY	4	2-1/2" x 22-15/16" (Bed panel upper rails)
ZZ	2	2" x 33-1/4" (Bed panel upper mullions)
AAA	2	2" x 23-1/2" (Bed panel lower mullions)
BBB	2	3/4" x 58" (Bed panel horizontal dividers)
CCC	4	2" x 16-1/2" (Door panel stiles)
DDD	2	2-1/2" x 12" (Door panel bottom rails)
EEE	2	2" x 12" (Door panel top rails)
FFF	1	3/4" x 600" (Edging)
3/4" POPLAR		
GGG	10	1-1/2" x 54-1/2" (Bed frame struts)
HHH	2	1-1/2" x 75" (Bed frame sides)
JJJ	2	1-1/2" x 14-3/4" (Bed header mounting cleats)
KKK	4	1-1/2" x 11-1/2" (Bottom shelf cleats)
LLL	4	1-1/4" x 11-1/4" (Middle shelf cleats)
MMM	2	1" x 17" (Top shelf front cleats)
NNN	4	1" x 11-1/2" (Top shelf side cleats)

the bed in place and keeping the cabinet steady.

With the bed cabinet and frame vertical, it's time to attach the gas springs. Snap the ends of the springs onto the ball stud plates on the bed frame and the cabinet verticals. The springs are marked with a "This End Up" sign; follow the directions carefully. Attach the bed stops from inside the cabinet. With the bed held in place by the gas springs, go ahead and move the cabinet up against the wall. Mark the stud locations just above the bed header and attach it with screws **(Photo 10)**.

Slide the bookcases into position, then attach them to the cabinet. Remount the crowns, and then add the tops **(Photo 11)**. Next, pull the frame down and swing the leg supports to the floor. The bed will want to close back up, so you'll need to add some weight to hold it down while you attach the two 1/4-in. plywood mattress supports to the inner frame. Finally, add the elastic retaining straps, and set the mattress in place.

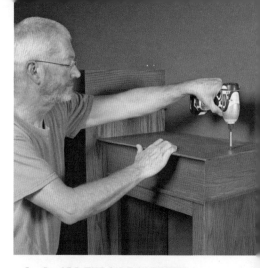

11 ADD THE SIDE CABINETS
Screw the side cabinets to the bed cabinet, hiding the screws behind the face frames and under the shelves. Fasten the cabinet tops and your Murphy bed is ready for guests.

We ordered the following supplies from rockler.com:

- Deluxe Murphy Bed Hardware Kit, Item No. 46025
- 96mm Arts & Crafts Pulls (2), Item No. 10988
- 96mm Arts & Crafts Backplates (2), Item No. 11014
- 3" Arts & Crafts Pulls (2), Item No. 10962
- 3" Arts & Crafts Backplates (2), Item No. 11001
- 1-1/4" Square Arts & Crafts Knobs (5), Item No. 10910
- 10" Series 757 100-lb. Slides (2 pairs), Item No. 48386
- 95° Thick Door Frameless Inset Hinges (2 pairs), Item No. 55879

Figure B Bookcase

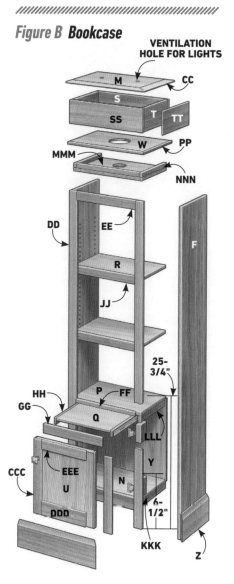

VENTILATION HOLE FOR LIGHTS

CLASSIC BUILT-IN BOOKCASE

NO COMPLEX WOOD JOINTS, NO TRICKY TECHNIQUES—YOU SIMPLY GLUE, SCREW AND NAIL ALL THE PARTS TOGETHER.

This handsome bookcase features the classic elements you may find in an old library—paneled wood, curved brackets, column-like partitions and crown molding. You can build the project as shown from our clear drawings and step-by-step photos, or use these techniques to modify the dimensions to fit the bookcase into your own space requirements. The partitions in **Photos 8** and **9** can be placed wall to wall as shown, or they can stop halfway into a room and then finish on the open side. Another option would be to extend the length by building additional partitions and shelves.

The bookcase is made from hardwood plywood, 2x6s, hardwood boards and standard moldings available at home centers and lumberyards. We

WHAT IT TAKES	
TIME 25-30 hours	**SKILL LEVEL** Advanced
TOOLS Basic hand tools, 18-gauge air nailer, circular saw, drill driver, jigsaw, level, power miter saw, random orbital sander, table saw	

Figure A Bookcase details

OVERALL DIMENSIONS: 95' H x 16" D x 142-3/4" W

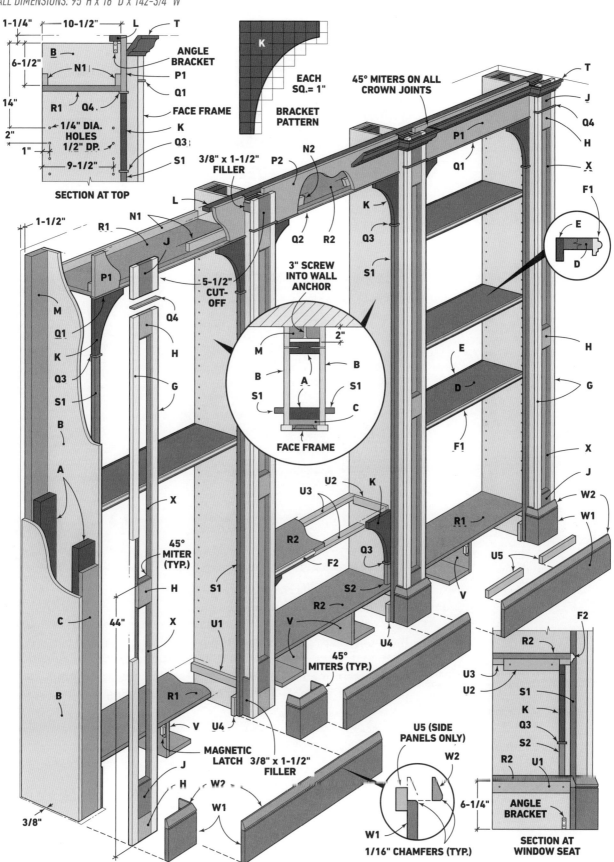

SECTION AT TOP

1-1/4" 10-1/2" L T
ANGLE BRACKET
6-1/2" N1 P1
Q1
14" R1 Q4 FACE FRAME
1/4" DIA. HOLES 1/2" DP. K
2" Q3
1" S1
9-1/2"

EACH SQ.= 1"
BRACKET PATTERN

45° MITERS ON ALL CROWN JOINTS

3/8" x 1-1/2" FILLER
P2 N2
L K
Q2 R2 Q3
S1

5-1/2" CUT-OFF
3" SCREW INTO WALL ANCHOR

1-1/2" R1 N1
J P1
M Q4
Q1 H
K G
Q3
S1
B
A
C
3/8"

44" H X
X
45° MITER (TYP.)
S1
U1

MAGNETIC LATCH 3/8" x 1-1/2" FILLER

2"
M
B B
A
S1 S1
C
FACE FRAME

U2
U3 K
R2
Q3
F2
S2
R2
V
V U4
45° MITERS (TYP.)

T
J
Q4
H
X
F1

E
D

P1 Q1 X
F1

H
G

E
D
F1

X
J
W2
W1
U5
V

W2
W1
U5 (SIDE PANELS ONLY)
W1
1/16" CHAMFERS (TYP.)

F2
R2
U3
U2 S1
K
Q3
S2
R2 U1
6-1/4" ANGLE BRACKET
SECTION AT WINDOW SEAT

H W?
W1

CUTTING LIST

KEY	QTY.	PART
A	8	1-1/2" x 4" x 95" center partition struts
B	8	3/4" x 12-3/4" x 95" plywood partition sides
C	4	3/4" x 4" x 95" plywood partition fronts
D	12	3/4" x 9-3/8" x 39" reinforced plywood shelves*
E	12	1/2" x 1-1/2" x 39" hardwood rear shelf supports*
F1	12	5/8" x 1-1/8" x 39" decorative edge molding*
F2	1	5/8" x 1-1/8" x 39-3/4" decorative edge molding*
G	8	3/4" x 1-1/2" x 95-1/2" partition face stiles
H	12	3/4" x 4" x 3-1/4" partition rails
J	8	3/4" x 5-1/2" x 3-1/4" partition rails
K	8	3/4" x 7-1/4" x 10" curved brackets
L	1	3/4" x 1-1/2" x 143-1/2" ceiling cleat*
M	4	1-1/2" x 4" x 95" wall cleats
N1	4	3/4" x 1-1/2" x 39-1/4" soffit cleats*
N2	2	3/4" x 1-1/2" x 42-1/4" soffit cleats*
P1	2	3/4" x 7-1/4" x 39-1/2" front fascia*
P2	1	3/4" x 7-1/4" x 42-1/4" front fascia*
Q1	2	1/4" x 1-1/4" x 39-1/4" left and right upper fillets
Q2	1	1/4" x 1-1/4" x 42-1/4" upper center fillets
Q3	8	1/4" x 1-1/4" x 1-1/2" under-bracket fillets
Q4	4	1/4" x 1" x 6-3/4" face frame fillets
R1	4	3/4" x 10-1/2" x 39-1/4" side base shelf and soffit (plywood)
R2	3	3/4" x 10-1/2" x 42-1/4" center base shelf, soffit and bench (plywood)
S1	6	3/4" x 1-1/4" x 78-1/4" bracket support molding
S2	2	3/4" x 1-1/4" x 3-1/4" seat bracket support molding
T	20 ft.	3-1/4" hardwood crown molding
U1	6	3/4" x 1-1/2" x 10-1/2" side and center base shelf supports
U2	2	3/4" x 1-1/2" x 7-1/2" side bench supports
U3	2	3/4" x 1-1/2" x 42-1/4" bench cleats (glued from underneath)
U4	6	3/4" x 1-1/2" x 4-3/4" base section stops
U5	4	3/4" x 1-1/2" x 12" side panel base cleats (glue to W1 and W2)
V	6	3/4" x 6-1/4" x 10-1/2" plywood center base shelf supports
W1	20 ft.	3/4" x 5-1/2" (1x6 base molding)*
W2	20 ft.	3/4" x 1-1/2" (bifold stop molding as base cap)*
X	30 ft.	1/2" quarter-round face frame trim*

* Cut pieces to fit

1 TAKE ROOM MEASUREMENTS

Measure the width of your room and the height of the ceiling. Also check the window placement. Our room was almost 12 ft. wide with an 8-ft. ceiling, and the window was very close to the center. If there's no window, just build shelves into the center section.

2 ASSEMBLE THE PARTITIONS

Glue and nail the plywood sides **(B)** to straight 2x6s **(A)** ripped to 4 in. wide. Leave a 2-in. gap at the back and a 3/4-in. gap in the front. Next, glue and nail the front 3/4-in. plywood piece **(C)** so it's flush with the sides. Make all four partitions exactly alike and be sure the pieces are all cut 1-1/4 in. less than your ceiling height. Let the glue dry for a couple of hours before assembling.

chose birch boards and plywood along with maple moldings and then used a gel stain to give the project a cherry wood appearance. You'll notice we also rubbed away stain to create highlights for an antique look. You can preassemble nearly all the parts of this modular-type project in your garage or shop and carry them into your room for assembly.

SANDWICH-STYLE PARTITIONS ARE KEY

Cut your plywood lengthwise to the dimensions in the Cutting

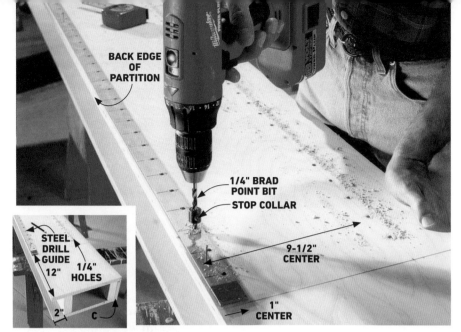

BACK EDGE OF PARTITION

1/4" BRAD POINT BIT

STOP COLLAR

9-1/2" CENTER

1" CENTER

STEEL DRILL GUIDE **1/4" HOLES** **12"**

2" **C**

3 DRILL HOLES FOR SHELF PINS

Measure 12 in. down from the top of your partition and drill 1/4-in. holes, 1/2 in. deep, every 2 in. to accept the shelf pins. Ensure accuracy by making a drill guide from a steel strip, available at a hardware store. Just mark and drill the strip with a 1/4-in. twist bit and you've got a great jig you can use for future projects. Mark one end with paint so you always know which end goes up, then drill three 1/16-in. holes evenly along the length so you can use brad nails to attach the guide to your work surface.

F

D

E

4 ADD HARDWOOD STRIPS AND DECORATIVE MOLDING

Glue and nail 1/2-in.-thick hardwood strips (**E**) on the backsides of the shelves (**D**) and 1-1/8 in. decorative molding (**F**) to the front. An 18-gauge air nailer is worth renting for this task. You can nail the molding as you align it without the possibility of it shifting, not to mention you'll be done in less than a tenth of the time required for ordinary nailing.

List to make your exterior partition skin. Equip your circular saw with a new thin-kerf 40-tooth carbide blade. Use a long cutting guide (available at home centers) clamped to the plywood sheet to guide your saw for straight cuts. Also rip straight 8-ft. 2x6s to 4-in. widths with your table saw for the core of each partition. **NOTE:** Buy your 2x6s about a week in advance, and bring them inside to dry out and adjust. You may have some that will warp or twist as they adjust to the dry environment inside the house, so buy a couple of extra pieces just in case.

Assemble the partitions on a flat surface as shown in **Photo 2** and then set them aside for the glue to dry. Once the glue is dry, drill the 1/4-in. holes for the shelf pins as shown in **Photo 3**.

Notice the 2-in. gap at the back of the sandwich. This is crucial. It'll allow you to slip the partitions over cleats attached to the wall with room to spare, as shown in **Photo 7**.

TIP: The extra 1/2 in. of space between the cleat on the wall and the recess in the partition is convenient for running wiring for low-voltage lights in the soffits of the bookcase. We were just storing books, so the lighting wasn't necessary.

PREASSEMBLE THE SHELVES

While the glue is drying on the partitions, it's a good idea to get

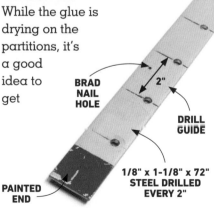

BRAD NAIL HOLE

2"

DRILL GUIDE

1/8" x 1-1/8" x 72" STEEL DRILLED EVERY 2"

PAINTED END

FACE FRAME DETAIL

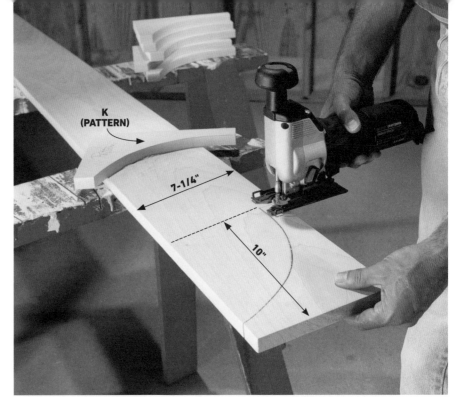

K (PATTERN)

7-1/4"

10"

5 CUT THE BRACKETS

Trace the brackets **(K)** from the dimensional grid in **Figure A** and cut them out carefully with a jigsaw. Sand the curve smooth with 100-grit sandpaper followed by 150-grit sandpaper.

other parts cut and ready to assemble. Start with the shelves. From measuring the room in **Photo 1**, you'll have a good sense of the shelf length. Make the shelves all about an inch or more too long, and trim them later for an exact fit. By doing this, you don't have to fuss with perfectly aligning the moldings on the fronts and backs of the shelves as you glue and nail them together. Also, save time by forming an assembly line.

NOTE: Don't make these shelves more than 42 in. long or they may noticeably sag. Our shelves are 39 in. long.

The 1/2-in. anti-sag cleat glued to the rear of the shelf is not a stock item, but you can make it on a table saw. First cut 1-1/2-in.-wide strips from a wider board. Then tip this piece on end and cut the 3/4-in. width down to 1/2 in. This step is called resawing and can be tricky because the workpiece gets narrow. Use a push stick to keep your fingers clear of the blade. If

6 ATTACH THE STILES TO THE RAILS

Cut the long stiles **(G)** of the face frame and nail them with 8d finish nails to the short rails **(H** and **J)**. Use a drill bit to make a pilot hole slightly smaller than the diameter of the nail. Set the nails and fill the recesses with matching putty later.

MATERIALS LIST

ITEM	QTY.
3/4" birch plywood	4
1x8 x 8' birch (fascia and bracket material)	2
1x6 x 10' birch base molding	2
1x6 x 10' birch (face frame parts)	4
1x6 x 7' birch bracket supports and fillet material	3
Bifold stop	20'
1/2" birch quarter-round	30'
3-1/4" birch crown molding	20'
1x2 pine cleat strips	24'
5/8" x 1-1/8" x 8' decra molding	7
1/4" steel shelf pins	48
3" deck screws	2 dozen
2" deck screws	2 lbs.
1-1/2" 18-gauge air nails	1 box
8d galvanized casing nails	1 lb.
Carpenter's glue	1 pt.
Magnetic cabinet latches	2

this is beyond your adventurous spirit, have the lumberyard folks cut it for you for a nominal fee and stick to the fun parts of the project. And don't forget, while you're resawing (or having someone else do it), make the **Q** parts.

TRACE THE CURVED BRACKETS

The partition faces are similar to super-narrow face frames on cabinets. Because they're so narrow and don't have to support weight as real cabinet face frames do, you can just nail the face frame parts together as shown in **Photo 6** and **Figure A**. Once they're nailed, you'll need to sand the fronts and backs completely flat to get the frames to lie nicely against the partition fronts. The tool of choice for this is a random orbital sander. You can start with 80-grit paper and finish with 150-grit.

ATTACH THE PARTITION CLEATS TO YOUR WALL

We're assuming you have wood or tile floors, but if you have carpeting, you'll need to roll it back, remove the tackless strip, and then stretch and trim it later. We're also assuming that you have drywall over wood studs, but if you don't, use the right anchor for your wall,

M — L

LEAVE 1-1/8" SPACE FROM SIDE WALL

4' LEVEL 1-1/2" x 4" WALL CLEAT

7 ADD WALL CLEATS

Fasten the wall cleats to the drywall with wall anchors and construction adhesive. We used E-Z Ancor with 3-in. No. 8 deck screws. Use a level to get the first cleat perfectly plumb, then a tape measure for the rest.

L

8 FASTEN THE PARTITIONS

Tip the column partitions into place and slip them over the wall cleats. Fasten the partitions to the cleats with 2-in. screws (3 and 6 in. from the ceiling and the floor, respectively). The screws will be hidden later by the upper soffit and lower base of the bookcase. Use a framing square to make sure the partitions are square to the back wall, then fasten them to the ceiling cleat with 2-in. steel angle supports.

L — P — N

ANGLE BRACKET

9 ADD THE FASCIA

Cut each fascia piece **(P)** to fit snugly between the partitions. Cut and fit the cleats **(N)** as well. Screw the fascia to the ceiling cleat with 1-5/8-in. wood or deck screws.

BRACKET AND UPPER PARTITION

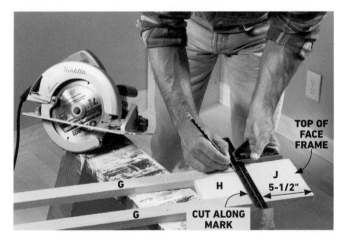

10 ATTACH THE FILLETS

Cut the fillets **(Q1-Q4)** on a table saw. Sand each piece (100 grit) to soften the sharp edges. Nail each piece into place with a small finish nailer. Glue and nail the brackets **(K)** below the fascia and fillet. Cut the lower bracket supports **(S)**, center them below the brackets and fillet, and glue and nail them to the partition sides with the air nailer.

11 CUT THE TOPS

Cut the tops off each face frame 5-1/2 in. from the top to make room for the column fillets **(Q4)**. Make the cuts perfectly square.

whether it's concrete, brick or plaster. If you have drywall with wood framing, you probably won't hit a stud as you try to screw the partition cleats to the wall **(Photo 7)**.

Before fastening the wall cleats, screw a 1x2 cleat to the ceiling so the front edge is 10-1/2 in. from the back wall. This cleat serves two purposes: It helps support the partition and it works as a cleat for the fascia **(Photo 9)**. Our ceiling joists ran perpendicular to the wall, so we could get a solid connection into the ceiling every 16 in. (your joists may be 24 in. on center). If your joists are running parallel to the back wall, you'll need to use anchors and construction adhesive.

Next, drill four 3/16-in.-dia. holes along the length of each wall cleat, plumb the cleat into position and then drive a nail through each hole to mark the anchor locations in the drywall. Screw in your wall anchors, and then smear construction adhesive

on the backside of the cleat and screw it to the wall. Measure top and bottom to the next cleat to ensure they'll be parallel. Install the rest in the same manner.

NOTE: Keep the end wall cleats 1-1/8 in. from adjacent side walls.

POSITION AND ATTACH THE PARTITIONS

Carry the partitions into the room and tip them up carefully to avoid scarring the ceiling. The partitions are fastened only at the top and

bottom, as mentioned in **Photo 8**, so the screw heads will be covered by other parts later. Once the partition is fastened to the cleat, screw the angle brackets to the partitions at the top and bottom 10 in. from the back wall as shown in **Photo 9**.

Use a framing square to ensure the partitions are perpendicular to the back wall. Once the partition is perfectly aligned, drive a screw through the bracket into the ceiling cleat and then into the bracket on the floor.

INSTALL THE FASCIA, SOFFIT AND BASE SHELF CLEATS

Before you screw the fascia pieces **(P)** between the partitions, screw a 1x2 cleat **(N1 and N2)** to the backside of each fascia 3/4 in. up from the bottom. Next, fasten the matching wall cleats parallel to the fascia cleat against the back wall. To finish the top of each section, cut the soffit pieces **(R)** and nail them to the cleats.

Screw 1x2 strips **(U1)** to the bottoms of the partitions and make center floor supports **(V)** from scrap plywood to support the lower base shelves **(Photo 15)**. If you have a floor heat register, remove the cover and install an extension boot **(Photo 17)**.

DRESS UP THE PLAIN BOXES WITH TRIM

Start by nailing the fillet trim **(Q1 and Q2)** on the bottom of the fascia. The fillet is wider than the fascia, so center it to extend equally on the front and back of

UPPER FACE FRAME SECTION

Q4

LOWER FACE FRAME SECTION

Q4

12 ATTACH THE FACE FRAMES
Center the face frames evenly on the front of the partitions, then glue and nail them to the plywood partition fronts. Glue the fillet **(Q4)** in place, then glue and nail the top section of the face frame to the top of the partition.

MITERED CROWN DETAIL

CROWN MOLDING (T)

18-GAUGE FINISH NAILER

CROWN RETURN PIECE

3/8" x 1-1/2" FILLET

13 ADD THE TRIM
Cut and nail the crown molding to finish the joints along the ceiling. Cut and glue small pieces of wood to fill the gaps on the sides of each partition behind the face frame.

14 CUT THE CROWN MOLDING UPSIDE DOWN
Cut crown molding safely and accurately by setting it upside down on the miter saw bed. Place the pieces so you can see the mark, and slowly cut through the piece. Let the saw fall through the molding. Don't force the saw or hurry the cut.

BOTTOM SIDE OF CROWN

the fascia. Next, glue each bracket **(K)** to the partition side, and nail it to the partition and to the fillet above. Working your way down the side, continue with the small fillet **(Q3)**. Glue this small piece to the bottom of the bracket with molding glue (a tackier woodworking glue) or carpenter's glue. Cut the bracket supports to fit between the fillet and the floor to support the curved bracket. These supports are designed to nestle the shelves and hide the gaps between the shelf ends and the partition sides. Cut the center seat **(Photo 17)** and fit the brackets and fillets underneath as shown in **Figure A** (the seat height is 22 in.).

Cut the partition face frames as shown in **Photo 11** and fasten them to the partitions. Notice that the plywood front of the partition becomes the background for the face frame. It's not necessary to get a tight fit against the ceiling because the crown molding will cover the ceiling joint and the exposed screws along the top of the fascia.

Crown molding can be fussy, so if you've never installed it before, buy an extra piece of molding

BASEBOARD DETAIL

15 INSTALL THE BASE MOLDING

Cut and nail the base molding to wrap around the face frame and partition sides. Note that you'll need small fillets to fill the gaps in the same way you did at the top under the crown molding returns. Screw in cleats **(U)** 6-1/4 in. from the floor on the side of each partition. Also screw the floor cleats **(V)** to the floor to support the center of each base shelf **(R)**.

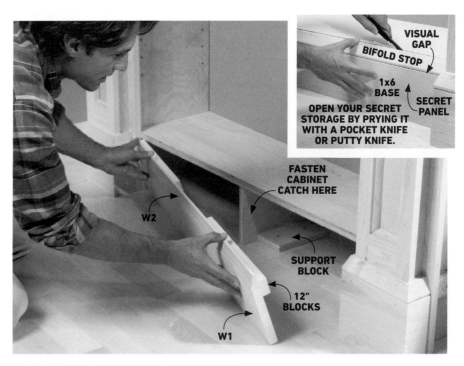

16 BUILD THE SECRET STORAGE BOX

Assemble the removable secret-panel base section to create a secret storage box under the base shelf. Keep the base panel in place by fastening a cabinet magnet catch to the side of the support piece **(V)**.

(you can always return the unused piece). We've installed miles of crown over the years and we still found the small pieces a bit challenging this time because the ceiling was somewhat irregular. The key is to cut the pieces uniformly. We like to draw a line right on the bed of the miter saw and always align the molding edge with the saw. Small gaps at the joints can be filled with putty and sanded, so don't drive yourself nuts seeking perfection against a ceiling that's not. Don't bother coping the crown pieces (**Photo 13**) because they'll be tough to fit; miter them instead.

FIT THE BASE AND MAKE A SECRET COMPARTMENT

This project will tie in with the rest of the room better if you replace your existing base molding and carry it through along the bottom of the bookcase. We made a two-piece base with 1x6 capped with bifold stop for the top member. To create a small gap between the two base pieces (**Photo 16** and **Figure A**), we chamfered the top edge of the 1x6 and the bottom edge of the bifold stop slightly with a block plane. This lends a traditional custom molding look.

To create the secret compartment panels, cut some 12-in. blocks, glue them to the backs of the 1x6 base pieces and nail the stop molding to the blocks (see **Figure A**). Glue a pair of small blocks to the backsides of parts **S** to create a stop for the secret panels. Install a magnetic cabinet latch to the center base shelf support (**V**) to hold the secret panel in place.

FILL NAIL HOLES, SAND AND FINISH

Sand the bookcase with 100-grit sandpaper followed by 150-grit.

EXTEND HEATING DUCT THROUGH BASE

SUPPORT BLOCK

17 BUILD THE WINDOW SEAT

Assemble the window seat by screwing cleats (**U2**) to the sides of each center partition and then nail the seat to the cleats. The seat is reinforced below by front and rear supports glued to the underside of the seat before it is nailed in place. Glue molding to the front of the seat, then nail the seat brackets and fillets in place as shown in **Figure A**.

Paint the bookcase if you'd like or create the handsome antique finish we did. We used Old Masters Gel Stain and mixed five parts Cherry to two parts Red Mahogany to one part Special Walnut. Blend these in a separate container and apply them to the sanded surface with a clean rag. Apply enough to cover, and remove the excess after a few minutes. Gently remove just enough stain to enhance the grain pattern. A dry brush works to get the excess stain out of the corners. You can rub a bit more aggressively if you'd like to reveal some

highlights or simulate wear. Let the stain dry and then finish the cabinet with two coats of polyurethane varnish.

SEAT WITH OPTIONAL CUSHION

WHAT IT TAKES

TIME
2 days

SKILL LEVEL
Intermediate to Advanced

TOOLS
Basic woodworking tools, biscuit joiner, drill driver, 35mm and 3/8-in. Forstner bits, miter or table saw, router with 3/8-in. rabbet bit

SECRET COMPARTMENT

MOTION SENSOR LIGHT

FRONT PANEL

The small compartment is a handy place to hide prescription medicine or jewelry. The front panel is held on with magnets. The battery-powered motion-sensor lights make the compartment look like a lighting valance.

MEDICINE CABINET WITH HIDDEN COMPARTMENT

ADD STYLE AND QUALITY AT A BARGAIN PRICE.

With medicine cabinets, the choices seem to be either high cost or low quality. And sometimes both! The medicine cabinet we designed is built from solid wood and good-quality hardware, so it will hold up to the rigors of everyday use. The materials aren't expensive. And it's relatively easy to build, making it a good project for an intermediate woodworker or an experienced DIYer.

This medicine cabinet has open shelves on the sides that can be used for display or storage. The mirrored door is mounted on self-closing cup hinges for maximum adjustability. There are adjustable shelves inside and even a hidden compartment disguised as a light valance. You can paint the cabinet, apply a clear finish to let the grain show through, or stain and varnish it.

We've kept the construction simple to allow even intermediate woodworkers to build this cabinet. The carcass is assembled with butt joints that are screwed together. We covered the screw heads with wood plugs, but you could substitute trim-head screws and just fill the screw holes with wood filler.

CUTTING LIST

KEY	QTY.	PART
A	2	1x6 board 3/4" x 5-1/2" x 29-1/2" Top and bottom
B	2	1x6 board 3/4" x 5-1/2" x 36" Sides
C	2	1x6 board 3/4" x 5-1/2" x 34-1/2" Dividers
D	4	1x6 board 3/4" x 5-1/2" x 5" Shelves
E	1	1/4" plywood Cut to fit Back
F	1	1x6 board 3/4" x 4-1/2" x 18" Compartment bottom
G	2	1x6 board 3/4" x 4-1/2" x 3-1/4" Compartment sides
H	1	1x6 board 3/4" x 4-1/2" x 17-7/8" Compartment panel
J	2	1x3 board 3/4" x 2-1/2" x 36" Door stiles
K	2	1x3 board 3/4" x 2-1/2" x 14-1/2" Door rails
L	1	Mirror Cut to fit (subtract 1/8")
M	1	1/4" plywood Cut to fit Mirror back

MATERIALS LIST

ITEM	QTY.
1x6 x 6' boards	4
1x3 x 8' board	1
1/4" x 4' x 4' plywood	1
3/8" flat-top wood plugs	32
1-1/2" multipurpose screws, 1-lb. box	1
1" nails, small box	1
Magnets	2
1/4" shelf pins	12
Screen fasteners, package	1
Full-overlay cup hinges	2
Mirror—cut to fit	1
Glass shelves—cut to fit	3
Mr Beams Night Lights (MB723)	1

SKILLS, TOOLS AND MATERIALS

Even though the joinery is simple, assembling the door and cabinet requires careful measuring, accurate cutting and attention to detail. We used a table saw fitted with a table saw sled to cut the parts, but a miter saw would also work for making the end cuts. The door is held together with wood biscuits, but you could use dowels or pocket screws instead. You'll need a router and a 3/8-in. rabbeting bit to make the recesses for the cabinet back and door mirror.

It's critical that you choose boards that are flat and straight, especially for the door. Sight down the boards and reject any that are twisted or crooked. The boards

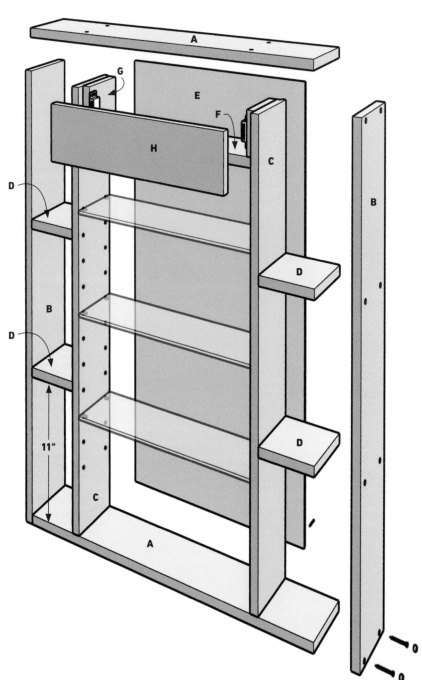

should lie flat when you stack them. We built this cabinet from inexpensive aspen, which looks great when painted. Pine or poplar would also be a good choice for a painted finish.

You'll find full-overlay cup hinges at home centers or woodworking stores, or you can

order them online. We purchased the mirror and glass shelves from a glass shop, but some full-service hardware stores also supply them. To save money, you could substitute wood shelves.

WOOD SCRAP

SIDE

DIVIDER

DIVIDER

SIDE

SHELF MARKS

FRAMING SQUARE

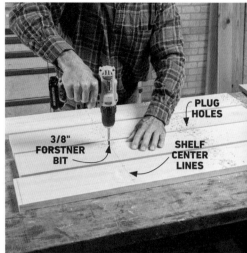

PLUG HOLES

3/8" FORSTNER BIT

SHELF CENTER LINES

1 MARK THE BOARDS FOR SHELVES AND SCREWS

Cut the cabinet box parts and arrange them as shown. Square the assembled boards by placing a framing square against the ends. Then use a scrap of the same wood to check the length of the dividers (C). If the dividers are the right length, the scrap will line up with the ends of the sides. Next, mark for the shelves using **Figure A** as a guide. Then flip the boards over and draw a single line to indicate the middle of the shelves. This is where you'll place the screws. Also mark screw locations for the dividers on the top and bottom boards.

2 PREPARE THE BOARDS FOR WOOD PLUGS

Mark screw locations 1 in. from each edge of the boards along the center lines you drew in the previous step. Then drill 3/8-in. holes about 3/8 in. deep at each mark. You'll glue wood plugs into these plug holes to cover the screws. For clean-edged plug holes, use a Forstner or brad point bit.

Figure B Door

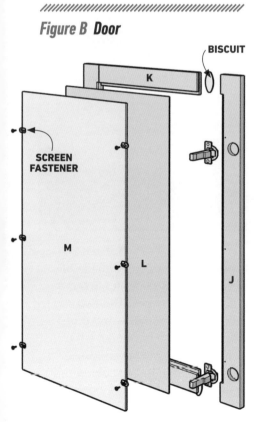

BISCUIT

K

SCREEN FASTENER

M

L

J

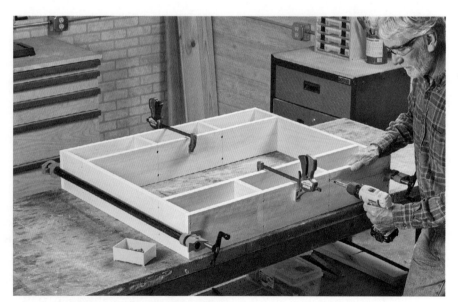

3 ASSEMBLE AND CLAMP THE PARTS

Arrange the parts with the shelf marks facing the inside. Line up the shelves with the marks and lightly clamp everything together. Tap the parts with a hammer to align the edges perfectly before tightening the clamps. Drill 3/32-in. pilot holes for each screw, using the divot left by the tip of the Forstner bit as a centering guide. Then drive 1-1/2-in. screws to hold the cabinet parts together.

4 COVER THE SCREWS WITH PLUGS

Apply a little glue to the edges of the plugs and tap them into the holes. Leave the plugs slightly proud of the surface so you can sand them flush later. For our painted medicine cabinet, we purchased flat-top wood plugs at a home center. If you plan to apply a clear finish, or a stain and clear finish, and want the plugs to be less conspicuous, shop for face grain plugs or cut your own plugs from the same wood you use to build the cabinet.

5 CUT A RECESS FOR THE CABINET BACK

Mount a 3/8-in. rabbeting bit in your router and set the depth to 1/4 in. If you don't already own one, consider purchasing a rabbeting bit with a set of interchangeable bearings that allow the bit to be used to cut several rabbet sizes. Place scraps of 2x6 alongside the cabinet to create a more stable base for the router. Cut slowly in a clockwise direction.

3/8" x 1/4" RABBET

SHARP CHISEL

BACK

1" NAIL

6 SQUARE THE CORNERS

The rounded corners left by the rabbeting bit need to be squared off so the plywood back will fit. You'll need a sharp chisel for this task. Start by marking the corner. Align a short straightedge with the edge of the rabbets and make pencil marks for the corner. Then carefully chisel out the wood to create the square corner.

7 NAIL ON THE BACK

Measure the height and width of the rabbet, and cut a piece of 1/4-in.-thick plywood to fit. Make sure the plywood is perfectly square by measuring diagonally from opposite corners. The two diagonal measurements should be equal. Run a bead of wood glue in the rabbet and insert the plywood back. Check to make sure the cabinet is square using the same diagonal measuring technique. If opposite diagonal measurements aren't equal, nudge the cabinet until they are. When you're sure the cabinet is square, attach the back with 1-in. nails placed about 6 in. apart.

BISCUIT JOINER TOOL

FAMILYHANDYMAN.COM For instructions on how to make biscuit joints, search for "biscuit joints" at familyhandyman.com.

NO. 20 BISCUIT

DOOR RAIL

BISCUIT CENTER MARK

BISCUIT SLOT

RABBET

DOOR

8 SLOT THE DOOR PARTS FOR BISCUITS

Cut slots to connect the door rails (top and bottom) to the stiles (sides). Becauses No. 20 biscuits are a little long, offset the slots so the biscuits protrude from the top and bottom of the door where they won't be noticeable after you cut them flush to the door edge. Make marks 1 in. from the top and bottom of the stiles and rails; center the biscuit slots on the marks. Glue biscuits into the slots and clamp the door, making sure it's square.

9 CUT A RABBET FOR THE MIRROR AND MIRROR BACK

Cut a 3/8-in.-deep rabbet to accommodate the 1/4-in. back and 1/8-in.-thick mirror. Use the same 3/8-in. rabbeting bit you used for the cabinet back. Make a first pass with the router set to about 3/16 in. deep. Then set the router to cut 3/8 in. deep and make the final pass. Square off the corners. Measure for the mirror. Subtract 1/8 in. from the width and height; take these measurements to a hardware store or glass shop.

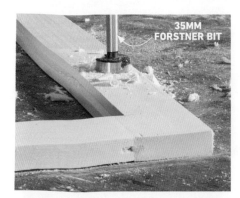

35MM FORSTNER BIT

CUP HINGE

HINGE PLATE

10 DRILL FOR THE CUP HINGES

Mark the hinge side and the top of the door to keep the orientation straight. Center the top hinge 8 in. from the top of the door and the bottom hinge 3-1/2 in. from the bottom of the door. Check your hinge specifications to see how far from the edge of the door to center the 35mm hole. Drill a 1/2-in.-deep hole with a 35mm Forstner bit for the cup hinge.

11 MOUNT THE CUP HINGES

Press the cup hinges into the hinge holes. Measure to make sure the centers of the hinge mounting holes are an equal distance from the edge of the door. This will ensure that the hinge is properly aligned. Then drive the included screws into the mounting holes.

12 MOUNT THE HINGE PLATES

Attach the plates to the hinges. Set the door into place on the cabinet, and align the top and bottom edges. Shim up the door with two thicknesses of thin cardboard. Mark the screw locations for the hinge plates. Remove the door and unclip the plates. Drill pilot holes at the screw locations. Then mount the plates to the cabinet with the included screws.

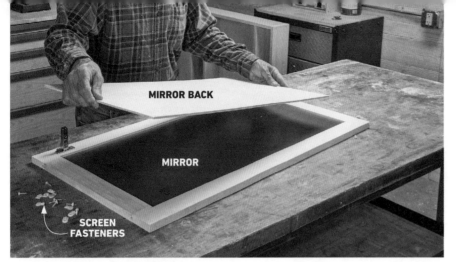

MIRROR BACK

MIRROR

SCREEN FASTENERS

MAGNET

13 INSTALL THE MIRROR

Cut a piece of 1/4-in. plywood to fit the rabbeted opening. Set the mirror into the frame and place the plywood on top. Secure the back with plastic screen fastener clips, available at home centers and hardware stores. For an easier and neater paint job, remove the mirror and all other hardware before painting the cabinet. Then reinstall them after the paint is dry.

14 BUILD THE HIDDEN COMPARTMENT

Build the compartment using **Figure A** as a guide. Attach magnets to the cabinet and metal plates to the removable cover to hold the cover in place. We mounted Mr Beams MB723 motion-sensor lights to the bottom of the compartment.

1/4" BIT

WOOD STOP

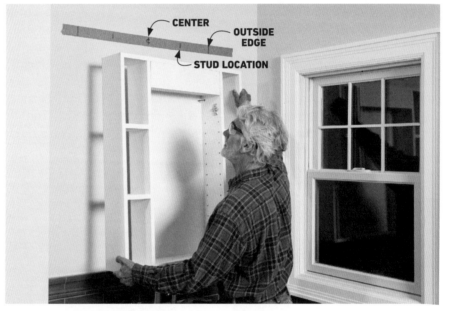

CENTER

OUTSIDE EDGE

STUD LOCATION

15 DRILL SHELF-PIN HOLES

Cut a scrap of 1/4-in. pegboard to 4-5/8 in. x 29-3/4 in., making sure the distance from the holes to the edges of the template is the same on the sides and on the top and bottom. This will avoid confusion by allowing you to position the template without regard to its orientation. For 2-in. hole spacing, draw lines across alternate sets of holes. Use a 1/4-in. brad point bit with a wood stop to limit the depth of the holes to 3/8 in. Press the pegboard against the back of the cabinet to drill the back holes. Clamp it flush to the front for the front holes.

16 INSTALL THE CABINET

Hang the cabinet by screwing through the back into one or two studs. Start by making two marks, level with each other and about 30 in. apart, to indicate the top of the cabinet. Apply a strip of masking tape to the wall so its bottom-edge aligns with these marks. Mark the cabinet center on the tape. Then measure out 15-1/2 in. in both directions and make marks to indicate the sides. Finally, use a stud finder or other means to locate any studs in the area where the cabinet will be mounted and mark them on the tape. Transfer the stud locations to the cabinet back to mark the mounting screw positions. If you hit only one stud, use toggle bolts or snap-toggle bolts to provide an additional hanging point. Prop or hold the cabinet in position and drive one screw at the top. Then use a level to plumb the cabinet sides before driving another screw at the bottom. Add the second set of screws or toggle bolts to complete the job.